QUESTIONING THE NEW PUBLIC MANAGEMENT

Questioning the New Public Management

Edited by

MIKE DENT, JOHN CHANDLER and JIM BARRY

ASHGATE

Published by
Ashgate Publishing Limited
Gower House
Croft Road
Aldershot
Hants GU11 3HR
England

Ashgate Publishing Company
Suite 420
101 Cherry Street
Burlington, VT 05401-4405
USA

Ashgate website: http://www.ashgate.com

British Library Cataloguing in Publication Data
Questioning the New Public Management
    1. Public administration - Great Britain 2. Civil service
    reform - Great Britain 3. National health services - Great
    Britain - Management
    I. Dent, Mike, 1944- II. Chandler, John III. Barry, Jim, 1950-
    351.4'1

Library of Congress Cataloging-in-Publication Data
Questioning the new public management / edited by Mike Dent, John Chandler and Jim Barry.
        p. cm.
    Includes bibliographical references and index.
    ISBN 0-7546-3397-7
    1. Public administration--Great Britain. 2. Administrative agencies--Great
Britain--Management. 3. Organizational change--Great Britain. I. Dent, Mike, 1944- II.
Chandler, John, 1954- III. Barry, Jim, 1950-

JN318.Q84 2004
351.41--dc22
                                                                2003063622

ISBN 0 7546 3397 7

Printed and bound by Athenaeum Press, Ltd.,
Gateshead, Tyne & Wear.

Contents

Part IV – New Public Management as Contested Terrain

Part V – The Limits of New Public Management

List of Contributors

Catrina Alferoff is presently employed as senior research assistant in the Department of Management at Keele University, working on an ESRC project investigating financial exclusion. While at Keele, she has researched knowledge management in call centres and the training and development of older workers. Previously, at Staffordshire University she worked on a number of Health Service Projects. She has published on equal opportunities, call centre work and direct mail, new technology and the problem of privacy.

Jim Barry is a political sociologist and Reader at the University of East London. He is currently Co-Director of the University's Organisation Studies Research Group based in the East London Business School and a member of the European Network on Managerialism and Higher Education. He is involved in two long-term research projects: one into gender and organisations with particular reference to managerialism in higher education; and another into gender, politics and urban governance in London and Mumbai (formerly Bombay). He is an Associate Editor of *Gender, Work and Organization* and has published on gender and politics, gender and public service, gender and organisations, gender and business ethics, gender and stress, gender and higher education, managerialism and higher education, and lone parenting and employment.

Elisabeth Berg is a Docent in sociology at Luleå University of Technology in Sweden with an appointment as Senior Visiting Research Fellow at the University of East London. She has been involved in several research projects into gender and organisations with particular reference to the public sector and is a member of the European Network on Managerialism and Higher Education. Her current research interests include gender and managerialism in higher education as well as the human consequences of recent changes in the public sector in respect of stress and burn-out. She has a number of publications, including *Kvinna och Chef i Offentlig Förvaltning* [Women and Leadership in Public Service], Stockholm: Liber, 2000.

Sharon C. Bolton is a lecturer in Human Resource Management in the Department of Behaviour in Organisations, The Management School, Lancaster University. Sharon started work in the department in August 2000 and prior to this was a Simon Marks Research Fellow in the Department of Sociology, University of Manchester. She completed her PhD in May 1999 in the Department of Behaviour in Organisations, University of Lancaster. Her research interests include the emotional labour process, public sector management and the nursing labour process.

Geraldine Catlow is a Research Associate at the University of Leicester Management Centre. Geraldine trained as a Chartered Accountant and worked in industry for a number of years until she took up the post of Senior Lecturer at University College Northampton. She left Northampton as Principal Lecturer and went to work for the Vocational Training Council in Hong Kong. When she returned to the UK in 1997 Geraldine joined Leicester Management Centre. Geraldine is currently completing her PhD and her research interests include public sector governance and accountability, financial reporting and gender issues in public sector management.

John Chandler is a Principal Lecturer and sociologist teaching Organisational Studies in the East London Business School at the University of East London. His current research interests include gender and managerialism in higher education and the 'new careers'. He is a Co-Director of the Organisation Studies Research Group in the East London Business School and is a member of the European Network on Managerialism and Higher Education. He has a number of publications, including *Organisation and Identities* (International Thomson, 1994) (edited with Jim Barry and Heather Clark) and *Organization and Management: a Critical Text* (International Thomson, 2000) (edited with Jim Barry, Heather Clark, Roger Johnston and David Needle).

Tony Cutler was, prior to joining the School of Management at Royal Holloway, University of London, Reader in Sociology, School of Social Science, Middlesex University, his books include *Keynes, Beveridge and Beyond* (1986), Routledge (with Karel and John Williams); *The Struggle for Europe*, Berg (1989) (with Colin Haslam, John and Karel Williams) and *Managing the Welfare State: Text and Sourcebook*, Berg (1997) with Barbara Waine.

Mike Dent is Professor of Health Care Organisation at the School of Health, Staffordshire University. He has been researching the professions for over twenty years and many of his publications have been concerned with accountability within health care, not only in the UK but also across Europe. His current research is on European hospitals, New Public Management, and the professions of medicine and nursing. He has recently edited two other books, one with Stephen Whitehead, *Managing Professional Identities* (Routledge, 2002) the other with Jim Barry and Maggie O'Neill, *Gender and the Public Sector* (Routledge, 2003). His latest book is *European Health Care Organisations* (Palgrave Macmillan, 2003).

Paul Michael Garrett is a Lecturer in Social Work at the University of Nottingham. He has published articles in a range of journals, including *Critical Social Policy, Social History, the British Journal of Social Work, Social Work Education, Practice*. A key area of interest is the question of how social workers' engagement with the users of services are being increasingly subject to regulation and monitoring. In addition, he is exploring how social work and more embracing academic discourses on 'race' and ethnicity fail to address the specificity of Irish people in Britain. In this context, he has examined historical responses to Irish birth mothers in Britain. He is currently the official advisor on social services to the All Party Irish in Britain Parliamentary Group.

Charles Harvey is Professor of Business History and Management at Bristol Business School, University of the West of England, UK. His main interests are in international business history, business elites and corporate governance, cultural production, and leadership, learning and change, particularly in healthcare organisations. He won the Wadsworth Prize for Business History with his first book, *The Rio Tinto Company: An Economic History of a Leading International Mining Concern* (1981) and again with *William Morris: Design and Enterprise in Victorian Britain* (1991). He has published widely in journals such as the *Journal of Management Studies, Human Relations* and *The Economic History Review*. He is joint editor with Professor Geoffrey Jones of the journal *Business History*.

Jeanette Henderson is a lecturer with the School of Health and Social Welfare at the Open University in the UK and has also practised as an Approved Social Worker with a local authority in the north of England. Her research interests are in mental health and mental health law, especially the meanings and constructions of 'care' for service users, their friends and families and professionals. Recent publications include papers on implementing change in mental health, and assessing Approved Social Worker's knowledge of mental health legislation.

Chris Howorth is a lecturer in Organisational Strategy in the School of Management at Royal Holloway, University of London. His research interests are in the fields of organisation studies, health care management, change management, strategy, and Equal Opportunities. He has published extensively on health care reform and management both in the UK and Germany and has carried out work on the education, recruitment and retention of ethnic minorities in a number of industries.

David Seth Jones is an Associate Professor, Department of Public Policy and Administration, University of Brunei. He has previously been an Associate Professor in Public Administration at the National University of Singapore having previously worked as a lecturer for the Overseas Development Administration of the UK in Southern Africa and as a professional officer in the Northern Ireland Civil Service. He has published extensively in the areas of public policy and administration, government budgeting and in Irish politics and government.

Linda Keen is currently Master of Keynes College, and lecturer in HRM and Public Sector Management at the University of Kent at Canterbury. She has written various articles and a book on local government management, and was an elected member on Canterbury City Council for eight years, in addition to sitting on the governing bodies/management committees of a number of local voluntary organisations.

Alison Linstead is Lecturer in Management and Organisation Theory in the Work, Organisation and Management group at Durham Business School. Before taking up this post Alison worked at the University of Essex and The University of Leicester Management Centre. Alison's research focuses on issues of identity in management and organisation with a particular focus on the processes of seduction, narcissism and resistance; gender and language; international diversity and retheorising gender from postfeminist perspective. Her publications appear in *Gender, Work and Organization*; *Organization* and *Culture and Organization*. Alison is currently editing two books *Thinking Organization* (Routledge) and *Organization and Identity* (Routledge) She is currently a board member of the *Standing Conference on Organizational Symbolism* and sits on the editorial board of the journal *Gender, Work and Organization*. Alison worked with Geraldine Catlow on a research project on women in the National Heath Service funded by the University of Leicester.

Beverly Metcalf is Lecturer in Human Resource Development and coordinator for the Management, Governance and International Development group at the Institute for Development Policy and Management at the University of Manchester. Her research interests are concerned with HR strategy in the public sector, international human resource development, gender and management, and feminist theory and organisation analysis, in particular Luce Irigaray. She is currently involved in a funded research project exploring gender and management in the Russian Federation and is writing a book entitled *International Human Resource Development* (Palgrave Macmillan).

Frank Mueller holds the Chair in Organisation Theory and International Strategy located in the Management Centre at the University of Leicester. His previous post was as Reader in the School of Management, Royal Holloway University of London. Before that, he held posts at Aston University Business School (Lecturer) and London Business School (Research Fellow). His research interests focus on: archetypal change in professional organisations, in particular health and engineering; theory and practice of human resource management and teamworking; comparative organisational behaviour and national business systems. He has published widely on these topics, including multiple publications in each of the following: *'Organization Studies'*, *'Human Relations'* and *'Journal of Management Studies'*. He is Co-founder and Co-organiser of the annual 'International Workshop on Teamworking' (IWOT).

Sally Ruane lectures in health policy at De Montfort University, Leicester. She studied Sociology and Social Policy at Durham University. She completed her PhD, which was on *Baby Adoption and the Social Construction of Motherhood* in 1990. Her research interests include maternal emotion and purchasing policies in relation to fertility treatments as well as the private finance initiative.

Janet Seden is a Lecturer in the School of Health and Social Welfare at The Open University. She has worked as probation officer, children and families field social worker, social worker/manager in a family centre, and lectured at Leicester University. She is the author of *Counselling Skills in Social Work Practice*, and has also published on the assessment of and provision of services for children and their families, social work processes, children and spirituality and practice teaching. Recent publications include: 'Family Assistance Orders: and The Children Act 1989' in the *International Journal of Law, Policy and the Family* (2001) and 'Underpinning Theories for The Assessment of Children in Need and their Families' in *Approaches to Needs Assessment* in Children's Services (2002). She also undertook a literature review on the underpinning theories for the 'Assessment of Children in Need and their Families' for the Department of Health in 1999, which was published in 2001.

List of Figure and Tables

Figure

Tables

Acknowledgements

There are a number of people that we wish to say thank you for their help and support with this volume – in addition to all the contributors. First, all those who were at the 'Dilemmas for the Human Services' conferences were these chapters were first presented, for their comments and encouragement. We have also really appreciated the good advice and patience from the folk at Ashgate. Thanks too are due to Lynne Skelton and Jackie Redhead, School of Health for providing really useful practical help with the production of the camera ready copy. Finally, we acknowledge the support of the School of Health (now Faculty of Health and Sciences), Staffordshire University and the Business School, University of East London.

MD, JC, JB.

Chapter 1

Introduction: Questioning the New Public Management

Mike Dent, John Chandler and Jim Barry

New Public Management (NPM) has enjoyed centre stage within the UK public services for well over a decade. There has been much written on the subject and much of it was concerned with establishing the presence and charting its development as well as considering the implications for the public sector (e.g. Hood, 1991, 1995; Ferlie, Ashburner, Fitzgerald and Pettigrew, 1996; Clarke and Newman, 1997; Exworthy and Halford, 1999; Hood et al 1999; Pollitt and Bouckaert, 2000). In this process there has been a tendency to see the NPM movement as a more integrated and uniform than it perhaps really is for we would argue that NPM is in practice not one unified set of practices but a theme which has distinct variations within the different sectors (e.g. health, education, social services): it varies *across* sectors, it varies *within* sectors and it varies according to the outcomes of specific management-professional settlements. Firstly, we contend that not only is NPM manifested in a variety of guises but also, its form varies across sectors. Beyond the general pressures to be cost effective, accountable and market-friendly the implementation of the NPM across, for instance, health, social services and education, has been quite variable. We would suggest, for instance, that schools were less directly affected by the introduction of the quasi-market than were hospitals, even if the rhetoric was similar. Conversely the impact of audits has had a far more direct and immediate effect earlier on within schools than in health care, although this has begun to change with the introduction of Commission for Health Improvement. Secondly, despite its underlying themes, NPM does not offer managers any 'magic bullet' or toolkit, for it is a *hydra-headed* phenomenon, not a single instrument but a collection of management tools that have been adapted and modified over time. During the early 1990s the disciplinary force of the 'quasi-markets' was expected to be, more or less, sufficiently effective. By the late 1990s, however, accountability and audits came to dominate NPM practice (Power, 1994; 1997; Jary, 2002) as it became clear that the quasi-market had failed to deliver and the model became politically less attractive in the wake of 'Blairism', or the 'Third Way'. Instead of quasi-market competition the emphasis was now even more clearly on managerialism, even so, the newer versions of NPM have continued to embrace private sector involvement as, for example, in the cases of public/private partnerships and the Private Finance Initiative (PFI). Thirdly, we would argue that NPM is very much a *contested terrain* on which a reconfiguration of management-professional relations has been forged. It has not offered an easy victory for managements, nor have the professions remained unscathed. Rather than the new managerialism undermining the public sector professions in any direct way what is to be seen is a reconfiguration of expertise and its management, a process that is redefining both managerial and professional work and their organisational relationship. Certainly this is a process that seriously challenges these professions but it is not a process that is leading to their 'deprofessionalisation' or 'proletarianisation' but instead, is redefining professional autonomy in ways that make it compatible with the new managerialism. Whilst many public sector professionals view NPM as a threat to their autonomy and authority they cannot openly condemn its implementation given the public claim that it will improve the service to the public/client/consumer. Instead, therefore, they broadly accept NPM and look for ways of ameliorating its impact. This, the professionals attempt to achieve in one or more of three ways:

1. *Colonisation*: claiming their professional right to take on the responsibility for the activity and thereby if not dictating certainly influencing the measures for success and failure. This is particularly evident within higher education
2. *De-coupling*: minimising the impact of NPM on their work by treating it as a formal requirement that has little practical importance for their real work (i.e. decoupled cf. Meyer and Rowan, 1991), for example in teaching and medical work. Doctors, for instance, have long adopted this technique in relation to medical audit (Power, 1997: 106).
3. *Reconfiguration*: a combination of both previous strategies in an attempt to retain control over the organisation and delivery of their services.

At the same time, some managers have felt threatened by the 'iron cage' of accountability and audits experiencing these as an attack on their traditional ethos of public service. But in general, management lacks a credible independent base from which to resist NPM and have to learn the new 'scripts' and adapt to the new ethos which increasingly draws on a revised form of professionalism which has more to do with the 'responsibilisation' of labour (Fournier, 1999) than with legitimating the autonomy of particularly groups of expert labour. All these issues are taken up within the chapters that make up this edited collection and together provide a critical assessment of the phenomena of New Public Management.

The authors draw on a range of sociological and organisational theories in their analyses of a range of case studies and evaluations. The body of the book starts, however, with a detailed and theoretical analysis of NPM and the public sector professions (Part I), provided my Dent and Barry. This is followed by three sections each one dealing with one of the characteristics of the NPM movement: variation; variability; contestability. Variation is the focus of Part II (*Variations Between Sectors*), which comprises of four chapters that relate to the issue of variation between sectors. It covers local government, social care management, social work and the police and each chapter documents the growing emphasis on the imposition of new 'standards' and chart the variation of responses across the public sector. While each report conflicts and dilemmas for managers and professionals the impact of NPM and the response to it varies considerably. In Keen's chapter on 'Best Value' in local government she draws on case study research to examine the range and variation of responses of middle managers to NPM and, in particular, the 'best value' policy initiative. Henderson and Seddon's study reports on the experience of first line managers in social care and the challenges they face in meeting the new demands to work in multi- and cross-disciplinary teams to provide the 'seamless care' promised by government. Garrett's study is of social work and emphasises more the challenges of standardisation within professional practice. He examines and analyses the increasing demands on social workers to work 'within centrally devised schedules, checklists and proforma' and the implications for social worker/ client relations. Metcalfe concludes this section with her study of an English police force and the challenges it faced in introducing a new performance appraisal policy. The study, which draws on a large survey as well as participant observation, identifies problems associated in introducing NPM-type organisational changes without taking sufficient account of organisational and professional cultures.

Variability is the subject of Part III (*Hydra-Headed NPM: The Case of the National Health Service*) and here there are four chapters each reporting on original research that demonstrate the variations of NPM and its implications within just one sector, the National Health Service (NHS). Linstead and Catlow open with a study of the experience of women in senior management and the extent to which the new managerialism has challenged the dominant discourse of masculinity. This contribution continues with concerns raised in the previous section and contrasts with the other three contributions, which focus on specific organisational and policy initiatives. Howorth, Mueller and Harvey draw on the concept of the 'learning organisation' in their study of the adoption of an NPM system of 'Patient Focused Care' within a hospital trust. Ruanne's case study examines NHS Trust managers' ambiguous perceptions of the Private Finance Initiative (PFI) while Alferrof and Dent's study of 'Out of Hours' care presents an account of the complexities and variations in the working relations between general practitioners and Accident and Emergency units in developing services that were consumer/patient focused.

The discussion of the contested nature of NPM is the subject of Part IV (*NPM as a Contested Terrain*) and it is here that the issues of adaptation, negotiation and struggle with NPM are examined. Berg, Barry and Chandler begin this section with a chapter reporting on studies that examines the insecurities and stress for academics within higher education in Britain. The chapter is as much a critique of the psychology of stress as it is a report on staff responses to work pressures and shows how the reach of management extends to the control of emotional responses. This is followed by Bolton's study that demonstrates how at least one occupational group resist the disciplinary mechanisms of NPM. The focus here is on a particular mode of resistance as employed by nurses – humour. Drawing on a longitudinal study Bolton demonstrates how humour can be applied as 'a potent negotiative device' one that can change the balance of power and defy the 'taken for granted' patriarchal assumptions of much of their work. In short, ensures the nurses retain their practical autonomy within the work terrain even in face of pervasive NPM driven organisational change.

Part V, *The Limits of NPM*, provides an overall assessment, comprising two chapters, each setting out a 'score card' for NPM. Jones provides an evaluation of the evidence from New Zealand and Singapore, countries selected because both are keen players in the NPM game. The chapter provides evidence that suggests the gains of the much-vaunted new managerialism are less easily won than many of its proponents had led us to expect. Finally, Cutler provides the coup de grace with an incisive critique of the rhetoric that has attached to the new managerialism in the public sector despite pre-existing evidence of poor performance within the private sector.

References

Clarke, J. and Newman, J. (1997), *The Managerial State*, Sage: London.

Exworthy, M. and Halford, S. (eds) (1999), *Professionals and the New Managerialism in the Public Sector*, Open University Press: Buckingham.

Ferlie, E., Ashburner, L., Fitzgerald, L., and Pettigrew, A. (1996), *The New Public Administration in Action*, Oxford University Press: Oxford.

Fournier, V. (1999), 'The Appeal of "Professionalism" as a Disciplinary Mechanism', *The Sociological Review*, 47(2): 280-307.

Hood, C. (1991), 'A Public Management for All Seasons?' *Public Administration*, 69: 3-19.

Hood, C. (1995), 'The "New Public Management" in the 1980s: Variations on a Theme', *Accounting, Organizations and Society*, 20, 2(3): 93-109.

Hood, C., Scott, C., James, O., Jones, G. and Travers, T. (1999), *Regulation Inside Government: Waste-Watchers, Quality-Police and Sleaze-Busters*, Oxford University Press: Oxford.

Jary, D. (2002), 'Aspects of the "Audit Society": Issues arising from the Colonization of Professional Academic Identities by a "Portable Management Tool"', in M. Dent and S. Whitehead (eds), *Managing Professional Identities: Knowledge, Performativity and the 'New' Professional*, Routledge: London.

Meyer J.W. and Rowan, B. (1991), 'Institutionalized Organizations: Formal Structure as Myth and Ceremony', in W.W. Powell and P.J. DiMaggio (eds), *The New Institutionalism in Organizational Analysis*, The University of Chicago Press: Chicago and London.

Pollitt, C. and Bouckaert, G. (2000), *Public Management Reform: a Comparative Analysis*, Oxford University Press: Oxford.

Power, M. (1994), *The Audit Explosion*, London: Demos.

Power, M. (1997), *The Audit Society: The Rituals of Verification*, Oxford University Press: Oxford.

PART I

CONTEXT AND THEORY OF THE NEW PUBLIC MANAGEMENT

Chapter 2

New Public Management and the Professions in the UK: Reconfiguring Control?

Mike Dent and Jim Barry

Introducing the New Public Management

Writing in the early 1940s the disillusioned ex-Trotskyist James Burnham warned of a managerial revolution, a 'major social revolution ... now in fact occurring [with] the [second world] war ... subordinate to the revolution, not the other way round' (Burnham, 1942: 8). In recent years a new variation has come to prominence, this time evolutionary rather than revolutionary, with academic commentators noting the emergence of a 'managerial reform movement' developing in the public sector, often referred to as the New Public Management (NPM), evident from the late 1970s onwards (Hood et al, 1999: 189-90). These commentators have, as with Burnham, also documented a growing international interest, albeit one which seems to have varied in its appeal (Hood, 1995). Some countries, including New Zealand and Sweden in addition to the UK, have adopted the reforms fairly readily while others have not. Germany and Japan are good examples of the latter category. As an early adopter Britain may even be something of a test case. Clarke and Newman (1997), sensing a managerial colonisation of the public sector, have argued that in Britain a 'managerial state' is in the making. Talk in Britain of a 'creeping managerialism' (Strong and Robinson, 1990) in relation to NHS reforms and the 'decline of donnish dominion' (Halsey, 1995) alongside the emergence of the 'McUniversity' (Parker and Jary, 1995) in academe, would appear to lend weight to this view.

The appeal of the NPM lies in the claim that it delivers improved public services and that it represents an empowerment of those it employs and those it seeks to serve. This siren call certainly seems to have found a ready and willing audience in senior public servants (Pollitt, 1990: 171-72), keen to better manage their unwieldy administrative machinery, and a fickle public who appeared to be losing faith in the 'bureau-professional regime' of the welfare state (Clarke and Newman, 1997: 12-13). Yet there is little in all this that appears to be new beyond a rhetoric concerning quality, shared values and empowerment in the service of a public now relabelled 'consumers'. Indeed, as a reading of the growing literature reveals, much of what constitutes the NPM is borrowed from private sector managerial techniques, themselves rooted in a long tradition founded on Scientific Management and Human Relations approaches (Pollitt, 1990: 11-27 and 187; Ranade, 1997: 121-26). Seen in this way, the legacy of control bestowed to erstwhile public sector servants is barely concealed.

Yet whatever it represents the 'new' managerialism, according to the literature at least, has spread widely. So too, in its wake, has the challenge to the professions, evident in Hood's (1991; 1995: 95-7) delineation of the NPM's various manifestations:

1. greater 'disaggregation' of public sector organisations into separately managed units;
2. enhanced competition; use of private sector managerial techniques;
3. emphasis on 'discipline and parsimony' in resource use;
4. greater 'hands-on management';
5. adoption of measurable standards of performance; and
6. use of 'pre-set output measures'.

In more recent work Hood – with others – (1999: 191-93) has argued that the NPM is becoming primarily concerned with the surveillance (increased 'oversight') and regulation of the public sector through mechanisms such as audit and inspection.

If fully realised of course the changes identified above, taken together, represent a substantial encroachment on professional autonomy. Yet things may not be quite as they seem. Perhaps there is in all this a substantial element of 'smoke and mirrors' or, to change the metaphor, 'myth and ceremony' (Meyer and Rowan, 1991). It is this possibility that we seek to examine through an exploration of the claims of the New Public Management (NPM) against the experiences of two professional groups in Britain: hospital doctors[1] and university lecturers. In this we draw on published academic sources as well as primary research undertaken by the authors.[2] We begin with a search for a theoretical framework to help us in our task. First by examining the contribution made by contemporary writers associated with the sociology of the professions, before moving on to a consideration of new institutional approaches.

Governmentality and the Institutionalisation of Expertise

Public sector services, particularly education and health, have played an important legitimising role within all capitalist societies (Habermas, 1976; Offe, 1984). The work of the professionals and managers in the public sector has acted as an important 'stabilising (or legitimating) function' in this process (Exworthy and Halford, 1999: 9). These services have been premised on the production of use values, 'however distorted' some may consider these to be (Thompson, 1990: 110), and not exchange values more commonly associated with the market. Nevertheless, the welfare state has in recent years been seriously challenged by the introduction of quasi-market principles, the impact of which should not be under-estimated. Yet it would be deceptively easy to interpret the growth of NPM as representing simply an abandonment of the public sector's legitimising role in favour of market economics. The NPM discourse is more complex. A consideration of concerns about pre-existing arrangements and the search for alternatives may provide some insight into why the NPM developed in the way it did and may help to identify a number of issues relevant for our analysis.

It certainly appears that interest in the NPM has been driven by a number of factors in addition to a preference for (quasi-) markets, not least the ideological factors associated with the politics of 'Thatcherism' in the 1980s. But there were also, crucially, criticisms from the left too. For example, the early critique of the lack of accountability of the social welfare professions documented in Paul Wilding's influential Fabian Tract (1981; see also Illich, 1977). There were also, and importantly, major concerns over the drain of public sector expenditure placed on international state-competitiveness (Figueras et al, 1998: 2-4). Indeed many forces appear to have been in play with implications for our analysis of professions and NPM – to which we return at different points later in the chapter – rendering easy answers problematic.

One possible means of unravelling the relationship between the professions and the NPM is to examine Foucault's concept of 'governmentality'. At its most general level it relates to the ensemble of institutions that ensure, more or less, the continuing reproduction of the self-regulating citizen-subject (Johnson, 1995: 12). It is concerned with the mechanisms by which governments govern in line with 'the personal and collective conduct of subjects' (ibid). This includes the modern professions who are part of the process of governing in a wider sense (Gane and Johnson, 1993: 9). In seeing the professions as a 'key resource of governing in a liberal-democratic state', which facilitates normalisation, Johnson (1995: 23) draws attention to the ongoing and transformative nature of the process being described. A disturbance to the existing state of affairs, one such being the Thatcherite reforms in Britain cited by Johnson (1995: 22), can thus:

> bring new jurisdictional claimants into being... [including] ... appraisers, auditors and monitors of expert services.

This is an argument for the emergence of what Power (1997) has called the 'Audit Society', or regulation in the case of Hood et al (1999).

The mechanisms by which such changes occur – or fail to occur – have been the subject of particular interest to the 'New Institutionalists' for some time. One of the purposes of this chapter is to explore the usefulness of this approach to explaining the changes impacting on the UK health and educational professionals. What the 'New Institutionalist' framework does offer is the opportunity, as Kitchener (1998: 73-4) points out, to break out of the 'insular and parochial' boundaries of much work on public sector organisations. In this approach, the work situation of health and HE professionals is conceptualised as part of an organisational 'field' (DiMaggio and Powell, 1991: 64-5). This will include a range of institutions and organisations that coalesce to form a framework in which to understand inter- and intra-professional, management-professional and state-professional relations as well as patients, students and other consumers and users of the professionals' services. In addition, the field will include key suppliers such as pharmaceutical companies and educational publishers. This configurational 'field' approach shares some of the qualities of Foucauldian post-structuralism, for the field is an ensemble of 'procedures, techniques, institutionalisations and knowledges' (Gane and Johnson, 1993: 9).

Another insight comes from Meyer and Rowan, who suggest (1991: 41) the 'formal structures of many organizations ... reflect the myths of their institutional environments instead of the demands of their work activities'. There is according to their arguments a 'de-coupling' of the formal organisation 'myth' from the reality. This acts as an uncertainty-absorbing arrangement that contributes to the legitimacy of an organisation and its survival. A good example of 'de-coupling' within the health system is the exercise of clinical judgement. Doctors (physicians) are able to follow the formal rules because these do not encompass in any detail this discrete area of autonomy within the clinic (Harrison, 1999). This 'de-coupling' is not simply another way of classifying the 'informal organisation', it instead identifies the ambivalent nature of professional, or specialist, judgement (discretion). Likewise university lecturers will follow course and complex modular degree regulations concocted by managers, as well as accept some increase in overall workload, providing they retain control of the design of the syllabi and the content of course modules. These remain the provinces of individual academic expertise. Meyer and Rowan (1991) argue that 'de-coupling' of this kind is part of the means by which complex organisations may legitimately and efficiently function, which would otherwise be impossible. It, moreover, provides the theoretical space to recognise the role knowledge/power discourses play within organisations. Nevertheless, Meyer and Rowan do underplay the impact of the (relative) autonomy of the professional. University lecturers and hospital doctors commonly have an allegiance to their professional association, an interest in their students/patients and possibly the management of the university/ hospital within which they work. These interests can and do conflict.

The analysis of Barley and Tolbert (1997: 98) may provide a way around this oversimplification. They suggest that new institutionalism can be usefully combined with structuration theory (Giddens, 1984). They utilise Barley's (1986) notion of 'scripts' as a substitute for Gidden's 'modalities'. These scripts are *'observable, recurrent activities and patterns of interaction characteristic of a particular setting'* (ibid: 98 emphases in original). This concept forms the basis of the 'four moments' of the institutionalisation process (Barley and Tolbert, 1997: 100-103):

1. 'encoding of institutional principles in the scripts used in specific settings' (a socialisation and internalisation process);
2. enactment of the 'scripts that encode institutional principles' (which 'may or may not entail conscious choice');
3. revising or replicating scripts (intentional alteration 'is more likely to lead to institutional change' than those which are made unconsciously); and
4. 'objectification and externalisation of the patterned behaviours and interactions produced during the period in question'.

This sequence indicates how social actors construct scripts that then become institutionalised but, equally, provide the means of institutional change. Changes are most likely to occur as a result of conscious intent, particularly in response to changes in the wider environment (ibid: 102). There remains the assumption that social interaction, within an organisational field, is 'constrained by histories and ritualistic patterning' (Barley, 1986: 107) and this leads to cumulative structuring and hence institutionalisation of new arrangements. At this point it is very important to emphasise that the four moments of 'encoding', 'enactment', 'revision' and 'objectification' are ongoing processes: 'institutionalization... is a continuous process whose operation can be observed only through time' (Barley and Tolbert: 1997: 100). It will, in our view, commonly be an *iterative process*. This is the case with the processes associated with NPM (e.g. Kitchener, 1998: 73). There will be a sequence of 'scripts' as the process of adapting to the demands for efficiency, effectiveness and accountability are turned from political rhetoric to organisational practice. This avoids any problem of reification as well as taking account of the processual character of the 'structuration' of institutions and action (ibid: 96-7). This model provides a useful framework, which we use here to explain the impact of managerialism on professionalism in higher education and the NHS hospital service.

Changing Scripts in Health and Higher Education in Britain

In education and health care, as well as in many other public sector organisations, there exists no set of unambiguous institutional principles. Wherever organised professionals are employed there is an organisational tension between professional socialisation and principles and managerial concerns with efficiency. Prior to the 'Thatcherite' reforms these tensions within the NHS were contained basically, according to Harrison (1999: 51-2), by the acceptance of three principles:

1. all governments were committed to clinical autonomy and the acceptance of medical dominance;
2. the formal organisation of the NHS was constructed to be consonant with clinical autonomy;
3. the practice of NHS management during this post war period was more a matter of diplomacy than management

(Harrison, 1999: 52-3).

The NHS health services, for the most part, were defined predominately by the doctors; and similarly, in universities, by academics. In both cases managers were there only to provide administrative support. At this time the universities looked to the state for funding rather than generating their own income, comfortable that the conventional wisdom inferred a 'direct relationship between university expansion and economic growth and that universities could be agents of social equality' (Parker and Jary 1995: 322). There were concerns but these, in line with other western societies, had been with reforming the system of higher education:

[transforming] the small elite university systems of the nineteenth and first half of the twentieth centuries into the system of mass higher education required to meet the growing demands both for wider access from segments of their societies, and for more highly trained and educated workers from their labour markets

(Trow, 1994: 11).

In Britain the binary divide between polytechnics and universities was abolished in 1992 and the number of universities more than doubled overnight. Only later did it become clear that the expansion to a mass or 'New Higher Education (NHE)' system (Parker and Jary, 1995: 319) was to be achieved in the name of efficiency (ibid: 322) and, so it was argued, the 'Taylorisation of intellectual labour' (Dominelli and Hoogvelt, 1996: 199).

One point of contrast between health and higher education is that the universities and polytechnics in their different ways appeared on the surface to be more reliant on 'bureau-professionals' (Newman and Clarke, 1994) or 'managerial-professionals' (Causer and Exworthy, 1999) than was the case in the health service. This may be a correlation of the difference between the work and institutional organisation of the two professional groups. The corporate influence of the British Medical Association and Royal Colleges was always much more influential than the lecturers' unions and professional bodies. On the other hand the 'managerial-professionals' of the university sector have been a powerful interest group, but they act in the interests of the universities as a set of institutions. They do not act, primarily, as a mouthpiece for the academic profession(s) but have fairly effectively defended the academic terrain at least of the pre-1992 (old) universities. Within these borders the professional 'community' of academics has been focused on day-to-day work arrangements. These include organising research, presenting papers, attending academic conferences and a range of other activities alongside their teaching. It is this that sustains the sense and reality of an occupational community of these professional knowledge workers. The configuration of interests between academics, other university occupations, student bodies and university management is nonetheless very different to that of hospital doctors and their equivalent actor-network. The majority of doctors work outside of universities just as a majority of academics work outside hospitals. There are then differences of organisational context that may be significant. But whatever the differences between the two groups the introduction of the new managerialism signalled a major revision of the organisational scripts for professionals in both health and higher education. On the face of it they were to be subordinated to a managerial rationality albeit dressed up in the guise of market competition. Drawing on Hood's delineation of NPM cited earlier in the chapter, as well as published sources; the changing scripts for health and higher education professionals in recent years can be reasonably summarised as follows.

1. In health there was a 'disaggregation' of organisations into separately managed units. The acute hospitals over about 3-4 years were transformed into organisationally autonomous hospital trusts. Professionals have of course

always been involved in managing (Exworthy and Halford, 1999: 12). But in higher education the emphasis on enhancing managerial power through Heads of Department recommended in the Jarratt Report (1985: 22 & 28), to better manage the major resource of universities – their staff – was quite marked. Here the stress was on management of staff, budgetary control and business generation (Parker and Jary, 1995: 320).

2. Relations between hospitals became defined in terms of competition: they competed for contracts with the district health authorities and local general practitioners. The role of market competition should not be overstated, however, often the term was a rhetoric for (political) conflicts over the distribution of scarce resources (Hughes, 1996; Dent, 2003a). Nevertheless, the rhetoric did coincide with the widespread introduction of private sector managerial techniques. This was particularly so in the area of quality management (Kirkpatrick and Lucio, 1995). In universities the emphasis on competition was also apparent, for students and the resources that followed them, as well as research. To this end emphasis was laid on the marketing of educational 'products', to ensure that courses were targeted at and appealed to segmented groups of student 'customers'. The introduction of league tables aided this process, not least in respect of research, which enabled the elite universities to maintain their lion's share of research funding. There was also a greater use of private sector managerial techniques, as in health, through so-called quality management of teaching and learning. The resultant paper trails, followed by quality auditors, and reviews, previously known as inspections, were the result.

3. There was an increasing emphasis on 'discipline and parsimony' in resource use. In health new systems of case-mix accounting were introduced to identify where the resources were being spent. Again, one must be careful not to overstate the case. Whilst there was much rhetoric surrounding the introduction of the 'internal market' and extolling the sophistication of the new case-mix systems that would identify the detailed DRG-based costs (Dent, 1996: 52-3), these had little direct impact on efficiency. Parsimony was achieved more by the crude imposition of budgetary constraints and the uncertainty surrounding the development of the purchaser-provider contracting system. In higher education from the late 1970s Thatcherite demands for efficiency (Parker and Jary, 1995: 322) led to ever-worsening staff-student ratios. This heralded the 'decline of donnish dominion' (Halsey, 1995: 99-100).

4. There was, nevertheless, a greater 'hands-on' management. No longer were hospital managers simply the adjuncts to the medical profession. Now they had to deliver results. The same was true of the universities. Heads of Department were exhorted to focus their energies on becoming effective middle managers even if this took them away from their academic leadership role, which could be delegated if necessary (Jarratt, 1985: 22 and 28). Lecturers generally were subjected to an array of managerial techniques, including appraisal, responsibility for such matters as the ratcheting up of student recruitment and ensuring a good score in any forthcoming review whether it be of teaching and learning, research or course validation.

5. The results were measured against new standards of performance, indicative of a decline of trust in professional expertise. League tables were used to assess both hospital and university performance, with the media 'naming and shaming' apparently poor performers. With evidence-based measures designed to track the ongoing health of patients and student 'wastage' rates, the pressure on professionals was to perform, not just consistently but increasingly over a wider range of tasks for which they were newly responsible.

6. There was increasing use of 'pre-set output measures' focused on predictability in the running of the new health and higher education organisations. Against the latter-day reliance on professional status, or rank, the emphasis switched to such techniques as performance-related-pay, in order to ensure the smooth running of organisations notable particularly in higher education as the new managers sought to ensure their targets through better organising the work of their junior colleagues.

The outcome, following the introduction of NPM reforms, would thus appear to have been considerable, with health and higher education professionals in Britain subjected to the rigours of the quasi-market and managerial colonisation as outdated bureau-professional regimes became less self-serving and more accountable. While it is clear that these changes have had a major impact on the organisation of hospitals and universities what is less so is the nature of their impact. The internal reconfiguration of relations between specialists and managers may not have been simply one of role reversal (doctors and lecturers now the adjuncts to managers rather than *vice versa* as previously) or role integration (professionals as 'new' managers themselves). The rewritten scripts are more complex as a reading of recent interview research on professionals in health and higher education reveals.

A Reconfiguration of Expertise?

Recent research on professionals in health and higher education makes for interesting reading. It reveals that in some cases they would indulge in nostalgia for a past remembered fondly, as shown in the following extracts. In health:

> You know, when you, you had a hospital administrator… you used to ring up and say 'Look I want to do this', they said 'Yes' or 'No'! Now, it has to go through umpteen committees and reports, and… you've got to have business plans and everything…it just slows everything up!
>
> (Surgeon, 1997).

While in academia:

> The job of a university lecturer is not what it was fifteen years ago…or thirty years ago and we've just got to accept it – it was lovely then, I can't remember it… but it must have been lovely then, it ain't lovely now, it's bloody hard work
>
> (Academic Head, Barry et al, 2001: 93).

Within the new organisational realities, however, doctors, at least, are as actively engaged in the new managerialism as they are its victims, as the following interview extract illustrates:

> The idea was... that one of us should become... chairman [*sic*]... of the group and would be the Clinical Director of Surgical Services... Then it transpired... that the job wasn't anything like... anybody... originally thought it was going to be. So now... I... have been transmuted into their boss...
>
> (Clinical Director, 1995).

Again, in academia, a concern about the possible excesses of managerialism enacted in university life was apparent. But living with the new reality is sometimes found to be uncomfortable:

> The policy has been to 'cut away' resources from higher education so the university ... [is short of funds and I'd hope that it is] ... making sure there is a fair distribution inside the university ... if we are teaching larger groups then everyone else is teaching larger groups – then there is equal misery...
>
> (Academic Head, Barry et al, 2001: 93).

In health, however, the autonomy of the individual directorates is not designed into the management structure but an outcome of its limitations. To quote a clinical director from another hospital:

> I don't [believe] the model of the clinical director... is a very good one... most clinical directors do it by default... Most doctors are not particularly keen on management issues, and certainly have no formal training...
>
> (Clinical Director, 1997).

But one should always be suspicious of accepting such claims at face value. By maintaining some role distance from management issues doctors as well as academics can more easily protect their autonomy, at least for the time being. A medical director illustrates this point when she explains how she carries out her (ambivalent) role:

> The medical director... is supposed to represent the interests of the doctors... not individual doctors... but to put forward the medical side. To give medical information... I mean ... it's difficult – *it isn't in the sense that she represents doctors' interests per se*, but she's supposed to be able to give medical direction, medical input. But obviously in doing that she cannot but represent the medics, the doctors' interests. Although at the end of the day, she's responsible to the Board as a Manager, rather than a doctor representative. So she has to go along with the Board, which may be in conflict with what her colleagues think
>
> (Medical Director, 1995. *Emphases* added).

There were very few occasions when medical and management interests clashed directly, not because they were so similar but because the relationship between medical work and hospital governance was very much one of 'loose-coupling' (Weick, 1976):

> The [Hospital Trust] Board is much more of a rubber stamp than I surmise... the Government wishes it to be. Not to be quoted to the 'Board' this but... it seems... to me however interested those parties are from outside [non-executive directors], they have even less knowledge about medicine than I do about my colleagues work... [T]hey will tend to accept much of what we say... The Board I think [will]... only say 'Stop' if we're going in [an] obviously totally wrong track
>
> (Medical Director, 1995).

Within the university sector, the impact of NPM has been seen by some observers as an undermining of academic autonomy and self-governance to be replaced, it would seem, by the McUniversity (Parker and Jary 1995). Prichard (1996; see also Prichard and Willmott, 1997: 299), for example, found evidence of:

> relations between deans and the senior team... based on aggressive and dictatorial relations overlaid perhaps with a concern for organisation targets, performance levels and efficiency
>
> (Prichard, 1996: 232).

Within medicine, the impact has been rather different, doctors have become used to the managerial discourse. Rather than finding themselves overwhelmed by new managerialism they are finding themselves able to engage actively in the discourse. But, we should not conclude from this that university lecturers differ significantly from health professionals in their adaptation to the NPM. Contrary to what might have been expected, academics on occasion express a preference for management, as reported in Barry et al (2001), at least of the kind that takes due account of their needs, is supportive and encourages collegiality. As one academic manager commented, with unintentional humour:

> I want to live with myself – I will not tread on people, if you have to do certain things to get somewhere I'm not prepared to do that. I have to live with me and more importantly with my wife, who is even more moral than I am
>
> (Academic Head, Barry et al, 2001: 96).

We should also note the comment by Prichard and Willmott that:

> [E]ach university is a mix of organizing practices which are historically located and variably resilient to being wholeheartedly overthrown by the 'new' managers
>
> (Prichard and Willmott, 1997: 299).

Possibly Prichard and Willmott underplay the role of resistance in their research but they do at least point to its possibility, others have taken up the issue in their studies of the impact of managerialism in academe. Goode and Bagilhole (1998), for example, reporting on one pre-1992 university also found evidence of variable reactions to managerialism, represented in the three stances adopted by their Head of Department respondents: *collaboration, transformation* and *resistance*.[3] Collaboration they argue did not mean unconditional support, but it did signify acceptance and some enthusiasm. Transformation by contrast represented 'attempts to play by the new rules at the same time as trying to change them'. Whilst resistance involved:

> holding on to former values and priorities and actively finding ways to 'create spaces' in which some degree of academic autonomy [could] be preserved
>
> (ibid: 154-57).

The passage of the NPM has thus not been as straightforward and untroubled as might have been supposed from a cursory reading of the literature, its transformative power perhaps assumed or overplayed. If encoding of principles and enactment of scripts, in Barley and Tolbert's (1997) sense, took place in establishing a managerial presence, then the conscious revision of scripts led to variable acceptance, in terms both of behaviour and the changing nature of taken-for-granted assumptions. The rewriting of scripts led, according to our evidence, not to a displacement of expertise but to its reconfiguration. Rather than becoming subordinated to the managerial logic of efficiency there is evidence that hospital doctors and university academics are beginning to learn how to manage managerialism.

Concluding Thoughts on Managing Professionals

In this chapter we have examined the role of the New Public Management (NPM) in health and higher education in Britain. In particular we have explored its impact on professionals' autonomy. We have argued, drawing on the notions of governmentality and legitimation, that there are limits to which the NPM can rationalise the work of doctors and academics. It is therefore hardly surprising that both groups have begun to adapt the new managerialist arrangements to their redefined requirements for institutional autonomy and 'loose-coupling'. Issues of accountability and financial constraints are now accepted in principle but the signs are that the professions want to be the main – if not the sole – arbiters of these issues; at least as far as they impinge upon their work situations. It is this process that we have attempted to analyse (at least in a provisional way) in exploring the impact of the NPM. We have done this drawing on the notion of 'scripts' as a means of conceptualising the way in which the new managerialist 'template' has been iteratively encoded, enacted and revised within hospitals and universities.

Academics and hospitals doctors have, in short, begun to learn to live with rather than be subordinated to the new disciplinary regime.

What our evidence suggests, perhaps above all else, is that the revision of 'scripts' will lead in turn to a greater objectification of the new role of medical/academic manager; one that has forced doctors and academics to take account of the resource implications of their decision-making than previously but one that has not, ultimately, meant their (clinical/academic) autonomy being fundamentally questioned. NPM has instead engendered a reconfiguration of professional dominance, not its demise, and this new configuration may mean even greater stratification within professions in Britain than hitherto, but not necessarily so. The varying responses to the NPM by hospital doctors and university lecturers may themselves be refracted by contexts of space and time. In this the different histories and organisational arrangements into which the NPM has been introduced may predispose those working in them to variable settlements, with some hospitals and universities experiencing a greater accommodation of its expert and intellectual labourers to the 'new' managerial demands than others.

Notes

1   The term 'hospital doctor' is used here as it is the usual term within the UK for a hospital clinician, whether surgeon or physician.
2   In respect of the primary research undertaken on health (Dent), we cite interview data drawn from the same research that formed the basis for a recently published case study, Dent (2003a), as well as interviews drawn from a later study carried out in preparation for a comparative study of European hospitals and health professions (Dent 2003b). In respect of higher education (Barry), acknowledgement is made to work undertaken with colleagues from the University of East London, some of which has been published (Clark, Chandler and Barry, 1999; Barry, Chandler and Clark, 2001).
3   The issue of gender cannot go unremarked in all this since Goode and Bagilhole's (1998: 157) respondents who opted for the transformation stance were all women, suggesting that there may be gender-related issues at play here which, although beyond the scope of this paper, may be significant. The interested reader is referred to Clark et al (1999) and Berg et al (2003).

References

Barley, S.R. and Tolbert, S. (1997), 'Institutionalisation and Structuration: Studying the Links Between Action and Institution', *Organization Studies*, 18(1): 93-117.
Barry, J., Chandler, J. and Clark, H. (2001), 'Between the Ivory Tower and the Academic Assembly Line', *Journal of Management Studies*, 38(1): 87-101.
Berg, E., Barry, J. and Chandler, J. (2003), 'Nice Work If You Can Get It?: The Changing Character of Academic Labour in Sweden and England' (2003), *Comportamento Organizacional e Gestão*, 9(2): 19-37.
Burnham, J. (1945), *The Managerial Revolution*, Penguin: Harmondsworth.
Causer, G. and Exworthy, M. (1999), 'Professionals as Managers Across the Public Sector', in M. Exworthy and S. Halford (eds), *Professionals and the New Managerialism in the Public Sector*, Open University Press: Buckingham.

Clark, H., Chandler, J. and Barry, J. (1999), 'Gender and Management in the Organisation of University Life', in P. Fogelberg, J. Hearn, L. Husu and T. Mankkinen (eds), *Hard Work in the Academy*, University of Helsinki Press: Helsinki.

Clarke, J. and Newman, J. (1997), *The Managerial State*, Sage, London.

Dent, M. (1996), *Professions, Information Technology and Management in Hospitals*, Avebury: Aldershot.

Dent, M. (2003a), 'Managing Doctors and Saving a Hospital: Irony, Rhetoric and Actors Networks', *Organization*, 10(1): 107-27.

Dent, M. (2003b), *Remodelling Hospitals and Health Professions in Europe: Medicine, Nursing and the State*, Palgave Macmillan: Basingstoke.

DiMaggio, P. and Powell, W.W. (1983), 'The Iron Cage Revisited: Institutional Isomorphism and Collective Rationality in Organizational Fields', in W. W. Powell and P. J. DiMaggio (eds), *The New Instituionalism in Organizational Analysis*, The University of Chicago Press: Chicago and London.

Dominelli, L. and Hoogvelt, A. (1996), 'Globalisation, the Privatisation of Welfare, and the Changing Role of Professional Academics in Britain', *Critical Perspectives on Accounting*, 7: 191-212.

Exworthy, M. and Halford, S. (eds), (1999), *Professionals and the New Managerialism in the Public Sector*, Open University Press: Buckingham.

Gane, M. and Johnson, T. (eds), (1993), *Foucault's New Domains*, Routledge, London.

Giddens, A. (1984), *The Constitution of Society: Outline of the Theory of Structurations*, Polity: Cambridge.

Goode, J. and Bagilhole, B. (1998), 'Gendering the Management of Change in Higher Education: A Case Study', *Gender, Work and Organization*, 5(3): 148-64.

Halsey, A.H. (1995), *Decline of Donnish Dominion*, Clarendon Press, Oxford.

Harrison, S. (1999), 'Clinical Autonomy and Health Policy: Past and Futures', in M. Exworthy and S. Halford (eds), *Professionals and the New Managerialism in the Public Sector*, Open University Press: Buckingham.

Hood, C. (1991), 'A Public Management for All Seasons?' *Public Administration*, 69: 3-19.

Hood, C. (1995), 'The "New Public Management" in the 1980s: Variations on a Theme', *Accounting, Organizations and Society*, 20(2/3): 93-109.

Hood, C., Scott, C., James, O., Jones, G. and Travers, T. (1999), *Regulation Inside Government: Waste-Watchers, Quality-Police and Sleaze-Busters*, Oxford University Press: Oxford.

Hughes, D. (1996), 'NHS Managers as Rhetoricians: a Case of Culture Management?' *Sociology of Health and Illness*, 18(3): 291-314.

Illich, I. (1977), 'Disabling Professions', in I. Illich, I. K. Zola, J. McKnight, J. Caplan and H. Shaiken (eds), *Disabling Professions*, Marion Boyars: London.

Jarratt Report (1985), *Report of the Steering Committee for Efficiency Studies in Universities*, CVCP.

Johnson, T. (1995), 'Governmentality and the Institutionalisation of Expertise', in T. Johnson, G. Larkin and M. Saks (eds), *Health Professions and the State in Europe*, Routledge, London.

Kirkpatrick, I. and Lucio, M.M. (eds), (1995), *The Politics of Quality in the Public Sector*, Routledge: London.

Kitchener, M. (1998), 'Quasi-Market Transformation: an Institutionalist Approach to Change in UK Hospitals', *Public Administration*, 76 (Spring): 73-95.

Meyer, J.W. and Rowan, B. (1991), 'Institutionalized Organizations: Formal Structure as Myth and Ceremony', in W.W. Powell and P.J. DiMaggio (eds), *The New Institutionalism in Organizational Analysis*, The University of Chicago Press: Chicago and London.

Newman, J. and Clarke, J. (1994), 'Going About Our Business? The Managerialisation of Public Services', in J. Clarke, A. Cochrane and E. McLaughlin (eds), *Managing Social Policy*, Sage: London.

Parker, M. and Jary, D. (1995), 'The McUniversity: Organization, Management and Academic Subjectivity', *Organization*, 2(2): 319-38.

Pollitt, C. (1990), *Managerialism and the Public Services: The Anglo American Experience*, Basil Blackwell: Oxford.

Power, M. (1997), *The Audit Society: Rituals of Verification*, Oxford University Press: Oxford.

Prichard, C. (1996), 'Managing Universities: Is It Men's Work?', in D. Collinson and J. Hearn (eds), *Men as Managers, Managers as Men*, Sage: London.

Prichard, C. and Willmott, H. (1997), 'Just How Managed is the McUniversity?', *Organization Studies*, 18(2): 287-316.

Ranade, W. (1997), *A Future for the NHS? Health Care for the Millennium* (Second Edition), Longman: London.

Strong, P. and Robinson J. (1990), *The NHS – Under New Management*, Open University Press: Milton Keynes.

Trow, M. (1994), 'Managerialism and the Academic Profession: The Case of England', *Higher Education Policy*, 7(2): 11-18.

Weick, K.E. (1976), 'Educational Organizations as Loosely Coupled Systems', *Administrative Science Quarterly*, 21: 1-19.

Wilding, P. (1981), *Socialism and Professionalism*, Fabian Tract 473, London.

PART II

VARIATIONS BETWEEN SECTORS

Chapter 3

Does 'Best Value' Represent Best Value? Local Government Middle Management Perspectives

Linda Keen

Introduction

The various New Public Management (NPM) models which have been adopted (to different degrees) by local authorities within England and Wales since the early 1980s, have all involved the attempted achievement of improved value for money in terms of the three E's: economy, efficiency and effectiveness. Latterly the emphasis has moved more towards the 'effectiveness' end of this spectrum with renewed interest, via, most recently, New Labour's Best Value (BV) policies.

Two broad perspectives can be identified in the BV research (Bartlett et al, 1999; Boyne, 1998; Boyne et al, 1999). It can be argued, on the one hand, that BV appears likely to stimulate the development of innovative, dynamic, consumer- and community-responsive services, empower local authority managers to meet more closely the more clearly identified needs of their local communities, and generally rejuvenate interest in local government. Alternatively, BV can be seen as representing a revised version of the ill-fated corporate planning initiatives of the 1970s (Keenan, 2000), with consequent unproductive increases in bureaucracy arising from the requirements placed on local authorities to meet a plethora of benchmarking and nationally set performance indicators within a context of increasing numbers of central inspection and monitoring agencies.

The Best Value Concept

Best Value formed the key element of the 1997 Labour Government's local government modernisation programme (Martin, 1999). Following the analysis of the results of a BV pilot programme launched in June 1997, immediately after the election, the Local Government Act (1999) imposed on UK local authorities the general duty of BV, to 'secure continuous improvement in the way in which its functions are exercised, having regard to a combination of economy, efficiency and effectiveness' (Local Government Act 1999, paragraph 3(1)). Essentially, BV requires local authorities to maximise the three E's of Economy, Efficiency and Effectiveness in all of their operations by going beyond the former Compulsory Competitive Tendering (CCT) prescriptions in order to review all of their services over five years within the framework of the 4C's: 'Challenging the purpose of its service, Comparing the local authority's performance with other providers, Consulting the community, and looking to Competition' (Institute of Sport and Recreation Management, 1998, p1; Leigh et al, 1999: v).

There is an emphasis on working across traditional service boundaries, across different agencies, working in partnerships with other organisations, including the idea of 'joined-up services' which are organised around users' needs rather than organisational convenience (Local Government Association, 1999). Authorities must publish their review findings and their planned improvements, including measures and targets, in an annual Performance Plan. This local performance planning takes place within a framework of comparison of each authority's achievements with those of the top 25 per cent of local authorities against national performance indicators concerned with quality, cost and efficiency. The Audit Commission BV Inspectorate publish reports showing how council services compare with those of other local authorities, including the inspector's answers to two overall questions: 'how good are the services? And will they improve in the way BV requires?' (Pike, 2000).

In terms of accountability (see Ferlie et al's [1996] model), the key elements of improvement sought within the BV context appear to centre around the improvement and amendment of accountability as an analytical framework: *accountability upwards* (to elected members in the local government context in the traditional participatory democracy model, and/or, ultimately, to ministers and Parliament); *accountability downwards* (mainly through various forms of consultation and participatory democracy); and *market-based forms of accountability* (market testing local authority forms of direct service provision against external providers). The primary mechanism for achieving these changes is focused around the identification of performance objectives to assess current performance and set targets for improvements - essentially to assess the extent to which a local authority's BV initiatives are maximising best value (Boyne, 1999). The *accountability upwards* model reflects a 'top down' policy-making process, which does not actively promote the active participation of users or consumers in decision-making. The levels of empowerment and effective citizenship participation advocated by BV require a 'bottom-up' policy (Prior et al, 1994, where users and the community have far more direct involvement in and influence over the design, delivery and review of local services within the performance management framework. This reflects the *downward accountability* model, which includes participatory democracy and consumerism. This new emphasis on local accountability involves: 'consultation with local people which is inclusive and systematic; services focused on, and involving, service users; transparency in decision-making; reporting back through the local performance plan; local solutions to suit local circumstance; published service standards and corporate objectives' (Local Government Association, 1998a: 4). But BV also clearly strengthens local authority *upward accountability* to central government, within a new framework of national performance indicators and standards, together with the creation of a new BV inspectorate within the Audit Commission, and an Inspectorate Forum to discuss common interests. The *market-based forms of accountability* model stresses the 'empowerment of users as customers... Central to this model has been an attempt to shift power from producers to consumers, by breaking up monopoly providers, or, where this has not been possible, to bring in new forms of regulation such as the setting of service standards...' (Ferlie et al, 1996: 211). Clearly, as mentioned above, the BV approach stresses the importance of direct accountability to 'customers' through the formal performance planning and monitoring requirements, and the continuing use of 'competition' as an 'essential management tool' (Local Government Association, 1999).

The Case Study Research

The case study authority was a Shire District Council in the South East of England covering a mixed urban and rural area, with a population of about 120,000, and employing about 600 staff. The authority was 'hung' with no party in overall control, and a new Chief Executive had recently been appointed. A bid had been made to become one of Labour's 'pilot' local authorities for testing out the government's BV ideas; although the bid was unsuccessful, the authority had nevertheless been strongly committed to the BV idea by the elected members and the senior management team who were already introducing some of the initiatives represented in the Local Government Bill then passing though Parliament. The study is clearly not statistically representative; it is intended to do no more than generate some initial insights into the early impact of 'New Labour's BV policies on a fairly typical 'middle England' local authority.

Semi-structured interviews were held in late 1998/early 1999 with a small sample of middle line managers employed within four different departments, providing both direct and support services, and including both purchaser and provider functions (Finance, Housing, Leisure and Planning). Particularly under the more devolved and decentralised management forms associated with the new public management models, middle managers – identified here as those managers located between first-line managers/supervisors or senior professionals/professional section leaders and more senior managers (Dopson and Stewart, 1990) - occupy a key role in implementing changes in service design and delivery provision (Keen and Scase, 1998). They are, therefore, in a good position to report on the extent to which the BV systems are achieving the desired best value results in terms of more efficient, effective and responsive service provision.

BV: Does it Represent Best Value-for-Money?

The success of the BV approach, in terms of achieving the government's overall objective of achieving more effective and responsive services, can clearly only be evaluated in the longer term. However, a number of case studies and reports have been produced to date which, together with the substantial body of earlier research evaluating the effects of the various 'New Public Management' models, are used here to structure the analysis of the respondents'' views about the general costs and benefits of the new BV accountability systems. (for example, Boyne, 1998, 1999, Vincent-Jones, 1999; Boyne et al, 1999; Wilson, 1999; Martin, 1999; James and Field, 1999; Bartlett et al, 1999; Cirell and Bennet, 1999a, 1999b). Much of the literature focuses on the contradictions which appear to be manifested within the BV philosophy and process between the increased bureaucratisation via the new performance planning and management systems, and the requirements to develop service innovations, which will transform council/community relations and usher in a new era of dynamic, inventive and responsive local government. Thus, Bartlett et al identify two possible scenarios:

> One possible fate is that BV will be a victim of its own success. A new relationship with service users will be created. Strategic decision-making capacities will be enhanced to the extent at which they will be hampered by the centrally imposed review criteria. The second possible fate is that BV will become the new local government industry. Every local authority will have completed, say, eight reviews in year one, and the real cost of the process will be realized with little evidence of real improvements
>
> (Bartlett et al, 1999: 117).

Similarly, in the context of welcoming the introduction of BV on 1 April 2000, Pike (2000: 16) comments: '[t]he words "bureaucracy" and "innovation" are rarely spoken in the same breath, but from this week the government is hoping to change this…'.

The extension of downward local accountability takes place within a potentially conflicting context of considerably strengthened upwards accountability to various central government agencies. Whilst market forms of accountability continue to generate the problems of split accountabilities identified by a number of authors (Walsh 1995; Stewart, 1993, 1996; Keen, 1997; Keen and Scase, 1998) - between the client or commissioning side (responsible for setting service specifications and targets and monitoring performance) and the Contractor or Provider side (responsible for service delivery against the targets) - particularly for professional services. However, the new BV emphasis on 'Partnership' suggests the possibility of achieving more innovative and less confrontational inter-organisational relationships, which:

may be contractually based, but the nature of the relationship should be trustful, co-operative and long term rather than distrustful, adversarial and short term....increased emphasis is likely to be placed on collaboration

(Wilson, 1999: 50).

Accompanying concerns focus increasingly around the costs of the BV (and other public sector) inspection and regulatory bodies and procedures (Timmins, 1997, 1999; Boyne, 2000). The costs of compliance with the new inspection systems and the Audit Report requirements were estimated originally to be around an extra £50 million per year 'which should be covered by the expected 2 per cent efficiency savings' (Local Government Association, 1999). In general, apart from the BV regulation, 'the rate of growth in regulator organisations (for the public sector) and the direct and indirect costs of regulation have accelerated markedly since Labour took office' (Timmins, 1999: 15). The respondents' views about the relative effectiveness and value-for-money (VFM) of the key BV elements are presented below in Table 3.1, categorised according to those who (a) considered that, overall, the new BV systems represented good VFM (b) thought it represented poor VFM (c) were uncertain.

Table 3.1 Overall, Does Best Value Represent Good Value For Money (VFM)?

Numbers of respondents within each response category:

	(a) Poor VFM	(b) Good VFM	(c) Uncertain
Departments:			
Finance (N=4)	2	2	-
Leisure (N=4)	-	2	2
Housing (N=4)	1	2	1
Planning (N=4)	2	-	2
Totals (N=16)	5	6	5

Source: Author

As the table shows, the respondents' views differed widely, with some interesting departmental differences. About a third considered that real benefits were being realised from the BV approach - through being much more rigorously and transparently accountable, and being able to tailor services more specifically (and hence more efficiently and effectively) towards more informed service users and the local community. About a third thought that the changes represented poor VFM in terms of the costs, such as officers' time, money and other resources, and in terms of inappropriate system design and implementation which meant that the benefits potentially available from the new systems were only very partially realised. About a third was uncertain, mainly on the grounds that the new systems were in their infancy, with some aspects not yet completed, and that it was simply too early to say whether or not, in the longer term, they would represent good or bad VFM.

'Good VFM' Responses

The respondents in this category focused strongly on identifying the extensive improvements and innovations in service planning and delivery, which, in line with central government expectations, were emerging from the BV systems. New performance management systems emphasised *'downwards accountability'* consultation with local users/community groups and clear service objectives and measures. They encouraged service planners and deliverers to 'focus on what we should be doing', to ask themselves, 'do we want to do this; do we need to; we don't have to'; such comments clearly equated to the first of the '4C's, 'Challenge purpose'. As a Finance manager commented:

> It makes everybody think about what we're doing. An example of that would be, we've got discretionary charitable rate relief, and we're looking at that at the moment. A report went forward - 'this is our approach but it's generous in comparison to other authorities. We don't have to give all this money away. Do you still want to?' So they set up a group and have been looking at it quite closely, and changing their attitudes...

Similar emphasis was placed on the importance of the third 'C', 'Consult Community', with several respondents stressing the importance of 'knowing what people want':

> I think it (BV) does represent good value for money because I don't think you can establish that you are providing good value for money unless you know that you're providing the sorts of things that people want. And the only way you can find out what people want is first of all to ask them. And then to give information back about what's been achieved... if you don't do these things, I don't think you could demonstrate that you're providing value-for-money. And BV makes you do it
>
> (Housing Manager).

They stressed the advantages of gaining valuable first-hand information about areas of weakness, which required improvement. More specific service objectives enabled more transparent decision-making processes, which clarified service levels and content for consumers, who consequently had more realistic expectations about the Council's role and function. A housing manager (the department had recently won a charter-mark award for its housing consultation and involvement strategies) pointed out some tangible benefits from such approaches:

there have been lots of mistakes made in social housing in the past where decisions are made by professional officers and members and not by the community generally. And then things go wrong. Estates go wrong. Design doesn't work. Lettings policies which concentrate people with the most difficult circumstances in particular geographical locations. Now, it's all about community involvement and empowering the community... it all takes a lot of time, to actually get tenants to be involved in a participative way, you have to put a lot of resources in. But in the end it's worth it - you get better decisions that benefit the whole community, that benefit everyone...

Two respondents also commented on the increased levels of 'upwards accountability' to local Councillors arising from the formal planning system, and the way in which increased knowledge about individual wards and community needs could enhance Councillors' relationships with their constituents, and reinvigorate their role - both in terms of their participation in the formal planning process and their 'casework' with individual electors.

Nearly half also focused on the BV approach in that accountability was seen as more than simply giving an account of one's activities; it was necessary to demonstrate clearly that one had made the best possible use of resources in the sense of meeting local needs as precisely as possible:

> ... probably the best example is the parable from the New Testament where the sons were given treasure and there was the one who put it in the ground who said 'Here it is. Here's what you gave me'. He hadn't stolen it but he hadn't made best use of it. And probably that's the best illustration of it. We are given resource to make the best use of, not to say 'I haven't stolen them, but I've not done anything with them'
>
> (Finance Manager).

As this, and other similar comments showed, these officers' ideas about accountability had clearly gone beyond the idea of simply showing that they had not 'broken the rules' to embrace the requirement that they should optimise, rather than 'satisfice', the output from their available resources to achieve maximum effectiveness - or BV. The differences between the four departments are also interesting It can be speculated that the BV requirements were impacting at the time more strongly on Finance officers, who were currently involved in CCT operations for some finance services as required by the legislation, and on Planning Officers who were involved for the first time ever in drawing up service plans in accordance with the BV initiative. Their counterparts in Housing and Leisure had operated for some time on a Commissioner/Client split, with formalised service specifications and monitoring systems, and were more accustomed to working within at least some of the elements of the BV approach.

Comments tended to be less effusive about the beneficial impact of the other 2 'C's - 'compare performance' and 'compete with others', but, again, departmental differences were important. Thus, two Leisure managers indicated that, perhaps because they had had some several years to get used to operating within the CCT system, they were beginning to move in the direction of the 'partnership approach' advocated by the government. They felt they had more opportunities for flexibility and service innovation within the contract specifications (mostly as a consequence of the clearer client side expectations and targets within the new performance management framework). Preset targets about relatively straightforward matters such as water quality appeared to free them to concentrate on more strategic service planning and innovations issues. But it was clear that a difference in primary orientation between the client and the contractor remained:

> We try to steer a middle course. As it (the Centre) is run as a contract, we have financial objectives - we want to manage the tender successfully and stay *in situ*... there is a lot of flexibility within the specification which would allow us to operate more lucrative activities - like monster work-outs with 60 or 70 customers as opposed to 5 badminton courts with up to 4 customer per court. But we don't want to upset the apple cart - we don't want a situation where we make more money but where the badminton customers would start complaining to us, the councillors, the Client... So we compromise
>
> (Leisure Manager).

These two managers also highlighted the development of more informal and collaborative 'partnership' relationships based on trust between the two sides. Some managers also welcomed the move away from CCT represented by the BV programme, which gave them the framework to prove that they provided 'good value':

> I think the Best Value *is* good value for money, it's taken away the crude threat of CCT for all services - it would never really have worked for planning... it takes that away, or it gives you two sides of the coin: one, that you can prove that you are - that you are good value rather than always having to compare yourself to the private sector...
>
> (Planning Manager).

However, even though they were generally positive about most of the BV initiatives, Finance managers were particularly resentful of the way in which, despite the advent of BV, they were still required to go through the CCT process for certain financial services, making the negative points represented in many academic evaluations of the application of CCT to non-manual service about the cost of the contractual bureaucracy. These and other negative points about BV's VFM are discussed further below.

'Poor VFM' Responses

Comments here can be categorised into (a) technical difficulties with various BV processes, including CCT (b) the undesirable extent of central government control, and (c) lack of analysis of the cost, including the opportunity cost, of the BV initiatives. As noted above, the respondents highlighted a number of (mainly) technical operating difficulties, which have been well reported in the literature on performance management and market systems in the public sector (for example, Walsh, 1995; Keen and Scase, 1998; Rouse, 1999). Thus, in relation to performance measures, they commented adversely on the excessive quantity and detail, and on the unproductive emphasis on process rather than outcome, on the quantitative at the expense of the qualitative.

> for example, we measure how quickly we can turn round correspondence, how quickly we register applications, how long it takes to determine them, how many applications as a percentage we seek improvements on, the number of phone calls we get, the number of letters coming in... we measure everything now - its unbelievable the amount of detail... you can measure how much a process costs compared with other people, although that's fraught with difficulty - but how do you actually measure whether the quality of the decisions is any good or no? Policy successes appeared on one we've got but it's very difficult...
>
> (Planning Manager).

One officer coined the term 'paralysis through analysis' to describe his frustration about the repeated incidences of such information gathering exercises without a corresponding emphasis on acting on the results. For example:

> the trouble with us over the last four years, we've been haunted by a series of these reviews, four audit reviews in the last six years....We're always being asked the question of what we're doing and how we're doing it rather than moving on to how you *do* improve it and then putting those improvements into practice. That's still to come...
>
> (Planning Manager).

Respondents also focused on the undesirable extent to which these measures were imposed by various central agencies such as the Audit Commission, CIPFA etc, and most respondents (across all three response categories) criticised the continuing, and undesirably high, levels of central government regulation over revenue raising, spending and service design. This was seen as conflicting directly with the key themes of BV - the importance of local service indicators for services, which were particularly appropriate for particular local needs - and thus directly diminishing the VFM of such exercises; such centralisation could also damage the morale and self-respect of the managers. As a Finance Manager pointed out:

The sad thing is that there is so much central government control, and it makes a nonsense of the thing about servicing the *local* community…it's good that we have some national standards to compare ourselves against but there should be much more local decisions. What people want here in Barset is different from, what, an inner city borough, and we should have the freedom to decide, and we haven't, there's still rate-capping… I don't mind, even, if someone gives me the targets and sets a cash limit, if they would only give me the credit for having enough nous to go and do it in the most efficient way - don't tell me how, let *me* be efficient please.

An allied point here was made about the perceived pointlessness of spending resources on identifying local need and wants without the corresponding powers to raise and spend money accordingly, free from central government 'capping' and other financial controls. About half of the respondents identified freedom from central government spending constraints as representing the most effective way of improving local accountability, and optimising BV. Putting all these points together, one Housing Manager commented succinctly on the poor VFM of:

spending money to find out what we already know about what customers want and then not being able to provide it because we don't have enough resources.

Several managers raised the question of the cost, in terms of resources, time, and money, of implementing these BV initiatives, querying whether anyone had actually 'done the sums'. They reflected concerns currently being expressed about the cost of both the national regulatory and inspection bodies, and the compliance cost to the local authorities of implementing and monitoring government directives. As one manager emphasised:

The problem with it all is, I think, the work that's entailed in actually doing the service plans, the service review and saying these are our performance indicators, is incredibly time-consuming. It takes a lot of time which means you can't get on with doing the important things, like actually delivering the service… the Service Manager doesn't deal with the big planning applications at all now, he spends all his time on writing a service plan, reviewing a service plan…

(Planning Manager).

As noted earlier, Finance and some Leisure managers were particularly critical of CCT methods of service delivery, focusing on the concerns expressed in the literature about unproductive 'contract bureaucracy', the cross-boundary tendering regulations which restricted the local authority 'contracting side' from competing freely on the open market, the inevitable conflicts between the client and contractor in terms of service provision because of their different orientations and roles, which prevented the more productive and trust-orientated 'partnership' relationships advocated by the government. One Leisure Centre Manager identified clearly an example of such a conflict between business (the contractor) and community (the local authority client) orientations:

> ...the client - he oversees the bowling centre as well, and they and other people would like to use this facility as a means of communicating their activity to the public, and that's what we should be doing, I suppose, from a social point of view... But we have a policy of not putting up anything for any other body because we have enough of our own publicity and it could confuse customers, and in any case, from a business point of view, why sell other people's activities? Instead of going swimming, they might go bowling instead!

The responses of those managers who were unsure about the VFM basis of the BV accountability initiatives tended to centre around the need for more time before making a firm judgement. They alluded to several of the points made by the managers in the first two categories, and focused on the possibilities of alleviating the problems and building on the strengths of the authority's BV developments to date.

Conclusions

The survey results suggest that the BV programme in the case study organisation was only partially realising the potential benefits available from BV approaches to service planning and delivery - of being able to tailor services more specifically (and hence more efficiently and effectively) to the more clearly identified needs and wants of service users and the local community (it is, however, important to note that change management programmes take time to yield good results; work had only just begun on the BV systems at this time.).

The problems experienced by the managers ranged from technical change management problems, found within any service sector, to those peculiar to the public sector (Keen and Scase, 1998). The latter concerned the essentially political and value-based nature of the ultimate outcomes of local authority activities, which make performance measurement in the public sector particularly difficult, in contrast to the relatively straight forward bottom-line profitability and other financial targets associated with private sector organisations (Stewart, 1993; Rouse, 1999). These peculiarly 'public sector' problems also included the complex issue of 'coercive autonomy' (Smith, 1990) - both within the authority in terms of limits set by elected member policies on managers' freedom to respond innovatively to user demands, and externally in relation to the paradoxical co-existence of BV requirements for *local* service planning and delivery alongside the ever more stringent *national* criteria for assessing BV progress within each local authority (Bartlett et al, 1999).

About half of the respondents identified freedom from central government regulatory and spending constraints as representing the most effective way of maximising BV, especially in relation to responsiveness to local consumer and community needs. Bartlett et al's (1999) possible scenario that BV could simply become a mechanical local government 'industry' did not appear, as yet, to be manifested within this authority; most managers seemed to be genuinely interested in fulfilling the spirit, rather than just the letter, of the BV requirements. But the managers' comments about the excessive amount of detail and repetition, and the associated diversion of time and money from direct service provision, sound warning bells reminiscent of the problems experienced with the old-style corporate planning systems of the 1970s, especially when, as one manager pointed out, contemporary IT systems enable the relatively easy collection of more data than ever before.

The apparent contradiction between the words 'bureaucracy' and 'innovation' (Pike, 2000: 16) was not alluded to by the managers, who acknowledged the need for formalised performance management systems to ensure effective and properly focused service delivery innovations which were focused on meeting real needs on a fair and equitable basis. On the other hand they deplored the lack of resources available, and echoed the concerns voiced increasingly in recent studies about the costs of the compliance with the new BV (and other public sector) inspection and regulatory bodies and procedures (Boyne, 2000) - especially the opportunity costs of time diverted from direct service provision activities. Recent research suggest similar conclusions:

> BV has had a positive impact on service quality and accountability but little effect on service costs and efficiency...the process is resource intensive in terms of staff time and service costs...improvements...dependent on receiving addition al financial resources to implement change
>
> (Boyne et al, 2001: 65).

Importantly, the research indicated significant and interesting differences between the views of respondents from different departments, and from different sides of the client/contractor relationship, reflecting the highly diversified nature of local authorities (Stewart, 1992; Keen and Scase, 1998). Thus, in relation to client and contractor roles, those managers occupying the client role (with greater job security and status) tended to be less critical of market forms of service delivery than the contractors, who occupied a slightly marginalised and less advantageous position. Similarly, some departments' activities lend themselves more easily to formalised performance planning and review systems than others, particularly in relation to setting ultimate performance outcomes as opposed to process measures. Basically, it is easier to set operational and strategic objectives and assess performance in a leisure centre that it is within a town-planning department. For maximum BV effectiveness, it can be argued that a significant degree of discretion or local autonomy is required - not just for individual local authorities but for departments as well.

References

Bartlett, D., Corrigan, P., Dibben, P., Franklin, S., Joyce, P., McNulty, T. and Rose, A. (1999), 'Preparing for Best Value', *Local Government Studies*, 25: 102-18.

Boyne, G. (1998), 'Public Services under New Labour: Back to Bureaucracy?', *Public Money and Management*, July-September: 43-50.

Boyne, G. (1999), 'Introduction: Processes, Performance and Best Value in Local Government', *Local Government Studies*, 25(2): 1-15.

Boyne, G. (2000), 'External Regulation and Best Value in Local Government', *Public Money and Management*, July-September: 7-12.

Boyne, G., Gould-Williams, J., Law, J. and Walker, R. (1999), 'Best Value in Welsh Local Government', *Local Government Studies*, 25: 68-86.

Boyne, G., Gould-Williams, J., Law, J. and Walker, R. (2001), 'The Impact of Best Value on Local Authority Performance: Evidence from the Welsh Pilots', *Local Government Studies*, 27(2): 44-68.

Cirell, S. and Bennet, J. (1999a), 'Best Value in Transition: Abolition and Adapting in an Altered Authority', *Municipal Journal*, 30 April: 16-18.

Cirell, S. and Bennet, J. (1999b), 'Best Value in Transition: Clarifying Contracts', *Municipal Journal*, 24 June: 13-15.

Dopson, S. and Stewart, R. (1990), 'What is Happening to Middle Management', *British Journal of Management*, 1: 3-16.

Ferlie, E., Pettigrew, A, Ashborne, L. and Fitzgerald, L. (1996), *The New Public Management in Action*, Oxford University: Oxford.

Institute of Sport and Recreation Management (1998), *Best Value Series – Issue 2: The Impact of Best Value*, Institute of Sport and Recreation Management: Melton Mowbray.

James, D.B. and Field, J. (1999), 'A Whole-Authority Approach to Testing and Developing Best Value', *Local Government Studies*, 25 120-38.

Keen, L. (1997), 'Markets, Quasi-Markets and Middle Managers in Local Government', *Public Policy and Administration*, 12(3): 42-58.

Keen, L. and Scase, R. (1998), *Public Sector Management: The Rhetoric and Reality of Change*, Open University Press: Buckingham.

Keenan, J. (2000), 'Just How New is Best Value?' *Public Money and Management*, July – September: 45-51.

Leigh, A., Mundy, G. and Tuffin, R. (1999), Best Value Policing: Making Preparations, *Police Research Series*, Paper 116, Home Office: London.

Local Government Association (1998a), *Best Value: An Introductory Guide*, Local Government Association: London.

Local Government Association (1999), *Circular 130/99*, London: Local Government Association.

Martin, S. (1999), 'Picking winners or Piloting Best Value? An Analysis of English Best Value bids', *Local Government Studies*, 25: 53-67.

Pike, A. (2000), 'Rewriting the Rule Book', *Financial Times*, 5 April: 16.

Pike, A. and Timmins, N. (2000), 'Local Emphasis Will Soon Be Talk of the Town Halls', *Financial Times*, 21 June: 9.

Prior, D., Stewart, J. and Walsh, K. (1994), *Citizenship: Rights, Community and Participation*, Pitman: London.

Rouse, J. (1999), 'Performance Management, Quality Management and Contracts', in S. Horton and D. Farnham (eds), *Public Management in Britain*, Macmillan: London.

Simon, H.A., Smithburg, D.W. and Thompson, V.A. (1950), *Public Administration*, Alfred A. Korpf New York.

Smith, V. (1990), *Managing in the Corporate Interest*, University of California Press: California.

Stewart, J. (1992), *Managing Difference: The Analysis of Service Characteristics*, Local Government Management Board: London.

Stewart, J. (1993), 'The Limitations of Government by Contract', *Public Money and Management*, July/September: 1-6.

Stewart, J. (1996), 'A Dogma of Our Times – The Separation of Policy-making and Implementation', *Public Money and Management*, July-September: 33-40.

Timmins, N. (1997), 'Who's Watching the Watchdogs?', *Financial Times*, 25 September 12.

Timmins, N. (1999), 'Another Inspector Calls', *Financial Times*, 12 August: 15.

Vincent-Jones (1999), 'Competition and Contracting in the Transition From CCT to Best Value: Towards a More Reflexive Regulation', *Public Administration*, 77(2): 273-91.

Walsh, K. (1995), *Public Services and Market Mechanisms*, Macmillan: London.

Wilson, D. (1999), 'From CCT to Best Value: Some Evidence and Observations', *Local Government Studies*, 25: 38-52.

Wilson, D. and C. Game (1998), *Local Government in the United Kingdom* (2nd edition), Macmillan: London.

Chapter 4

What Do We Want From Social Care Managers? Aspirations and Realities

Jeanette Henderson and Janet Seden

Introduction

The practice of management in social care and the contexts in which managers operate have been the focus of much recent interest. Standards are being developed for managers in particular settings (such as residential care homes), and training for managers in registration and inspection services is a current government pre-occupation. The papers *Modernising Health and Social Services: developing the workforce (Department of Health, 1999a)* and *Modernising Health and Social Services: national priorities guidance* (Department of Health, 1999b) require investment in training, especially for managers to implement the related Quality Protects Programme. As a result of these and other initiatives, the role of the first line manager is being scrutinised. At the same time the role is changing rapidly as managers seek to find ways of responding to a spate of new policy agendas. For example, as social work mental health teams join with colleagues from health to form new multi- and inter-disciplinary teams, professional alliances and identities are being questioned. In children's services, managers are seeking to respond creatively to improve services for looked after children and those in the community. Such creativity requires changes to structures, networks and ways of practising. Writing in *Community Care* recently, Frances Rickford (2000) suggests that managers are 'first in line for blame...but not always first in line for training' and as one of our interviewees remarked managers have 'responsibility without power. There is a growing realisation that effective services require managers to be better at what they do and better equipped to do it. Many first line managers have no management training, and it can also be argued that some management training that is available does not equip them for the challenges of delivering social care in current contexts.

> The transition from practitioner to frontline manager is probably the most difficult career transition in social services – people struggle with how to do the job and we would strongly argue for formal pathways
>
> (Kearney, 1999).

However, a manager with a social work *and* management qualification commented that 'no training or qualification could have prepared me for the management role I undertook.' In the research upon which this chapter is based we set out to identify the day-to-day challenges managers – and to some extent their organisations and agencies – face under the constant pressure to deliver services according to standards and frameworks developed by central government. We were particularly interested to find out whether social care qualifications or management qualifications were seen as most important for employers, and whether expectations and qualifications addressed or compounded the dilemmas that individual managers encounter. There is little in the way of management training in the DipSW, a small amount in community work education and none in nursing training. Management qualifications seek to apply traditional management models to social care settings. This misses the complexity of managing in social care. A discourse of customer care, for example, does not fit easily with service users who are being compelled to receive services in child protection or mental health.

We present two strands of our research in this chapter. Firstly, we obtained the particulars of forty posts from advertisements, reflecting a wide range of social care settings. From these and government papers we constructed our understanding of expectations. We argue that what employers want from managers, is that they manage the dilemmas, constraints and challenges which face them, with limited opportunity to become the well-qualified, professionally developed people aspired to in job descriptions and person specifications. In other words, they may be nicely set up for blame and certainly are operating in a situation of meeting conflicting requirements with little opportunity for the professional development of themselves or others. Having thus set the context for managing in the second part of the chapter we compare these aspirations with the realities for first line managers. To make this comparison we discuss the results of a series of individual and group interviews undertaken between October 1999 and June 2000 with managers, practitioners and users of services to consider the tasks and roles of first line managers. A diverse group of individuals representing a large range of voluntary private and local authority settings were invited to contribute their views. The questions to which all participants were invited to respond were about the lived realities, roles and responsibilities, experiences and dilemmas, and training/training needs of managers. Becoming a manager is a steep learning curve:

> the transition to management was de-skilling in the sense that I came to a new unit ... I needed to build up networks, but was seen as the manager, who is the ultimate boss, and yet I felt completely out of my depth when the staff were talking about a family or child who they knew well, but where I couldn't even picture them in my head. You are supposed to be organising the whole unit, but you don't yet know about your staff's skills, abilities, histories or strengths and that's hard
>
> (First Line Manager).

This chapter sets out our developing ideas about the links and tensions between the operational, strategic and professional components we have regularly heard managers talk about.

Great Expectations: A Survey of Forty Job Descriptions and Person Specifications for First Line Management Posts

Over two months in late 1999 we obtained details of forty jobs. These were selected to represent the diversity of first line management posts in social care and were in the salary range of £12-30K. They included fourteen local authority fieldwork management positions; four voluntary fieldwork management posts; seven social care managers for projects in local authorities; four local authority residential care management posts; seven voluntary sector residential care management appointments and four social care management posts based in NHS trusts. The data gathered enabled the formation of our preliminary ideas about what employers were expecting from a range of managers in a variety of levels of post and settings, and informed the structure of our subsequent fieldwork.

The information from the application packs was organised under the following headings: job title; to whom accountable; aims and purposes of the post; qualifications (essential/desirable); experience (essential/desirable); main duties and responsibilities; attributes/abilities/knowledge (essential/desirable); salary and other. All the job application forms fitted into this kind of framework although some were much less clear than this, jumbling attributes, knowledge and qualifications in longish lists under person specification. What emerged was a complex picture, in which five kinds of requirement seemed to predominate. Managers were expected to:

1. *Operate in the space between more senior managers and a range of other practitioners*: all the employers expected the manager to be accountable to a more senior manager and also supervise the work of other staff. This dual accountability, a bridging of diverse interests, emerged as a key function and dilemma for managers in a range of social care settings. This is especially the case in multi-disciplinary settings where a manager may not manage all members of her team.

2. *Possess varied kinds of specific professional qualifications and experience:* only three of the posts did not require the potential candidate to have a social care qualification. These three (all voluntary sector) asked for a good general education or relevant degree. The other 37 wanted a qualification relevant to the service user group and the agency function. Essential qualifications included CSS, DipSW, CQSW, NVQ3-5; 'relevant social care qualification'; nursing; occupational therapy. Desirable qualifications named were PQ (2), Practice Teacher Award (3) and NVQ assessor (2). The importance of NVQs were also highlighted in our interviews where one middle manager noted:

Managers should also be involved in staff development – especially in relation to competency-based training. A lot of manager's posts – if not now but in the future – will require D32 and D33 assessor qualifications. There's a role for [managers] in monitoring and measuring quality standards, national standards as well.

3. *To fulfil a wide range of duties and responsibilities within strategic, operational and professional dimensions including across agency boundaries*: the lists of main duties and responsibilities were detailed and long. For example, a post of residential care manager listed twenty-eight key tasks, and a post of fieldwork manager listed twenty-four. It was of note that the more operational the post, on the whole, the longer the list. The numbers of requirements also appeared to be in inverse ratio to salary.

4. *To have a multiplicity of skills, abilities and knowledge and attributes*: these were usually linked to the client group and the main roles and tasks of the job (for example, skills and abilities in communication; recording; counselling; or IT). Knowledge expectations were closely related to the client group and role (for example, knowledge of transition for a care home manager; child care knowledge for children's settings; housing law for a housing project; knowledge of equal opportunities policies for local authorities). Attributes encompassed a diverse set of requirements, but often included attitudes and values, as well as skills.

5. *To have certain kinds of personal qualities*: here, lists of requirements usually included traits such as commitment, flexibility, and the willingness to work in own time. Occasionally there are curious and hopeful expectations that the applicant will show that they are a 'can do person' and have 'creativity' or 'passion'.

When asking for *qualifications*, employers mostly sought professional and task related qualifications. There was little evidence of employers prioritising management expertise rather than professionally defined skills, abilities and experience. To manage in social care, applicants need above all to have demonstrated they are able to do the job. In this sample of forty only three posts required a management qualification as essential, although ten listed it as desirable. Five post specifications listed a willingness on the part of the applicant to undertake management training as essential and four specified a willingness to undertake management training as desirable. More important was proven *experience* of managing. Experience was essential for 22 posts, ranging from 1 year (3), 2 years (4), 3 years (3), 5 years (4) to unspecified amounts of time (8). Four other posts listed experience as desirable. This range largely reflected the seniority of the management position advertised (the more senior the post, the more experience requested). It also demonstrated the reality of employer expectations and their knowledge that few candidates with professional *and* management qualifications would be forthcoming from the bank of people who have 'acted up', deputised or gained hands-on management experience and who might well be looking for management posts. There is a recognition that in-service training will need to be provided. This also confirmed the evidence of our consultation with practitioners that they became managers 'in service', often being promoted from an existing practitioner post. Some then enrolled on management diplomas and certificates to remedy what they quickly found was a deficit in their professional training, some had in-service training but for many it was a 'sink or swim' scenario.

When it comes to delineating main tasks and responsibilities, the picture changes. Professional qualifications based on team function and lists of professional competencies fill the abilities, aptitudes, skills and knowledge lists of requirements and desirable elements for posts. When it comes to the main tasks and responsibilities listed for candidates to fulfil if appointed, however, there is a bias towards management skill, with strategic, operational and professional dimensions, which usually include an element of work with other agencies. The list below is a typical of the kinds of main duties and responsibilities listed:

- effective liaison with other agencies
- supervising and supporting staff
- maintaining records
- writing reports to senior management
- promoting the agency externally
- managing the budget and other resources
- implementing policies as directed by senior managers
- monitoring the implementation of equal opportunities policies
- providing information
- responsibility for evaluating practice
- promoting consumer involvement
- responsible for recruitment, induction, appraisal
- supervise staff and carry out disciplinary procedures where necessary
- institute policy reviews
- manage change
- prioritise and allocate the team's work
- implement health and safety legislation
- know the work of other agencies and develop partnerships
- monitor service level agreements
- provide strategic direction to the team

For most posts the list of main roles and responsibilities was even longer and more detailed and extensive than the above example suggests. The language of the activities wanted is extensive. What employers want first line social care managers to do is to access, account, act, adhere to policies, analyse, arrange, assess, assist, advise, budget, chair meetings, coach, commit, communicate, consult, contribute, co-ordinate, delegate, decide, deliver, demonstrate, deploy, deputise, develop, discipline, ensure, establish, evaluate, facilitate, gather, grasp, identify, induct, influence, initiate, instigate, integrate, join-up, lead, liase, maintain, monitor, motivate, negotiate, network, organise, oversee, participate, plan, prepare, present, prioritise, produce, promote, purchase, provide, pro-act, provide, record, recruit, resolve, be responsible, review, supervise, support, teach, think, train, undertake training, work, and write. So, it can be argued from these examples, that when employers write job and person specifications and advertise to recruit a social care manager, they are not sure that potential candidates will have management qualifications and training. They are also uncertain as to whether this can be undertaken while 'on the job'. In terms of doing the job of manager, however, employers do know that what they want is a person with a wide range of professional competence, and skills to undertake the complex and multi-faceted roles and responsibilities of managing. Thus they cite practice abilities, skills, knowledge and attributes and then add a set of management roles and responsibilities. Managers are employed to be:

> *operational*: 'to ensure that the care services are effectively managed and adhere to departmental objectives to resolve operational problems'
> *strategic*:   'to develop strategies, systems and procedures to meet the overall objectives'
> *professional*: 'take responsibility for managing all domestic and ancillary staff which includes their induction, supervision, training and development and appraisal. Ensuring staff are empowered, consulted and involved in decision-making and effective supportive, corrective or disciplinary action is taken'…
> 'implement anti-racist and ethnically sensitive services in accordance with legislation and council policy'

Hard Times: First Line Manager Group and Individual Interviews

We chose to look at the lived reality of managers from three different, but interrelated viewpoints. The geographical focus of the locality based consultation sessions is in line with moves towards partnership working in specific localities required by various documents (Department of Health, 1999c, 2000). Managers must develop and take part in partnerships with service users, other agencies and organisations on local and regional levels and so we wanted to find out what partnership means for some of the people involved. Single agency groups were structured according to participant's role in the organisation to give an indication of perceptions and expectations of first line managers from various places within the same organisation. Lawler and Hearn, (1997) consider management from the perspectives of senior managers in social services, Balloch et al (1998) looked at a range of views within agencies. This study seeks to make comparisons within and between agencies and settings. So, in the single agency sessions participants were split into middle manager, first line manager and practitioner groups. Workshops were held in three organisations. The first had integrated adult social work and health services several years ago, the second was moving towards integration in two areas – mental health and learning disabilities (as well as planning for joint review) and the third workshop was held with managers, practitioners and service users selected on a regional basis to represent local authority, voluntary and private agencies. This group also evidenced their pre-occupation with cross-agency and 'joined up' work. The third strand of the fieldwork was a series of in-depth semi-structured interviews with managers from social services and voluntary sector organisations. In total 26 participants in residential and day-care settings as well as fieldwork projects were interviewed. Of these, 14 had social work qualifications and 11 had other social care professional qualifications. All were actively managing units, projects and teams. Only four had management qualifications although ten had undergone in-house training. All group sessions and interviews were recorded and transcribed. These interviews together with the group consultations form the basis for this section of the chapter.

The similarities between groups were marked. One theme echoed through the workshops and interviews very clearly indeed. The role of the manager in social care is in a state of change and confusion with a plethora of policies and procedures, but no real recognition of the day-to-day management challenges of implementing policy and procedural changes – the lived realities for managers. This section, therefore, draws out some of those day-to-day challenges and dilemmas for managers – and the people with whom they work. We have structured our discussion around the areas identified by the participants as central to their experience – the operational, strategic and professional aspects of management, as these were divisions made by the participants themselves.

Operational

There is a strong tension between the operational aspects of the management role and the first line manager's involvement in strategic developments and decision-making. On the one hand, first line managers focused on the operational component of their management role – the day-to-day support and supervision, work allocation, developmental and enabling role working with team members. On the other hand, middle managers recognised the difficulties faced by first line managers, but saw the strategic aspects of the first line manager task as priority:

> I've just appointed two temporary team managers [in child protection] to cover for people who aren't there. I would love to have said to those two people, you just concentrate on looking after those teams for the next 3-6 months. If I did that I had to decide who was going to take on our statutory function in the Education Action Zones, the Sure Start initiative, the Health Improvement Group and pick up the chair of the Parenting Skills strategy group ... There's just four things I had to allocate to those two people in the first few weeks. And they're not things I could say 'That's not a priority at the moment'
>
> (Middle manager, Social Services).

The operational challenge of managing multi-disciplinary teams was seen as linking all aspects of the management role. Implementing the move at an operational level held profound challenges for first line managers:

> You've got to allow people to maintain their own professional identity but at the same time to manage them and that's a very difficult balance ... otherwise there's no point in having a multi-disciplinary team
>
> (First Line Manager, Social Services).

And this has impacted on the manager's own position:

> A manager needs to be positive and constructive about multi-disciplinary working to staff – at the same time as having concerns myself ... it wouldn't be fair for them to take on board my anxieties
>
> (First Line Manager, Social Services).

Participants referred to the first line manager as a bridge or translator many times in workshops and interviews. This was seen as a central operational role, although we argue that it crosses into strategic and professional arenas. The manager communicates with and mediates between groups and individuals about policies, practices and strategies that are often very new to the manager herself.

The importance of communication and relationships was stressed by service users who thought that the more distant from practice a manager becomes, the less the manager was aware of the very real effects of decisions. Practitioners also felt that managers were becoming more remote and removed from the day-to-day work of the team. It was felt generally that managers were often away from the office on 'strategic business', unavailable to deal with many of their operational or team demands:

> Time management is difficult, because you have to be out of the building sometimes up to half the week at meetings, manager's days and other projects that you are working on and it's difficult to keep up to speed with what's happening in the unit
>
> (First Line Manager).

This includes being available to offer support or guidance to staff on practice and statutory matters. It is proving difficult for team managers adequately to support staff who work with distressed people in demanding situations. The importance of relationships with people appears, as one first line manager commented, to be forgotten 'in our focus on competencies'. Managers found staffing issues could take much of their time:

We are fully staffed now, but struggle between posts, we are able to represent the population in that over half the practitioners are Asian, but there are restrictions on appointing at the moment and you know it will be difficult if anyone leaves or is sick

(First Line Manager).

Decision-making was identified as another important operational task. Some practitioners felt that managers were not always able to make difficult decisions:

... managers don't like making difficult decisions – I think they often run away from it and that frightens the life out of me

(Social Worker).

Managers saw the complexity of their decisions:

All of a sudden people come to you for a decision, and you have to stand by it and think of the long term effects of it. If I make this judgement it will mean certain things, but if I do the other thing there are different implications... so I have to try and look at everyone's needs and think of the welfare of staff and users.

The types of decisions managers make are affected by their work setting. One middle manager spoke about a decision-making course he had attended where:

people were trying to make a distinction between operational and strategic decision making. They said that they're on a spectrum really – operational decision-making being the day to day but relatively inconsequential type of decision... but in the social work profession (it was a health course) some of the day to day decisions that may be operational and not to do with great strategic plans or the long term view, are very consequential to people's lives.

Managers in voluntary sector projects have more freedom to undertake their operational tasks. A manager of a voluntary sector project for young people, for example, is able to take chances with her management approach:

My style of managing is very much hands off ... this style of management probably has the most risks – to let people make mistakes...

The same manager's management committee had agreed to external management supervision that focused on structures, people and relationships within the project. Although there were more demands on the manager in relation to assuring quality within the project, a new worker had been employed to work on funding, financial issues and grant applications. This appears to be at odds with the experience of most first-line managers who are expected to incorporate greater budgetary and strategic planning into their role as well as fulfil other duties. It is one of several examples which demonstrate some of the operational creativity and flexibility to be found in the voluntary and private sector:

> The benefits of this agency are informality, quick decision-making, tight adherence to our professional standards ... being a small agency it is easier to identify staff needs and develop and build expertise in identified areas
>
> (Private Agency Manager).

The focus in the voluntary sector is on the importance of the operational aspects of the first line manager's role and is further illustrated by a line manager from another voluntary sector project who noted:

> I have three workers who are using a very different [therapeutic] approach and I need to keep up to scratch with that – even though I don't offer therapeutic supervision.

This is in sharp contrast to some statutory sector managers who are finding that the supervisory components of their role are being taken over by newly introduced senior practitioner posts.

Strategic

While first line managers identify operational issues as their priority, middle managers consider that the first line manager has crucial local knowledge that is vital in strategic planning. First line managers feel overwhelmed by so many policy initiatives over which they have no control or influence and by the development of procedures and standards that do not take implementation time into account. New policies and procedures appear from national government and from City or County Hall at a frightening pace. Managers do not have time to consolidate the information or practice with their partners and teams before the next new procedure comes along:

> There were lots of new initiatives and everyone was feeling overloaded... at the centre it's the way in which you sell things to people ... if you can see the positives to new things...
>
> (Family Centre Manager).

and

> ...information bombardment and making it mean something for staff...
>
> (Children's Home Manager).

Of particular note are the changes in children's services in relation to Quality Protects and in adult services in relation to moves towards multi-disciplinary teams. Within many agencies there appears to be a lack of clarity and continuity about what constitutes a manager's role. The role has expanded over time (as opposed to changed) to the point that expectations of managers have become unrealistic within available time frames:

> I worry that I will lose what I came into social work for because the management task becomes so difficult
>
> (First Line Manager).

and

> keeping up with government agendas and quality standards as well as managing the work is a *challenge*
>
> (Carers Project Manager).

Although some authorities have focused on time management courses the problem, however, appears to be a finite amount of time with an infinite amount of expectations that no amount of training will address. Clarity about role may help in this respect:

> It isn't actually fair to say to people 'if you're going to be a team manager simply be the manager of a team'. Maybe we're saying we can't do that. What we are doing is recruiting people to manage operational, day-to-day demands in a busy social work team and at the same time be involved in the development of services within their locality in partnership with other agencies and the wider department. We shouldn't suggest to people that it's anything else but that
>
> (Middle Manager).

Another middle manager pointed to the implications of:

> Management styles, management speak, competencies and inspection are influential – things can get very mechanical

The rate and intensity of development, especially in relation to procedures and standards, was noted in all of the groups:

> It's as if we're driven by a machine that actually records information at the expense of service users
>
> (First Line Manager).

and

> we seem to be performance managed to death these days, rather than having realistic targets to aspire to
>
> (First Line Manager).

This was an area thought to have a negative impact on practitioners who felt criticised and undermined by the performance tables being used:

> Quality and measuring has become a dilemma. How do you implement standards and know that you are attaining them? What do you ask? Social Services will ask about the numbers of families who have received a service, but what do the families think? When reviewing the toddler group the children's views of quality might be different from the adults...you can't say whether everyone is satisfied or whether the service is oppressive...how do you judge the standard of the service?
>
> (Family Centre Manager).

So again we have the manager as translator, this time in a strategic sense – between the wider department and team members, between policy and practice and between people from different agencies and backgrounds. Communication within organisations does not appear to be growing alongside strategy and consultation as the following three quotes – all from members of the same department – illustrate:

> There is lip service paid to consultation and we do have managers come round and talk to us so on paper it looks like [consultation] is happening – but somehow it isn't effective
>
> (Practitioner).

Managers don't feel listened to (First Line Manager).

> Middle managers keep consulting with and asking managers, but don't seem to listen to the response
>
> (Middle Manager).

A barrier to developing effective strategic partnerships was identified as a lack of real delegated power to managers. Decision-making is important in partnership working but there may be constraints in this area:

> We may go to a meeting with health managers and come away having to get authorisation to do something which health managers could give approval to on the spot. So you have people trying to develop partnerships but feel they don't have equal levels of authority
>
> (Middle Manager).

The challenges of developing partnership working and the cultural changes and challenges this involves are complex and time consuming. There is a lack of understanding within other organisations and agencies about the nature of social services and this adds to the difficulties for managers and several participants mentioned the lack of a shared language between partners.

Professional

This is an area of some anxiety for first line managers and practitioners – especially in adult services – although less so for middle managers. Moves towards integration of health and social work teams and the development of multi-disciplinary teams within some specialisms brought the issue to the fore for many participants:

> It can cause quite a bit of resentment being managed by someone who is not of your profession
>
> (Practitioner);

although others felt:

> having a multi-disciplinary team gives us the right skills mix and the ability to talk to other agencies in the right language as well. It makes a difference
>
> (Children's Home Manager).

Teams developed without a professional identity and practitioners were concerned that their own professional identity was being diluted. As a result of service integration, one social worker we spoke with had joined BASW and a nurse had become involved with a nurses action group fighting to preserve their professional identity. Both people said that they would not have joined profession specific groups prior to integration.

A background in social care was seen as essential by service users and managers alike although experience of a particular specialism such as learning disabilities or mental health was not as important:

> social care context and values are inherent and shouldn't differ
>
> (First Line Manager).

When it came to the move from practitioner to manager, participants felt there was little in the way of preparation or support. There are more opportunities for staff to take part in development and project work – as a form of preparation for possible future management roles – but at some cost for remaining team members who must then take on extra work. Management development programmes are often only available after someone has taken post as a first line manager.

Managers need increasingly to direct team members' attention away from their professional backgrounds towards a single system of care management and planning. As a result managers may find themselves torn between their own practice and professional background and organisational and policy requirements and expectations. Within and between specialism and levels of management, participants considered that hybrid cultures are developing. These are about a person-centred approach to management and a 'hard' business management approach. Participants from one organisation considered that a culture of blame was developing where performance tables are (a) not measuring quality and (b) not using the correct data for quantitative measurements. In some instances this is resulting in a survival culture where the process of evidence collection appears to hinder practice. The need for accountability and enforcement as components of the first line manager's role was however, recognised.

Discussion

Managers identified many dilemmas and challenges that impacted on their day-to-day management task. These ranged from the operational (being available for consultation with staff) to the strategic (developing plans for service development in their localities) to the professional (working in a manner consistent with social work ethics and values). It is not possible in this paper to consider all of these in detail and so we have focused on one from each area. These are the operational dilemma of the introduction of senior practitioner posts, the strategic dilemma of developing partnerships, and the professional dilemma of appropriate training. Themes identified included the uneasy transition from practitioner to manager, running to keep up with the pace of change, the fit (or lack of it) between organisation, identity and profession, balancing the responsibility for buildings, health and safety, budgets and staff management with the need to devote time to multi-agency planning meetings and strategic functions. In Syrett's (1997) study participants felt that managers did not see the real issues for practitioners and service users. Our research shows that managers see the operational issues all too clearly but feel unable to respond because of strategic demands on their time. The tension between operational and strategic functions discussed above is being addressed by several organisations through the introduction of senior practitioner posts to oversee many of the day-to-day operational matters within teams. In some cases this includes the very areas of management that attracted first line managers to the role in the first place – staff supervision and support, workload allocation and day-to-day team maintenance. On the one hand this is seen as an essential support for first line managers and as an opportunity for staff to gain some experience of managerial roles. On the other hand it may also serve further to distance a manager from her staff and may place the senior practitioner in an invidious position of being neither practitioner nor manager. Vanstone (1995, p.124) argues that the distance between practitioners and managers may foster mistrust in 'besieged managers'. He goes on to note that the situation – for all concerned – is influenced by:

> The degree to which managers are actually, as well as seen to be, in touch with the experience and concerns of practitioners.

In practice the opportunities for practitioners to develop management interests or skills are unplanned. People usually become managers without any formal preparation often by 'acting up'.

Some middle managers recognise the difference between what they did as new managers and what managers now undertake. However, they continue to look at the first line manager job in terms of skills rather than look at the job itself. This would seem to support Lawler and Hearn's (1997) finding that senior managers saw their own social work experience as giving them credibility with staff, but having little or no relevance otherwise. The focus of middle managers in our study was clearly on the centrality of the strategic function of management. Middle managers spoke rather grandly about the role of the manager being to 'prioritise in the light of changing demands' but not about the reality of doing so when the needs of practitioner and department are in competition or when strategic aims clash with operational realities. The comment noted earlier by the manager who spoke about being 'performance managed to death' is illustrative of Newman and Clarke's (1997) argument that searching for quality in the form of the latest charter mark or award may be 'as much about external legitimacy as it is about effectiveness' (p.4). This is an illustration perhaps of the competing demands upon the line manager and how the rhetoric of social care management bears little relationship to its realities. Inter-agency liaison was a challenge for managers in adult and children's services, as well as statutory and voluntary sector settings:

> Difficulties come when you work with agencies who don't listen to young people for whatever reason
>
> (Young People's Project Worker).

> Inter-agency boundaries are still quite tricky...the care co-ordination project is about a joint co-ordinated approach for under 8s and we have one child to whom it applies, one care plan travels with the child regardless of the setting they are in...
>
> (First Line Manager).

Both practitioners and managers find the role of translator between people and agencies challenging, especially in relation to language in multi-disciplinary teams:

> There isn't a shared language – a vocabulary to express what I had been trained to express in the way I had been trained to express it... over time I don't think it's changed. I think I've got more used to it and can accommodate it more perhaps
>
> (Practitioner).

> Managing multi-disciplinary teams is a big threat because you don't have understanding of their professional expertise or language
>
> (First Line Manager).

In the absence of the 'magic bullet' for management effectiveness, we are led to wonder if the introduction of the Babel fish as a management tool would be at least as useful as yet more communication strategies.   As *The Hitchhikers Guide to the Galaxy* tells us:

> The Babel fish is small, yellow and leech-like, and probably the oddest thing in the universe... the upshot is if you stick a Babel fish in your ear you can instantly understand anything said to you in any form of language

(Adams, 1979: 48-49).

Conclusion

First line managers are pivotal in ensuring client, worker, departmental and governmental needs are met. This may feel overwhelming especially as expectations on first line managers continue to grow. As one manager commented, the fast pace and overwhelming amounts of change are such that 'we're making our own histories'. Delegation has implications for team members who may feel pressure to accept extra work in an attempt to support the team manager, and prioritisation is difficult when, as one participant noted, 'they're all priorities'. This manager went on to say that a member of her team 'shouldn't have to say she feels sorry for me'. Our research has indicated that the lived realities of first line managers in social care are taking place in 'Hard Times' indeed. The 'Great Expectations' of managerial discourse are able as Clarke (1998) argues, to claim the moral high ground of quality and efficiency. None of the participants in our study disputed the importance of improving the quality of social care. What they argued for was a closer relationship between the aspiration and the reality.

References

Adams, D. (1979), *The Hitchhiker's Guide to the Galaxy*, Pan: London.
Balloch, S., McLean, J., Fisher, and M., (eds) (1998), *Social Services: Working Under Pressure*, The Policy Press: Bristol.
Clarke, J. (1998), 'Thriving on Chaos? Managerialism and Social Welfare', in J. Carter (ed), *Postmodernity and the Fragmentation of Welfare*, Routledge: London.
Department of Health (1999a), *Modernising Health And Social Services: Developing The Workforce*, Department of Health: London.
Department of Health (1999b), *Modernising Health And Social Services: National Priorities Guidance*, Department of Health: London.
Department of Health (1999c), *The Relationship Between Health And Social Services* (CM 4320), The Stationery Office: London.
Department of Health (2000), *Guidance on the Health Act Section 31 Partnership Arrangements*, Department of Health: London.
Kearney, P. (1999), *Managing Practice: Report On The Management Of Practice Expertise Project*, NISW: London.
Lawler, J. and Hearn, J. (1997), 'The Managers Of Social Work: The Experiences And Identifications Of Third Tier Social Services Managers And The Implications For Future Practice', *British Journal of Social Work*, 27: 191-218.

Newman, J. and Clarke, J. (1997), 'An Unstable State? Managerialism And Social Welfare', *Social Services Research*, 2: 1-10.

Rickford, F. (2000), 'First In Line For Blame', *Community Care*, 9th August, 20-21.

Syrett, V., Jones, M., and Sercombe, N. (1997), 'Implementing Community Care: The Congruence Of Manager And Practitioner Cultures', *Social Work and Social Sciences Review*, 7(3): 154-69.

Vanstone, M. (1995), 'Managerialism And The Ethics Of Management', in Hugman, R. and Smith, D. (eds), *Ethical Issues in Social Work*, Routledge: London.

Chapter 5

'Have You Seen My Assessment Schedule?' Proceduralisation, Constraint and Control in Social Work with Children and Families

Paul Michael Garrett

Introduction

This chapter will examine two sets of documentation devised for social workers interactions with children and families in Britain. First, the *Looking After Children* (LAC) system, which was devised from the late-1980s onwards and which began to be used by local authorities in the 1990s (Parker, Ward, Jackson, Aldgate and Wedge, 1991). These 'tools' for social work practice do not have to be used by local authorities, but most opted to utilise them in some form, on account of the likely adverse consequences if they had failed to do so on occasions of inspection and audit. Second, the *Framework for the Assessment of Children in Need and their Families* that was introduced by the Blair administration in April 2000 (Department of Health, Department for Education and Employment, Home Office, 2000).[1] This latter package is issued under section 7 of the Local Authority Social Services Act 1970 which requires local authority social services to act under the general guidance of the Secretary of State. As such the Framework lacks the full force of statute, but will be complied with 'unless local circumstances indicate exceptional reasons which justify a variation' (Department of Health etc, 2000: Preface). In practical terms, therefore, the Framework is likely to become mandatory.

The discussion will begin by putting into place a theoretical foundation for the analysis of LAC and the Framework. Here, it is suggested that it is conceptually helpful to have regard to comments made by Zygmunt Bauman (2000) and contemporary theorising associated with 'governmentality'. After briefly discussing more general changes connected to professionals and expertise – and social workers specifically – the focus will narrow in order concentrate on aspects of both LAC and the Framework. The imposition of both packages, it is suggested, is likely to present field social workers with a range of dilemmas centred on responding to, even resisting, proceduralisation.

Fleeing 'Procedural Execution' and the Return to 'Ethical Impulses'

As an activity 'social work' is historically and culturally unstable. Baron-On, for example, (1999: 9) is his discussion on the development of social work in Africa, points out that social work training in Botswana originally took place in 'an agricultural college where students were taught 'cooking, knitting, vegetable gardening and the like'. In short, the activity constructed and identified as 'social work' is here entirely abstracted from a preoccupation with 'competencies' (see also Edwards and Usher, 1994; Clark, 1995) and was partly shaped and determined by the context in which it took place and evolved. This is not, however, to argue that the 'ways of seeing' promoted by primary definers in Britain and the United States and the operational modalities, which these visions give rise to, do not have consequences further afield. Indeed, the plethora of protocols, schedules and assessment 'tools', devised in both Britain and the United States, are apt to become exports, that is to say, cultural artefacts, which are promoted and used in other national settings. The LAC materials, for example, are presently being used, we are advised, with 'Aboriginal peoples in Western Australia and the Inuit of Labrador' as well as being used with children and families in Canada, Sweden, Hungary and Russia (Ward, 2000: 134).

Turning specifically to the West, Bauman (2000) commenting on the 'proceduralisation' of social work has expressed concern that 'daily practice' is becoming 'ever more distant from its original ethical purpose' (Bauman, 2000: 9) He reminds his readers that 'social work, whatever else it may be, is also the ethical gesture of taking responsibility for the fate and well-being of the Other' (Bauman, 2000:10). He goes on:

> Clarity and unambiguity may be the ideal of the world in which 'procedural execution' is the rule. For the ethical world, however, ambivalence and uncertainty are the daily bread and cannot be stamped out without destroying the moral substance of responsibility, the foundation on which the world rests.

In a liberal and humanistic sense, therefore, this tension between the 'original ethical impulse' and 'procedural execution' might be viewed as the focal point for a range of dilemmas which confront social workers (and, perhaps, others in social care and health fields), particularly in a context when the components of micro–engagements with the users of services are increasing being plotted by centrally devised assessment schedules. Although being outside the scope of this discussion, this development also presents problems and dilemmas for social work educators who increasingly have their teaching mapped out by 'systems' and 'frameworks' which qualified practitioners are expected to use (see also Jones, 1996). The arid format, for example, of the *Action and Assessment Records* (AARs) which are part of the LAC system implicitly defines social work with children and their families and conveys powerful messages to students about its key tasks and functions.

It might, however, be argued that Bauman's magisterial overview – although welcome because his comments run counter to the hegemony of managerialism and the practitioner cynicism it is apt to engender inside of welfare bureaucracies –

is not entirely convincing on account of the way he perceives the 'original' ethical purpose of social work. In Britain, for example, it could be argued that the motivations, impulses and preoccupations of the Charity Organisation Society in the late-nineteenth century were more complex than his analysis would seem to suggest (see Bosanquet 1895; Woodroofe, 1962; Rooff, 1972; Jones, 1983). To be sure, there was a concern of *about* 'the Other', but how the recipients of services were constructed – in the language of the day as the 'industrial residuum' (Dendy, 1895) – suggests a project far less benign and more regulatory and disciplinary. From these early days, social work interventions were also intent on reinforcing *particular* economic and gender relations. During this period, which marked the beginning of professional social work, there was also an early fixation with proceduralisation (see Richmond, 1917) and the 'case'. In short, current technologies of intervention are the products of historically rooted tendencies, reflecting aspects of Foucault's (1977: 184-94) 'examination... surrounded by all its documentary techniques' making 'each individual a "case"'. More provocatively, it has also been maintained that there is no 'ethical' foundation, existing outside of power relations, in which social work can locate and embed itself.

No Help Outside of Governmentality?

Part of this understanding, or standpoint, can be related to the idea that social work can be perceived as part of the assemblage of micro-practices which comprise contemporary modes of government. For Foucault, 'government' needed to be conceived in the broad way in which it was viewed in the sixteenth-century. During this period 'government', therefore, did:

> not simply refer to political structures or the management of states; rather it designated the way in which the conduct of individuals or states might be directed: the government of children, of souls, of communities, of families, of the sick...It did not cover only the legitimately constituted forms of political or economic subjection... To govern, in this sense, is to structure the possible fields of action
>
> (Foucault cited in Harris, 1999: 30).

This conceptualisation and its 'analytics of government' identifies social work as a particular 'regime of practices' which is informed by various forms of knowledge and expertise which produces 'programmes' and operational modalities (see Dean, 1999 for a fuller account). Social work is, therefore, complicit in the strategies of governance (see also Johnson, 1993). In this conceptual context, it is asserted, despite the claims of 'radical social work' throughout the late-1970s and early-1980s (Jones, 1983), there is no 'space of innocence', which permits the choice of being 'an agent of social change or being an agent of social control' (Rossiter, 2000: 32). Problems are further compounded because social work has 'barely begun the work of understanding its construction *within* power' (emphasis added). Hence, it continues to seek to rely on 'notions of innocent helping to legitimate its presence' despite there being 'no help... outside of governmentality' (Rossiter, 2000: 32-33).

The autonomy of experts and expertise is, however, important for governmentality theorists. Rose and Miller (1992: 180), for example, argue that:

> [l]iberal government identifies a domain outside of 'politics' and seeks to manage it without destroying its autonomy. This is made possible through the activities and calculations of a proliferation of independent agents [including social workers].

Here, 'political forces' also:

> seek to utilise, instrumentalise and mobilise techniques and agents other than those of 'the state' in order to 'govern at a distance'
>
> (Rose and Miller 1992: 181).

Expertise and experts 'embodying neutrality, authority and skill' fulfil a crucial role, because they hold out the hope that the problems of regulation can remove themselves from the disputed terrain of politics and relocate into the 'tranquil seductive territory of truth' (Rose and Miller, 1992:188). More recently, Rose, (1993: 285) in articulating the concept of 'advanced liberal rule' has stressed the relocation of experts within a 'market governed by the rationalities of competition, accountability and consumer demand' (see also Rose, 1996: 40-41). Here, it might be countered that expertise and experts are no longer, in a 'risk society', unquestionably accepted as possessing unimpeachable attributes of authority and skill (see Beck, 1998) Rose (1993: 295) has, in part, acknowledged this shift in that his conceptualisation of 'advanced liberal rule' recognises the 'dialectic of hope and suspicion today attached to experts and their truths'. For him, this development can also be associated more with a:

> reconfiguration of the political salience of expertise... [and] a new way of 'responsibilizing' experts in relation to claims made upon them other than those of their own criteria of truth and competence
>
> (Rose, 1996: 55).

A number of writers, not associated with the governmentality approach, have looked at how these developments have had an impact on the professions and professional identities (see Hanlon, 1998; Hanlon, 2000) and some have specifically examined the implications of 'responsibilizing' for the welfare professions as a whole (Foster and Wilding, 2000; Malin, 2000), or particular fields of welfare (see for example, Ball, 1994; Nellis, 1999). In the next section, the aim is to outline how these processes might specifically relate to social work.

Maligned and Directed 'Experts'

Social work is, perhaps, a 'special' case in its claim to an 'expertise' status. Since the days of the Charity Organisation Society, for example, there has been a 'long standing anxiety' about the 'volatility and precariousness of social workers hold on the dominant line' (Jones, 1996: 16). Moreover, there has also been the related debate concerned with whether or not social work can legitimately be regarded as a 'profession'. In 1915, for example, Abraham Flexner – in an influential speech which was to have major implications for the social workers self-perception in the United States – suggested that it was appropriate to 'view social work as in touch with professions rather than as a profession in and by itself (in Pumphrey and Pumphrey, 1961; see also Aldridge, 1996; Harris, 1998). Public perceptions of the role of social workers have also been shaped by inquiries into the deaths of children, such as Victoria Climbie, which – albeit filtered by the media – have appeared to highlight a manifest lack in 'expertise' and 'professionalism' (Department of Health, 2001; see also London Borough of Brent, 1985; London Borough of Greenwich, 1987; London Borough of Lambeth, 1987; Secretary of State for Social Services, 1988). Furthermore, revelations about the institutional abuse of children have had a further impact on the public perception of social work and social workers (Waterhouse, 2000). Importantly, the notion of 'governing at a distance' and expert autonomy is also highly questionable when applied to local authority social work in the early twenty-first century given the concerted attempts to render the 'invisible trade' (Pithouse, 1998) and the 'outcomes' it generates more visible. Consequently, as LAC, the new Framework, and the whole 'competencies' approach central to social work education indicate, social work practice is, perhaps, more industrialised (Fabricant, 1985) with centrally devised modalities being used to 'Taylorize the labour process and impose technological controls over the work' (Dominelli and Hoogfelt, 1996: 55).

For eighteen years, social work was also shaped by the political project of the right wing of the Conservative Party (see Gledhill, 1989), which set out to 'sanitise social work' (Jones, 1996a) and to rid it of any oppositional or 'ideological' infection. By the late 1990s and with the fall of the Major administration, the language of market forces and market imperatives had infiltrated the theory and practice of social work and had especially come to characterise the formulations of its senior managerial, policy making and educative tiers (see Edwards and Usher, 1994; Dominelli, 1996; Dominelli and Hoogvelt, 1996; Humphries, 1997). On this terrain, the 'social services supermarket' (Smale, 1993: 4) came to be eulogised even if this type of rhetoric was juxtaposed, not always happily (Singh, 1997), with historically and professionally rooted notions such as 'traditional social work values' (BASW, 1996) and 'anti-oppressive practice' (Froggett and Sapey 1997: 47-48). Equally important, there have been attempts by both the previous Conservative administrations and the current Blair government to change the culture of public sector bureaucracies such as local authority social services departments (see Hall, 1993; Hall, 1998; Powell, 1999; Powell, 2000). Here, the aim has been to instil new norms and perceptions that mirror those of the private sector (see Wilson 1999). These efforts are, for example, reflected in the New

Labour administration's modernisation project (Department of Health, 1998; see also Nellis 1999; Garrett, 2002a; Garrett, 2002b). My aim below is to narrow the focus and to concentrate just on two packages of materials for the assessment of children and families. Both the LAC system and the new Framework may be perceived as technologies of government and (to use the language of the governmentality theorists) these 'humble and mundane mechanisms' (Rose and Miller, 1992:183). Although significantly different from each other, they are illuminating in terms of what they reveal about processes and techniques of governance.

The 'Looking After Children' System and Action and Assessment Records

Action and Assessment Records are to be used with children in public care, or 'looked after' by local authorities (see Parker, Ward, Jackson, Aldgate and Wedge, 1991; Corrick, Jones and Ward, 1995; Jackson and Kilroe, 1996; Ward, 1995; Jackson, 1998; see also Knight and Caveney, 1998; Garrett, 1999; Garrett, 2002c). Other LAC related materials are also available, forming a 'package' of documentation, but it is the AARs which will be the main focus of this part of the discussion since they constitute the centrepiece of the LAC system. These assessment schedules are designed to enable social services departments and the Department of Health to track developments in seven key areas, or 'dimensions' of a child's life: their health, education, emotional and behavioural development, family and social relationships, self-care skills, identity and social presentation. They enable social workers, therefore, to assess 'looked after' children's progress from birth into young adulthood by means of what the LAC Training Guide refers to as 'a series of questions which seek *objective answers*' (Department of Health, 1995: 58, emphasis added). Specific schedules are, moreover, available for children and young people located in six different age-bands; under 1, 1-2, 3-4, 5-9, 10-14 and 15 and over.

The 'official' literature on the LAC scheme states that the AARs are 'designed to set an agenda for meaningful conversation' (Corrick, Jones and Ward, 1995: 26). However, the AARs seek to expunge any lingering notion that that the micro-dimension of social work engagement and interaction with children and young people should be non-directive and empathic (Rogers, 1980; see also, in this context, Parton and O'Byrne, 2000). Each AAR has been produced as an A4-size booklet with, for example, the schedule for use with those young people aged 15 and over spanning 60 pages and containing approximately 375 questions and an accompanying menu of multiple choice answers. This format cannot, of course, lend itself to ease of dialogue between a social worker and a young person because it is structured in such a directive and interrogative way. Furthermore, children's subjective experiences and right to identify relevant issues *for themselves* are entirely marginalised. The checklist format with multiple-choice answers is alienating for children and young people and overly directive. During the limited piloting of the AARs, for example, some 'adolescent' service-users simply 'refused to participate' and the non-participation of these young people can, perhaps, be connected to the arid, interrogative format of the schedules (Parker, Ward, Jackson, Aldgate and Wedge, 1991: 124). 'Assessment forms consisting of lists of questions can inhibit open participation' and evidence is slowly beginning to emerge of young people's dissatisfaction, even anger, about the LAC system (see Shemmings and Shemmings, 2000). Indeed, their response is also attributable to the way the AARs can be interpreted as objectifying children and young people. In the Cleveland Inquiry (Secretary of State for Social Services, 1988) it was, for example, famously remarked that the child at the centre of a child protection investigation was 'a person and not an object of concern'. Yet the LAC system appears, in many respects, to invert this maxim.

How particular questions are grouped is also of concern (see also Shemmings and Shemmings 2000: 94). The AAR schedule for those aged 15 and over rushes through potentially emotive questions on sexuality, alcohol and drug use in just four pages. Questions connected to a young person's sexual orientation are, moreover, rendered medical matters by being placed in the section headed 'Health', as opposed to 'Identity'. Dangers also exist in that the impersonal technocratic rigour of the AAR approach could prove counter productive to its stated aims by reinforcing the sense of stigma and 'abnormality' a young person might already feel whilst in public care (see Merrick, 1996: Appendix). More fundamentally the entire approach appears to be characterised by a somewhat crude endeavour to produce children who will *fit* when they become adults (see particularly, Kilroe, 1996; also Garrett, 1999).

A completed AAR, has an alienating lettering and numbering system that lends itself to inputting onto a computer database. The 'outcome' of social work interventions becomes over a period of time, albeit in crude terms, easier to 'measure' and, significantly, the social worker risks becoming a mere gatherer of 'data' (see also Poster, 1990). Such an interpretation has been officially countered with the claim that AARs are not intended to be used mechanistically with children and young people. Despite such an assertion, the *form* in which the AARs are presented is likely to structure and contain the process of engagement. In short, because of the *content* and the *form* of AARs both the social worker and user of services are being contained, shaped and regulated.

The Assessment Framework and the 'Family Pack of Questionnaires and Scales'

The Framework for the Assessment of Children in Need and their Families, pictorially represented in the form of a triangle or pyramid with the child's welfare at the centre of its 'conceptual map', is to be used by social workers and other social care professionals to 'understand what is happening to children in whatever setting they may be growing up' (Department of Health, 1999: 26; see also Department of Health, 2000; Department of Health, 2000a; Department of Health etc 2000; Department of Health, Cox and Bentovim 2000). The social work assessment of children and their families should, we are advised, take into account 'three systems or domains whose interactions have a direct impact on the current long-term well-being of a child' (Rose, 2000: 32). These are identified as a child's developmental needs (based on the seven LAC dimensions referred to earlier), the parenting capacity and the family and environmental factors (Department of Health etc 2000: Ch. 2). Here, however, the aim is simply to concentrate on *The Family Pack of Questionnaires and Scales* (Department of Health, Cox and Bentovim 2000), which are to accompany the new Framework. These are comprised of: *The Strengths and Difficulties Questionnaire*; *The Parenting Daily Hassles Scale*; *The Home Conditions Scale*; *The Adult and Adolescent Well-being Scales*; *The Recent Life Events Questionnaire*; *The Family Activity Scale* and *The Alcohol Scale*. Here again we have an assertion concerning design objectivity since *The Family Pack* has been constructed 'to provide *objective*, structured information that will help practitioners approach with greater confidence complicated issues' (Ward, 2000: 136, emphasis added). The questionnaires and scales 'widely used in psychology and psychiatry' were, moreover, found to be 'helpful', even 'useful' when piloted in five social services departments in 1998/99 (Department of Health 2000: 118). They can be used 'following a process of familiarisation', but do not 'require any formal training' and will provide 'a clear evidence base for judgements and recommendations' (Department of Health 1999: 70). Elsewhere, it is confided, a little glibly, that: 'Good tools cannot substitute for good practice, but good practice and good tools together can achieve excellence' (Department of Health 1999: 66). We are incessantly advised that social workers in the piloting authorities found them 'easy to administer and of immediate benefit' (Department of Health, Cox and Bentovim 2000: 4), yet what is oddly jarring – and perhaps disingenuous given the Framework's 'evidence-based' discourse – is the actual lack of any evidence. No data is furnished in respect of social workers, or service users' receptiveness to these 'instruments', only the occasional anecdote (see Department of Health, Cox and Bentovim 2000). Related to the question of evidence, a good deal of the research that is marshalled in order to substantiate the validity and utility of the 'instruments' is unsatisfactory, moreover, references to underpinning research for *The Adult and Adolescence Wellbeing Scales* date from the 1970s and early 1980s. Similarly, research for *The Recent Life Events Questionnaire* and *Family Activity Scale* is from the mid-1980s. Some of the research foundation, such as that which informed the development of the *Parenting Hassles Scale*, is also questionable in that it only involved mothers (see Crnic and Greenberg, 1990).

The importation of these 'instruments' into the social work assessment of children and families may represent a tilt toward a more positivistic and psychiatry-led orientation. Perhaps of particular note, in this connection, is the attachment of the 'instruments' to methodologies, which seek to 'screen' for emotional and behavioural disorders via 'scoring' techniques. So, for example, with *The Strengths and Difficulties Questionnaire* 'the scales can be scored to produce an overall score which indicates whether a child/young person is likely to have a significant problem. Selected items can also be used 'to form subscales for Pro-Social Behaviours, Hyperactivity, Emotional Symptoms, Conduct and Peer Problems' (Department of Health, Cox and Bentovim, 2000: 16). Here, the concern must be about potentially pre-emptive and inaccurate diagnostic labelling, particularly in the wider social context where many are primed and alert to a deficit in 'pro-social' behaviour in certain groups of children and young people – and the application of anti-social behaviour orders and child curfews become more common (see Coppock, 1996; James and Jencks, 1996; Garrett, 1999). Significantly, during the piloting of the *Strengths and Difficulties Questionnaire* 'over half the children assessed scored above the cut off indicating a problem disorder' (Department of Health, Cox and Bentovim, 2000: 16). The risks of this happening are, moreover, multiplied within a discipline where 'psychiatrists come to diagnostic decisions quickly and direct their attention to confirm their hypotheses' (Birlson, 1981: 75; see also Rose, 1985; Rose, 1989). Historically, the 'psy complex' (Rose, 1985) – which these questionnaires and scales represent the ascendancy of – has also been enmeshed in more embracing discourses centred on crime and social disorder (see Birlson, 1981: 86). The search for 'crimino-genic' tendencies remains, moreover, bound up with policies directed at young people in contact with social services (see Garrett, 1999).

The tone of the 'tools' and their accompanying commentary might also be viewed as insulting and patronising toward the children and families using social services. We are advised, for example, that:

> even when there are crises there are times when professionals are consulting with each other and carers or children are waiting. Appropriately presented a questionnaire can help carers or children feel they are still active partners, and that the professionals are still listening
>
> (Department of Health, Cox and Bentovim 2000: 5).

Whilst also highlighting the separation of the designers from social work practice, such comments risk seeming to infantilise parents and other carers. Problems are compounded by the language used in the various 'instruments'; for example, items featured in the various questionnaires might 'seem daft' in terms of what is asked about 'the kids' (Department of Health, Cox and Bentovim 2000: 12). Related to this, *The Family Pack* might be perceived as being at odds with an 'inclusive' orientation (Department of Health etc, 2000) in that it continually hints at an entrenched class prejudice. For example, *The Home Conditions Assessment,* includes a check for 'stale cigarette smoke' and *The Family Activity Scales,* which is supposed to include 'information about the cultural and ideological environment in which children live' (Department of Health 1999: 72) asks if the family have recently attended a 'county show' or 'fete' (Department of Health, Cox and Bentovim, 2000: 24; 40). Young people, under 11 years old are not, moreover, permitted to self-evaluate with *The Strengths and Difficulties Questionnaire* because 'parents reports of their children's emotions and behaviours are usually more reliable than those of children themselves' (Department of Health, Cox and Bentovim 2000:16).

Turning to the impact on the *process* of social work, a sub-textual theme appearing throughout *The Family Pack* is a fixation with the time in which it will take to complete each questionnaire and scale; normally within ten minutes. Along with the new time limits introduced under *Quality Protects* to regulate assessments (Department of Health 1998a; Department of Health 1998b), this suggests that a new-time discipline is being constructed for social workers micro-engagements with children and families (see also Harvey, 1990: Ch. 4; Ennew, 1994). This has potentially major implications for the process of social work and might also be viewed as an echo of more pervasive cultural trends centred on what Virilio (1997) has identified as the 'tyranny of unrelenting acceleration'. The ascendancy of a rational-technical orientation also reflects contempt for the centrality of 'talk' and 'conversation' in social work interactions (see Parton and O'Byrne 2000). Again related to shifts in the process of social work, these 'tools' illuminate the fact that social work activity is increasingly being contained by a plethora of pro-formas. This is reflected in the materials associated with the LAC system, discussed earlier, and the *Young Offender Assessment Profiles (ASSET)* developed by the Centre for Criminological Research at the University of Oxford. Furthermore, there are potentially far reaching implications in terms of how the Framework's 'instruments' will come to be used and deployed. Will, for example, social work managers begin to ask questions, in professional supervision, about the quantities of questionnaires and scales completed? Similarly, will managers want to know about particular 'scores' achieved by individual children and families? Will 'scores', or assessments derived from questionnaires and scales, begin to feature in child protection case conference reports and will professionals begin to use these 'instruments' to calibrate risk? Will judges and magistrates begin to seek from social workers the 'certainties' which 'hard' data appears to provide? These questions could, therefore, prompt a range of practice dilemmas. More fundamentally, the questionnaires and scales, perhaps also reflect a hankering for 'certainty', a seeking to 'define out' the notions of 'ambiguity, complexity and uncertainty', which are the 'core of social work' (Parton, 1998: 23). Ultimately, this type of documentation and the orientation that it represents could also lead to the shaping of new welfare 'subjects', new professional subjectivities and to the 'emptying out' (see Lash and Urry 1999:15) of social work relationships.

Conclusion

The proliferation of assessment schedules and 'instruments' is likely to prompt a number of dilemmas for social workers involved with children and families. Importantly, the LAC system, developed under Conservative administrations and the new Framework, launched by New Labour, are different types of documentation, which, in part, reflect differing social and political preoccupations (Garrett, 2002c). However, with both packages it is a powerful alliance comprising the Department of Health, senior civil servants, senior managers within social services departments as well as academics (with a seemingly validated and 'objective' knowledge base) who are promoting these new ways of working. Nonetheless, these various 'systems', 'frameworks' and 'instruments' need to be examined in some analytical and critical depth. Clearly, there should be cause for concern about the calibre or 'quality' of social work available for children and families, yet the history of child welfare reform is ordinarily 'written simply as progressive narrative' and 'interrogative questions appear ungracious' (Hendrick,

1994: Preface). This is despite the fact that 'the history of child care in Britain is littered with solutions that subsequently emerged as creating problems themselves' (Knight and Caveney 1998: 31).

In theoretical terms, specifically in relation to the utility or otherwise of governmentality theory, the implementation and operation of LAC and the Framework could be interpreted as evidence of *translation*, that is to say, the translation of thought and action from a 'centre of calculation' into a diversity of locales (Rose, 1996: 43). This encompassing analytical approach also acts as a useful counterweight to some of social work's more facile, sentimental and optimistic ruminations on power relations. Currently, this discourse in social work and social care is apt to pivot on 'empowerment' (Rose, 2000: 334-35; see also Forrest, 2000). Nonetheless, theorising encased within govermentality paradigm(s) can provide a theoretical and intellectual cover for a more practical willingness to merely acquiesce and to reach an accommodation with managerialism and proceduralisation (see also Harris, 1999: 27). More fundamentally, because of an antipathy for anything resembling a grand narrative and a preference for scholarly moderation, some of the leading intellectual interventions associated with governmentality appear to rule out the possibility of human agency and fail to appreciate the significance of counter-discourses and oppositional practices (see, particularly, Dean 1999: Ch 3). Foucault referred to the State as a 'mythological abstraction' and for governmentality theorists it remains a 'somewhat obscure concept' (Dean, 1999). However, it might be argued that the role of the State and political forces have been crucial in terms of the orchestration and implementation of the various assessment tools and schedules (see especially, Garrett, 2002c), hence, the endeavour to centralise and supervise social work's professional task and operational modalities. This trend is apparent in the creation of the a new social work degree (Department of Health, 2002), a new post-qualifying award in child care practice and a more entrenched and successful bid to rein in the independence and radicalism within social work education (see Webb, 1996). In terms of actual practice, despite the references to social worker autonomy and judgement, the LAC system (specifically the AARs) and Framework (specifically the *Family Pack of Questionnaires and Scales*) provide little 'space' for the practitioner. Clearly, for social workers, some 'spheres of discretion' (May and Buck, 1998) can still be recaptured, but in the new procedurally-driven world of social work and social care it is becoming increasingly difficult to find and safeguard these autonomous locations and to practice in them.

The assessment 'tools' discussed are evidence, we would suggest, of a regulatory impulse which is driven, in part, by a lack of trust in social work and in individual social worker's ability and commitment to adequately assist in the task maintaining the social order necessary for the process of capital accumulation. These 'tools' are also like to further deepen the process of social work's de-skilling and fragmentation; characterised by complex tasks being broken down into discrete components and facilitating 'social work' being undertaken by less qualified staff, such as 'family support workers', 'outreach workers', or sessional and agency staff receiving lower rates of pay providing, possibly, evidence that the West is indeed undergoing 'Brazilianization', on account of the spread of temporary and insecure unemployment (Beck 2000).

To conclude, the 'systems', 'frameworks' and 'instruments', which social workers involved with children and families are expected to use are likely to proliferate. Social workers will need, therefore, both individually and collectively, to decide to what degree they are going to allow centrally devised documentation to structure their engagement with children and families. Clearly, social workers are not 'automata', yet because of a fear of management reprisals there is, perhaps, a pervasive inclination to 'keep to the official definition of the situation and not to move beyond the constraints imposed by protocol and procedures' (Spratt and Houston, 1998: 320). Critical analysis and creative work will, therefore, need to take place in order to resist proceduralisation and to resist bureaucratic constraints, which are seeking to produce both 'competent' social workers and compliant users of services.

Note

1. Referred to throughout as Department of Health etc, 2000.

References

Aldridge, M. (1996), 'Dragged to Market: Being a Profession in the Postmodern World', *British Journal of Social Work*, 26: 177-94.

Ball, S.J. (1994), *Education Reform: A Critical and Post-Structural Approach*, Open University: Buckingham.

Baron-On, A. (1999), 'Social Work and the "Missionary Zeal to Whip the Heathen Along the Path of Righteousness"', *British Journal of Social Work*, 29: 5-26.

Bauman, Z. (2000), 'Am I My Brother's Keeper?', *European Journal of Social Work*, 3(1): 5-11.

British Association of Social Workers (BASW) (1996) *A Code of Ethics for Social Work*, Birmingham: BASW.

Beck, U. (1998), *The Risk Society* (6th Edition), Sage: London.

Beck, U. (2000), *The Brave New World of Work*, Blackwell: Oxford.

Birlson, P. (1981), 'The Validity of Depressive Disorder in Childhood and the Development of a Self-Rating Scale: A Research Report', *Journal of Child Psychology and Psychiatry*, 22: 73-88.

Bosanquet, B. (1895), (ed), *Aspects of the Social Problem*, Macmillan: London.

Clark, C. (1995), 'Competence and Discipline in Professional Formation', *British Journal of Social Work*, 25: 563-81.

Cochran, M.M. and Brassard, J.A. (1979), 'Child Development and Personal Social Networks', *Child Development*, 50: 601-16.

Coppock, V. (1996), 'Mad, Bad or Misunderstood?', *Youth and Policy*, 53: 53-66.

Corrick, H., Jones, J. and Ward, H. (1995), *Looking After Children: Good Parenting, Good Outcomes. Management and Implementation Guide*, HMSO: London.

Crnic, K.A. and Greenberg, M.T. (1990), 'Minor Parenting Stresses with Young Children', *Child Development*, 61: 1628-37.

Dean, M. (1999), *Governmentality: Power and Rule in Modern Society*, London: Sage.

Dendy, H. (1895), 'The Industrial Residuum', in B. Bosanquet (ed), *Aspects of the Social Problem*, Macmillan: London.

Department of Health (1995) *Looking After Children: Good Parenting, Good Outcomes Training Guide*, HMSO: London.

Department of Health (1998), *Modernising Social Services*, HMSO: London.

Department of Health (1998a), *Objectives for Social Services for Children*, HMSO: London.

Department of Health (1998b), *Quality Protects: Framework for Action*, HMSO: London.

Department of Health (1999), *Framework for the Assessment of Children in Need and their Families: Consultation Draft, Department of Health: London.*

Department of Health (2000), *Assessing Children in Need and their Families: Practice Guidance*, Stationery Office: London.

Department of Health (2000a), *The Child's World: Assessing Children in Need – Reader*, Department of Health: London.

Department of Health (2001), 'Milburn Orders Inquiry into the Death of Victoria Climbie', Press Notice, 12th January.

Department of Health (2002), 'New Social Work Degree will Focus on Practical Training', Press Release, 22nd May.

Department of Health, Cox, A. and Bentovim, A. (2000), *Framework for Assessment of Children in Need and their Families*, Stationery Office: London.

Department of Health, Department for Education and Employment, Home Office (2000), *Framework for the Assessment of Children in Need and their Families*, Stationery Office: London.

Department of Health, NSPCC, University of Sheffield (2000), *The Child's World: Assessing Children in Need – Trainer Modules*, Department of Health: London.

Dominelli, L. (1996), 'Deprofessionalizing Social Work: Anti-Oppressive Practice, Competencies and Postmodernism', *British Journal of Social Work*, 26: 153-75.

Dominelli, L. and Hoogvelt, A. (1996), Globalisation and the Technocratization of Social Work, *Critical Social Policy*, 16(2): 45-63.

Edwards, R. and Usher, R. (1994), 'Disciplining the Subject: the Power of Competence', *Studies in the Education of Adults*, 26(1): 1-15.

Ennew, J. (1994), 'Time for Children or Time for Adults?', in J. Qvortrup (ed), *Childhood Matters: Social Theory, Practice and Politics*, Avebury: Aldershot.

Fabricant, M. (1985), 'The Industrialization of Social Work Practice', *Social Work*, 30(5): 389-96.

Forrest, D. (2000), 'Theorising Empowerment Thought: Illuminating the Relationship between Ideology and Politics in the Contemporary Era', *Sociological Research Online*, 4(4) <http://www.socresonline.org.uk/4/4/forrest.html>

Foster, P. and Wilding P. (2000), 'Whither Welfare Professionalism?', *Social Policy & Administration*, 34(2): 143-59.

Foucault, M. (1977), *Discipline and Punish*, Penguin: Harmondsworth.

Froggett, L. and Sapey, B. (1997), 'Communication, Culture and Social Work', *Social Work Education*, 16(1): 41-54.

Garrett, P.M. (1999), 'Producing the Moral Citizen: the Looking After Children System and the Regulation of Children and Young People in Public Care'. *Critical Social Policy*, 19, 3: 291-311.

Garrett, P.M. (2002a), 'Encounters in the New Welfare Domains of the Third Way: Social Work, the Connexions Agency and Personal Advisers', *Critical Social Policy*, 22(4): 592-615.

Garrett, P.M. (2002b), 'Getting a Grip: New Labour and the Reform of the Law on Child Adoption', *Critical Social Policy*, 22(2): 174-202.

Garrett, P.M. (2002c), 'Yes Minister: Reviewing the "Looking After Children" Experience and Identifying the Messages for Social Work Research', *The British Journal of Social Work*, 32: 831-46.

Gledhill, A. (1989), *Who Cares?* Centre for Policy Studies: London.

Hall, S. (1993), 'Thatcherism Today', *New Statesman and Society*, 26 November: 14-17.

Hall, S. (1998), 'The Great Moving Nowhere Show', *Marxism Today*, November/December: 9-15.

Hanlon, G. (1998), 'Professionalism as Enterprise: Service Class Politics and the Redefinition of Professionalism', *Sociology*, 32(1): 43-63.

Hanlon, G. (2000), 'Sacking the New Jerusalem? The New Right, Social Democracy and Professional Identities', *Sociological Research Online*, 5(1) <http://www.socresonline.org.uk/5/1/hanlon.html>

Harris, J. (1998), 'Scientific Management, Bureau-Professionalism, New Managerialism: The Labour Process of State Social Work', *British Journal of Social Work*, 28: 839-62.

Harris, P. (1999), 'Public Welfare and Liberal Governance' in A. Petersen, I. Barns, J. Dudley, J. and P. Harris (eds), *Poststructuralism, Citizenship and Social Policy*, Routledge: London.

Harvey, D. (1990), *The Condition of Postmodernity*, Oxford: Blackwell.

Hendrick, H. (1994), *Child Welfare. England 1872-1889*, London: Routledge.

Humphries, B. (1997), 'Reading Social Work: Competing Discourses in the Rules and Requirements for the Diploma in Social Work', *British Journal of Social Work*, 27: 641-58.

Jackson, S. (1998), 'Looking After Children: a New Approach or Just an Exercise in Form-Filling ? A Response to Knight and Caveney', *British Journal of Social Work*, 28: 45-56.

Jackson, S. and Kilroe, S. (eds), (1996) *Looking After Children: Good Parenting, Good Outcomes Reader*, HMSO: London.

James, A and Jencks, C. (1996), 'Public Perceptions of Childhood Criminality', *British Journal of Sociology*, 47(2): 315-32.

Johnson, T. (1993), 'Expertise and the State', in M. Gane and T. Johnson (eds), *Foucault's New Domains*, Routledge: London.

Jones, C. (1983), *State Social Work and the Working Class*, Macmillan: London.

Jones, C. (1996), 'Anti-Intellectualism and the Peculiarities of British Social Work Education', in N. Parton (ed), *Social Theory, Social Change and Social Work*, Routledge: London.

Jones, C. (1996a), 'Regulating Social Work: A Review of the Review', in S. Jackson and M. Preston-Shoot (eds), *Educating Social Workers in a Changing Policy Context*, Whiting and Birch: London.

Kilroe, S. (1996), 'Social Presentation', in S. Jackson and S. Kilroe (eds), *Looking After Children: Good Parenting, Good Outcomes Reader*, HMSO: London.

Knight, T. and Caveney, S. (1998), 'Assessment and Action Records: Will they Promote Good Parenting?', *British Journal of Social Work*, 28: 29-43.

Lash, S. and Urry, J. (1999), *Economies of Sign and Space* (Third Edition), Sage: London.

London Borough of Brent (1985), *A Child in Trust: The report of the Panel of Inquiry into the Circumstances Surrounding the Death of Jasmine Beckford*, London Borough of Brent: London.

London Borough of Greenwich (1987), *A Child in Mind: Protection of Children in a Responsible Society. The Report of the Commission of Inquiry into the Circumstances Surrounding the Death of Kimberley Carlile*, London: London Borough of Greenwich.

London Borough of Lambeth (1987) *Whose Child? The Report of the Public Inquiry into the Death of Tyra Henry*, London Borough of Lambeth: London.

Malin, N. (ed), (2000), *Professionalism, Boundaries and the Workplace*, Routledge: London.

May, T. and Buck, M. (1998), 'Power, Professionalism and Organisational Transformation', *Sociological Research Online*, 3(1) <http://www.socresonline.org.uk/3/2/5.html>.

Merrick, D. (1996), *Social Work and Child Abuse*, Routledge: London.

Nellis, M. (1999), 'Towards "the Field of Corrections": Modernising the Probation Service in the Late 1990s', *Social Policy & Administration*, 33(3): 302-23.

Parker, R., Ward, H., Jackson, S., Aldgate, J. and Wedge, P. (1991), *Looking After Children: Assessing Outcomes in Child Care*, HMSO: London.

Parton, N. (1998), 'Risk, Advanced Liberalism and Child Welfare: the Need to Rediscover Uncertainty and Ambiguity', *British Journal of Social Work*, 28: 5-28.

Parton, N. and O'Byrne, P. (2000), *Constructive Social Work*, Macmillan: London.

Pithouse, A. (1998) *Social Work: the Social Organisation of an Invisible Trade* (Second Edition), Ashgate: Aldershot.

Poster, M. (1990), *The Mode of Information: Post-structuralism and Social Context*, Polity: Cambridge.

Powell, M. (2000), 'New Labour and the Third Way in the British Welfare State: a New and Distinctive Approach?', *Critical Social Policy*, 20(1): 39-61.

Powell, M. (ed) (1999), *New Labour, New Welfare State?* Policy Press: Bristol.

Pumphrey, RE and Pumphrey, M.W. (1961), *The Heritage of American Social Work*, Columbia University: New York.

Richmond, M.E. (1917), *Social Diagnosis*, Russell Sage Foundation: New York.

Rogers, C. (1980), *A Way of Being*, Houghton Mifflin: Boston.

Rooff, M. (1972), *A Hundred Years of Family Welfare*, Michael Joseph: London.

Rose, N. (1985), *The Psychological Complex: Psychology, Politics and Society in England 1869-1939*, Routledge & Kegan Paul: London.

Rose, N. (1989), *Governing the Soul: The Shaping of the Private Self*, Routledge: London.

Rose, N. (1993), 'Government, Authority and Expertise in Advanced Liberalism', *Economy and Society*, 22(3): 283-300.

Rose, N. (1996), 'Governing "Advanced" Liberal Democracies', in A. Barry, T. Osborne and N. Rose (eds), *Foucault and Political Reason*, UCL Press: London.

Rose, N. (2000), 'Government and Control', *British Journal of Criminology*, 40: 321-39.

Rose, N. and Miller, P. (1992), Political Power Beyond the State: Problematics of Government' *British Journal of Sociology*, 43: 173-206.

Rose, W. (2000), 'Assessing Children in Need and their Families: An Overview of the Framework', in Department of Health (2000a) *The Child's World: Assessing Children in Need – Reader*, Department of Health: London.

Rossiter, A. (2000), 'The Postmodern Feminist Condition: New Conditions for Social Work', in B. Fawcett, B. Featherstone, J. Fook and A. Rossiter (eds), *Practice and Research in Social Work: Postmodern Feminist Perspectives*, Routledge: London.

Secretary of State for Social Services (1988), *Report of the Inquiry into Child Abuse in Cleveland*, HMSO: London.

Shemmings Y. and Shemmings D. (2000), 'Empowering Children and Family Members to Participate in the Assessment Process, in Department of Health' (2000a), *The Child's World: Assessing Children in Need – Reader*, Department of Health: London.

Singh, G. (1997), 'Developing Critical Perspectives in Anti-Racist and Anti-Oppressive Theory and Practice – into the New Millennium', unpublished paper presented to the *National Organisation of Practice Teachers (NOPT) Annual Conference*, 9-11 July.

Smale, G. (1993), *Empowerment, Assessment, Care Management and the Skilled Worker*, National Institute for Social Work/HMSO: London.

Spratt T. and Houston, S. (1999), 'Developing Critical Social Work in Theory and in Practice: Child Protection and Communicative Reason', *Child and Family Social Work*, 4: 315-24.

Virilio, P. (1997), *Open Sky*, Verso: London.

Ward, H. (ed) (1995), *Looking After Children: Research into Practice*, HMSO: London.

Ward, H. (2000), 'The Development Needs of Children: Implications for Assessment' in Department of Health (2000a), *The Child's World: Assessing Children in Need – Reader*, Department of Health: London.

Waterhouse, R. (2000), *Lost in Care: Report of the Tribunal of Inquiry into the Abuse of Children in Care in the Former County Council Areas of Gwynedd and Clywd since 1974*, Stationery Office: London.

Wilson, F. (1999), 'Cultural Control Within the Virtual Organization', *Sociological Review*, 47, 4: 672-95.

Webb, D. (1996), 'Regulation for Radicals: the State, CCETSW and the Academy', in N. Parton (ed), *Social Theory, Social Change and Social Work*, Routledge: London.

Woodroofe, K. (1962), *From Charity to Social Work*, Routledge & Kegan Paul: London.

Chapter 6

New Police Management, Performance and Accountability

Beverly Metcalfe

Introduction

The rhetoric of new public management (NPM) and managerialism has been, and remains, a highly significant trend within western governments (Leishman et al, 1995; Jones and Newburn, 2002). In the UK in particular NPM ideology is seen as having significantly impacted the design and delivery of public services (for example, Flynn, 1999, 2001; Exworthy and Halford, 1999; Pollitt, 1993; Hood, 1991). However, throughout the 1980's and 1990's unlike other public agencies the police have successfully resisted public sector managerialism (Loveday, 1999; Reiner, 2000), although there is now mounting evidence that this is beginning to change (Metcalfe, 2001). Drawing on performance management literature, a management strategy often cited as part of the NPM repertoire (Sanderson, 2001), this chapter focuses on the way in which discourses of accountability and its implementation technologies have attempted to transform police management and organisation. It is argued that performance management ideology as part of the *new police management* has brought with it a new principle of police accountability. The new accountability gives emphasis to managerial rather than legal or public interest issues, favours external and centralised control over self-regulation and promotes risk management rather than rule enforcement. This shift in accountability discourse and control style is partly a response to the failure of traditional legal and disciplinary procedures to control police misconduct and a 'post-social' government rationality which favours the adoption of private sector techniques for the administration of state agencies. The experience of a large English police force, *ForceCo,* will be used to examine the limits of such strategies, focusing in particular on the analysis of the introduction of performance management techniques. I draw on survey data, interviews and ethnographic field notes to reveal the different ways in which individuals responded to *new police management* discourses. I will suggest that attempts to introduce *new police management* have not necessarily been successful in holding the police more accountable, nor indeed in providing measures to monitor and improve police effectiveness. I show how discourses of accountability and police performance help to symbolically constitute *new police management* ideologies as well as reveal how employees resist these disciplinary controls.

I will begin the chapter by discussing what is meant by 'accountability' and 'performance management' in a policing context. This is followed by a case study of *ForceCo*, describing the Home Office's new accountability structures, performance appraisal policy and the implementation of performance appraisal in *ForceCo*. I then consider these results in relation to old and new forms of accountability and police performance. In conclusion I will argue that the new accountability technologies are having limited impact on police governance and performance, primarily due to a lack of coherence in police accountability strategy, and also police managements ability to resist these new police technologies.

Accountability and Performance in the Police

Accountability is a term that has two competing meanings in the police literature. On the one hand accountability is seen as ultimately concerned with control over the police (Reiner, 2000; Loveday, 2000); on the other hand it is said to be about 'requirements to give accounts' or explanations of conduct (Reiner, 2000). These competing meanings are reflected in Marshall's distinction between two approaches to accountability: the 'subordinate and obedient model', and the 'explanatory and co-operative' model which requires decision makers to provide information about their decisions (in Chan, 1999: 250-53). The dichotomy however between these two approaches is not so great when you consider that both models are concerned with *evaluation*. As Chan states, citing Schelnker, accountability has recently been defined as:

> Being answerable to audiences for performance up to certain prescribed standards, thereby fulfilling obligations, duties, expectation, and other charges. When people are accountable, they can be made to explain and justify their conduct, and their behaviour can be scrutinised, judged and sanctioned by audiences

> (Chan, 1999: 253).

As part of *new police management*, then, accountability, becomes inextricably intertwined with performance monitoring at both the individual and organisational level, though it is only recently that this as been acknowledged in the literature (Metcalfe, 2001; Metcalfe and Dick, 2002).

Historically, assessment of police behaviour and conduct was principally concerned with specific police activities, rather than how well they performed them, so that police accountability is often conceptualised in relation to the rule of law, police powers and police corruption (Reiner, 2000; Jones and Newburn, 2002). Hence, police practices have been governed by departmental rules, which are enforced by the courts and police hierarchies respectively. The predominant mode of control tended to be 'deterrence through legislation and rule making, investigation and enforcement, criminal sanction and organisation discipline' (Chan, 1999: 254). This type of police administration rested on policing strategies, which focused on law enforcement, or reactive policing techniques. Many police and criminological scholars have written extensively of the failures of reactive policing techniques, since it is widely believed amongst senior police and Home Office policy advisors that reactive strategies are inefficient in allocating scarce police resources, as well as being ineffective in tackling the social problems that cause crime (see especially Bennett, 1998; Rosenbaum, 1998; Waters, 2000; Leigh et al, 1998; Rogerson, 1995; Correia, 1999). The primary reasons cited for the failure of reactive techniques have been a police occupational culture which excuses and encourages abuses of power (Reiner, 2000); the rising costs of police services in the 1980's and 1990's (Collier, 2001; Rogerson, 1995); as well as mounting concern in the public eyes about the police's ability to manage crime effectively (Leishman et al, 1995; Redshaw et al, 1998; Loveday, 1999).

The repeated failures of the old accountability and its limited impacts for effective reforms have paved the way for a new way of thinking about police accountability. The new accountability has a distinctive discourse and an associated set of technologies in line with a governmental rationality, which is committed to the ascendancy of the managerial prerogative. This includes greater financial accountability and the development of a range of efficiency measures by which individuals, and police organisations are judged. These developments have also heralded the move towards more proactive policing strategies, namely community policing and 'intelligent' lead policing initiatives (Rosenbaum, 1998; Correia, 1999). A strong focus of the NPM discourse has been the desire to introduce new disciplinary technologies designed to inculcate the police with new managerial attitudes and new values (Pollitt, 1993; Flynn, 1999; Exworthy and Halford, 1999). This was against a background of rising crime levels throughout the 1980's and 1990's and a series of reports questioning police management structures and their efficient use of resources (for example Sheehy, 1993; Redshaw et al. 1998). Above all government philosophy emphasised the importance of greater police accountability so that individual constabularies now find themselves open to evaluation, as well as having to justify their policies and procedures to a greater extent than was previously the case (Reiner, 1992; 1998, 2000; Leishman et al, 1995; 1996). This shift in accountability and control structures is a reflection of modern society's concern with the documentation and management control of risks in both government and private institutions (Chan, 1999: 254) and it is the features of this performance discourse that I now turn.

Performance Discourse

Performance accountability embraces a theory that public agencies have failed the tests of effectiveness and efficiency (Leishman et al, 1995; Hood, 1991), and to correct this deficiency they need to adopt private sector management techniques as well as introduce competition under market or quasi market conditions. NPM is often presented as the transference of private management techniques to the public organisation and incorporates:

> ...cost control, financial transparency, the autonomization of sub-units, the decentralization of management authority, the creation of market and quasi-market mechanisms separating purchasing and providing functions and their linkage via contracts, and the enhancement of accountability to customers for the quality of service via the creation of performance indicators
>
> (Power, 1997:43).

Flynn (2001) and Osbourne and Plastrik (2000), in particular, have noted that the process of performance evaluation involves establishing definitions of service delivery and associated 'output' performance indicators. Within the policing environment performance standards encompass *inter alia*: crime management, public order management, and call management, and are primarily assessed on 'crime clear up rates' and 'associated costs' (Loveday, 2000: 215). However, while the rise of NPM is acknowledged as one of the most 'striking international trends in public administration' (Hood, 1991: 3) it is fair to say that the impact of NPM has had much less impact on police organisations, especially in the UK (See Loveday, 1999; 2000). A good example of resistance to performance controls is evidenced by Leishman et al's early review of the police response to the Sheehy report. They state:

> NPM constituted an attack on the entrenched interests of many actors within the policing policy network. Reforms opposed by the police (especially ACPO [Association of Chief Police Officers]) were largely blocked and diluted; while reforms favoured by the more powerful ACPO were left relatively unscathed
>
> (1995: 35).

They do note however, that NPM will 'eventually' restructure the way that the police are managed as the government appoints the 'right people'; 'buys' some people off, and continues to 'erode the solidarity' amongst different police associations (ibid, 1995: 35). In the following I suggest that policies relating to police performance standards are now taking on a much stronger managerialist turn (Pollitt, 1993; Exworthy and Halford, 1999), as already evidenced by the use of terms such as 'competencies', 'best value' and 'best practice' in addition to the traditional aspiration of *new police management* and professionalism (Waters, 2000: 276-80).

Technologies of Performance

The new accountability is presented as involving a shift in regulatory style away from centralised control towards a combination of self-regulation and external oversight. Implementing a new accountability involves a range of technologies and accounting devices to measure performance and make decisions auditable. Within the police in the UK this has involved the strengthening of public bodies whom are responsible for monitoring all aspects of police performance. In addition guidelines have been developed which are intended to govern micro-processes of police behaviour and conduct. In this chapter I am mostly concerned with examining the micro-processes of performance regulation. In the following I briefly focus on the new accountability systems that have been implemented throughout the 1990's and which help frame the background for my focus on individual performance management in the police. I then turn to consider the performance management framework, which was established by the Sheehy report in 1993 and the 'Home Office Circular 43 on Performance Appraisal' in 1996.

Since the 1990's new accountability measures have been put into place to scrutise police performance in all aspects of crime management (Leishman et al, 1995; Cope et al, 1997; Leigh et al, 1998; Loveday, 1999). The introduction of the Police and Magistrates Courts Act (1994) provided the Home Secretary with statutory responsibility for the 'efficiency' of police services. This involves directing police forces in the development of 'national key objectives', which all police agencies are expected to pursue (Waters, 2000). Although the Home Office Circular 114 of 1983 (See Reiner, 2000: 191, and Waters, 2000) established the Audit Commission to ensure that existing resources were being used 'efficiently effectively and economically' (the 3 E's) it was not until a series of hard hitting reports in the 1990's aimed at enhancing value-for-money (for example Audit Commission 1993; 1996),[1] that the Audit Commission was really taken seriously by police agencies. Closely linked to the rise of the Audit Commission has been the rise of Her Majesty's Inspectorate of Constabulary (HMIC). The HMIC annual inspection of all police forces now forms the basis for the development of performance improvement strategies at both the individual and national level.[2]

In addition to the growth in importance of the Audit Commission and HMIC in recent years the Home Office has also encouraged ACPO (Association of Chief Police Officers) to become the pivotal body for harmonising policies between forces (Reiner, 2000: 219). The resultant effect of this policy co-ordination role has served to substantially influence the role of ACPO (Metcalfe, 2001). There has been extensive debate as to whether these new accountability structures have been effective in discharging these responsibilities (See Jones and Newburn, 2002; Loveday, 1999, 2000). Indeed, one of the most interesting features of the current monitoring arrangements remains the complete dependence of the police authority on the information provided by the police force for which they have ostensible oversight (Loveday, 2000: 216).[3]

From the forgoing discussion it is clear that there is now a greater involvement by central government in police management and service delivery to a degree not countenanced a decade ago (Loveday, 2000: 226). The thrust of government policy has ostensibly been concerned with introducing more stringent measures of monitoring and control while at the same time arguing that police strategy development is to be directly managed by local representatives. As Leishman et al have argued, national policing strategy 'substantially shifts the balance of power away from local government towards central government' (1996: 21). This centralising influence is also evidenced in the way that the government is introducing guidelines by which police agencies should develop human resource and employment systems and it is to this that I now turn.

Policing Performance

A unique feature of police agencies is the level of discretion that they have historically had in the management of police personnel (Metcalfe, 2001). Personnel departments in police agencies have traditionally been directed by time served police officers with little or no personnel training or qualifications. The personnel department's role was chiefly administration, overseeing payroll, grievance and discipline and training and development. Three key influences can be identified as having a direct impact on personnel management policy. Firstly, the NPM agenda has undoubtedly raised concerns about the professionalism and lack of strategic orientation amongst police personnel departments (Metcalfe, 2001). Secondly, ACPO has pushed for harmonisation of personnel procedures across forces, as well as promote the adoption of 'best HR' practices in police agencies. Finally, the HMI inspections conducted yearly for each police force introduced 'Leadership and Management' performance indicators from 1996. This has meant, as Leishman et al (1995) predicted, that police restructuring has assisted the reconstitution of police management roles and identities.

The Sheehy report published in 1993 focused specifically on trying to enhance the performance of police forces, as a whole, as well as individual officers, regardless of rank and specialism. Its broad objectives covered the evaluation of rank structures, remuneration, and conditions of service. The review included an analysis of key policing skills for each operational and management level and set out in detail how an annual appraisal would evaluate these core skills and rate officers on a ranked grid ranging from 'outstanding' to 'unsatisfactory'.[4] However, it was not until the publication of the Home Office Circular (HOC Number 43 September 1996) entitled '*Staff Appraisal: The Performance Development Review System*' which 'instructed' police agencies to define and measure core policing responsibilities and implement administrative controls for a performance and development review system,[5] that police agencies began to enact the recommendations in Sheehy. From 1997 all of the UK police agencies have begun the process of designing and implementing a performance development review programme though there is no available data to assess the progress of this.

The Sheehy Report and Home Office Circular (1996) were committed to strong administrative controls, stressing the importance of measuring outcomes and controlling behaviour - in essence, the *hard* aspects of performance management (Guest, 1987, 1998; Storey, 1995; Winstanley and Stuart-Smith 1996), rather than be concerned with cultural and human resource development techniques (See for example Stiles, 1997; Armstrong and Baron, 1998). Sheehy states that in: 'a results orientated role the achievement of objectives may be more important than the way it is achieved' (1993: 53 para 6.39). At a broader level this *hard* focus is shown by police commitment to a range of quantitative performance measures and 'output controls' (Pollitt, 1993, Rogerson, 1995; Sanderson, 2001; Collier, 2000); this is further evidenced by the growing number of Audit Commission and HMIC reports which highlight police management and organisation as prioritising the development of 'performance culture' and 'stringent performance controls' (for example see Audit Commission, 1998; HMIC Manchester, 1998, 2000, HMIC, Kent, 1998). As Loveday comments (1999: 357-35) there is an implicit assumption within HMIC that the 'culture of performance' can become a feature, which can be 'identified, encouraged and measured'. These observations are significant for if the police are rebranding themselves as a 'service' in tackling the social problems that cause crime (along with other community agencies), and not as a 'reactive' force, performance measurement will continue to be problematical (See Bennett, 1998; Rosenbaum, 1998; Rogerson, 1995).

Unlike other public agencies the consequences of the new accountability technologies for police management have not been reported on in detail in the UK, especially when considering assessment of individual officer performance. With the 'audit' explosion in the UK Power (1997) found two types of unintended consequences, which can be applied to the policing context. Firstly, a situation of 'decoupling' can emerge whereby external units are deemed as chiefly responsible for monitoring accountability requirements. Both Loveday (1999; 2000) and Reiner (2000) have suggested external accountability controls are largely symbolic. The second type of unintended consequence is 'colonisation', which occurs when organisations become dominated by the accountability process to manage their own performance. This is significant since inspection and audit do not passively monitor, but shape the standards of the performance in crucial ways. As Jary notes 'audit' reshapes professional subjectivities and demonstrates the 'colonizing power of audit' (2002: 39). Undoubtedly as Loveday (2000) has argued these 'consequences' both attend to some form of 'image management'. The following case study data lends support to this observation and discloses how dominant discourses of performance management are rooted in symbolic constructions of service and quality improvement. I show that through colonisation, dominant discourses of performance have reconstituted policing identities, although these are fraught with tension and instability and are continually renegotiated and contested.

A Case Study

To explore the technologies and consequences of the new accountability I will draw on the experience of a large English police force. The discussion draws on an ongoing research project examining the nature and effects of HRM strategies, specifically performance management on a large shire police force – *ForceCo*. In this chapter I selectively use data from a force-wide attitude survey and ethnographic data collected over a period of two and a half years. *ForceCo* is split into ten geographical divisions and employs 3,828 employees. My ethnographic research was located in the two largest divisions, one city, one rural, although I did visit all the divisions of the force. To help structure the survey semi-structured interviews were held with a cross sample of operational and management staff which assisted me in unravelling relevant organisational and managerial themes. The survey question areas relevant to this chapter relate to the employees understanding of the strategic direction of *ForceCo*; the relationships between line supervisor and employees; and employee responses to the implementation of the Performance Review System. The police population was 3,828, with 1,675 returns for the survey (46 per cent return rate).

In addition, as part of my ethnographic study I undertook sixty-two interviews with police officers and managers. All of the interviews were conducted by the author and lasted between one and three hours. Individuals were self-selecting for interviews, indicating a willingness to discuss police performance issues. In addition information was also collected from senior police (The Chief and Assistant Chief Constables) and police union representatives. Forty-nine of the interviewees were men on account of the dominance of men at all ranks.

The methodological approach thus combines quantitative and qualitative data. However, the author acknowledges that survey techniques do not unravel 'within group' differences and presents interview data so as to focus on the shifting meanings given to performance management and police identities. The interview material presented here is not comprehensive, nor is it intended to present 'pure' data but acknowledges the way performance scripts are socially constructed allowing for the potential to read and interpret police and performance dynamics in fluid and diverse ways (see Metcalfe and Dick, 2002). The intention was to encourage a critical re-reading of the survey data so as to provide accounts of the social and contextual nature of police employment relations (See also Jones and Newburn, 2002).

Performance Review System (PRS): Design and Implementation

Following Sheehy and the Home Office Circular the *ForceCo* version of the PRS model was implemented in June 1998. The central aim of the PRS system was to 'encourage the best possible performance from individuals', though emphasis was placed on 'enhancing communication, enabling honest, two way discussions between appraisees and their immediate supervisors, providing regular feedback and the opportunity for development' (Chief Constable – Personnel Bulletin No 183 1998). The PRS process incorporated assessment of core policing skills and competencies (ethics/integrity; communication; self-motivation; decision making; creativity and innovation), and the achievement of specific objectives (to be linked to departmental policing objectives). Participants would be graded A-E in each of the competency areas, while objectives achieved would be assessed on a scale including outstanding, commendable, satisfactory, and unsatisfactory. The reviews were to take place at least once annually, though personnel recommended two to three assessments per year, which is what is recommended for most performance management schemes (Storey, 1995; Armstrong and Baron, 1998).

To communicate the policing priorities *ForceCo* published a strategy document entitled 'Forward Together' which introduced objectives for how policing duties were to be carried out. This included 'vision' statements that stressed commitment to improving police services; the importance of community partnerships in tackling crime; and the ethical approach that *ForceCo* will take when dealing with all aspects of police work. The document also claimed that it is *ForceCo's*:

> ...aim to continually provide better services by the more appropriate use of resources in *a Performance Management Culture*
>
> (*italics* my insertion).

This was to be achieved by 'measuring effectiveness qualitatively and quantitatively'. The following discussion reveals that performance was constructed in terms of quantitative indicators, what I term the 'hard' policing discourse. I also show that this dominant discourse causes tensions and ambiguities in terms of how individuals construct and reconstruct their police role.

Hard Policing Discourse

A key concern with the performance management literature has been that employees should be able to identify with the goals and values of the organisation (Bevan and Thompson, 1992); personnel should be aware of the aims of the performance scheme (Armstrong and Baron, 1998); and there should be openness and honesty between employees. Table 6.1 reveals that the substantial majority of employees agreed or strongly agreed with questions relating to their knowledge of the strategic priorities of the force. Table 6.2 clearly reveals that the majority of respondents agreed or strongly agreed with the questions about attitudes to performance improvement. These findings reflect the dominant performance discourse that reflects commitment to improvement and quality enhancement. A strong element of this has been the promotion of 'professional' managerial subjectivities (See Townley, 1994; Exworthy and Halford, 1999) as evidenced in the *ForceCo* PRS police 'skills and competencies' described above.

For some officers the hard performance discourse was an important aspect of them being able to perform in their job:

> I strongly see the PRS scheme and the division's overall performance closely linked. I want to see how my shift are [*sic*] performing. I want to see clear indicators because that is something that the Chief can easily see, and I will get rewarded on it. If I can show that burglary detection rates are up in my division then that looks good. No-one pays attention to what you're doing and how you're doing it – it's the results that count
>
> (Chief Inspector Operations, Rural Division).

Table 6.1 Employee Perceptions of Policing Strategies

	SD (%)	D (%)	Neut (%)	A (%)	SA (%)
I am aware of the goals of Forward Together	1	7	12	65	14
I understand the links between the Police Authority's plan and my divisional plan	4	17	28	42	10

SD = strongly disagree
D = disagree
Neut = neither agree nor disagree
A = agree
SA = strongly agree

Table 6.2 Employee Perceptions of Performance Improvement

	SD (%)	D (%)	Neut (%)	A (%)	SA (%)
Generally my division/department Is taking actions to improve the quality of its work.	2	10	17	54	17
The service we provide and possible improvements are regularly discussed by myself/ colleagues/supervisors.	5	14	15	52	15

Similarly the Chief Inspector (Operations) in the City Division stated:

> We are pushed to improve police services with lower manpower, and ultimately lower costs. That means we have to prioritise policing strategies, decide what resources to use where, so measuring what each division and each individual in that division is important – it's just what I have to do. It's now part of the system, The HMIC wants it, so the Chief wants it, so we do it.

And a probationary officer:

> You've got to put yourself around, show you know about strategies, targets, let people know when you score, you can't just quietly do your stint like the old days, everything's about performance. I don't mind it but the older guys don't like it.

The focus on measurement and assessment is perceived as part of the new police management role – 'it's part of the system', and is clearly tied to the broader accountability structures – 'the HMIC wants it, so the Chief wants it, so we do it'. Indeed the Chief Constable commented that the PRS:

> ...will change the way that we manage, it will provide the opportunity to identify both blocks to performance and permit joint problem solving
>
>   (Commanders meeting, 1998).

PRS then as it is constituted within the broader performance discourse facilitates 'the spread of a distinct mentality of administrative control, a pervasive logic which has life over and above specific practices' (Power, in Jary, 2002: 38). However, at the operational level the hard performance discourse is contested:

> There's a feeling that measuring everything is going against what the police job is actually about – protecting the public. The preference for MBA-type police managers rather than those who have street experience ignores all this community consultation stuff – how do you measure that?
>
>   (Community Sergeant, Rural).

A special police officer said:

> I really want to make a difference but I know my performance is about how many arrest rates, and clear-ups I get.

A Chief Inspector of Personnel (Rural Division) states:

> I really looked after them – always there, supporting them. Now it's about resourcing, deployment, less money, no overtime and better performance.

The 'hard' performance discourse thus poses a challenge for how real police work is individually constructed. The Chief Inspector of Personnel clearly articulates tensions in his role as one expected to promote 'hard' human resource management rather than 'soft' human resource management agendas (Guest, 1987; 1998; Storey, 1992; 1995). He suggests that the promotion of professional and managerial subjectivities confronts traditional notions of police performance. This is supported further by the Sergeant who questions whether hard performance measures can meaningfully evaluate 'community consultation stuff'.

The concerns and tensions about appropriate disciplinary technologies are also revealed when we consider employee responses to survey questions relating to the PRS scheme itself. Table 6.3 shows that 52 per cent strongly disagreed or disagreed with the statement that the PRS is understood by employees. Only 15 per cent agreed or strongly agreed that the PRS process enabled them to contribute to organisation performance. So while employees clearly see performance improvement an everyday aspect of police work (Tables 6.1 and 6.2) there is disagreement over what disciplinary technologies are used to measure police performance. While the social texts presented above reveal tensions and ambiguities over how individuals carve out their policing role it is clear that the hard performance discourse has colonised managerial and organisational practices. I do not have space in this chapter to unveil the numerous tensions and discomfort with the formation and reformation of new subjectivities offered by the discourses of NPM, but turn instead to focus on the 'colonisation' of performance as an organisation and managerial resource.

Table 6.3 Employee Perceptions of the PRS

	SD (%)	D (%)	Neut (%)	A (%)	SA (%)
The PRS system is understood by employees	21	31	32	23	2
The PRS has improved my contribution to the performance of my division	17	28	40	13	2

Colonising Performance

While the PRS scheme was purportedly concerned with evaluating personal development issues this was not the experience in practice. Assessment was largely based on the achievement of individual objectives and tended to be (indirectly) linked to divisional objectives which were largely numerical and related inter alia to arrests, car crime and burglary detection rates. This was true of assessments at all levels in the hierarchy but especially at superintendent level which tended to use divisional crime detection rates as a measure of individual effectiveness. It was clear the importance of quantitative measures and hard indicators were embedded within existing management and cultural practices. Overall *ForceCo* demonstrated an instrumentalist approach to the management of employees. As Storey argues, hard HRM emphasises 'the quantitative, calculative and business strategic aspects of managing the headcount resources in as rational a way as for any other factor of production' (1992: 92; See also Townley, 1994). Performance dialogue was informed by reference to rational and structuralist accounts of organisation theorising, namely achievements and outcomes, and the objective measurement of these (Pollitt, 1993; Power, 1997; Bruijn, 2002). Drawing on theoretical accounts of performance management (Bevan and Thompson, 1992; Storey, 1995; Armstrong and Baron, 1998), *ForceCo* conceptualised the nature of performance development and performance strategy in terms of a *hard* systems approach.

Individual resistances were articulated in the way that the scheme was interpreted and procedures carried out. Perhaps the best reflection of resistance is shown by the fact that after 18 months in operation only 48 per cent reported in the survey that they had participated in the new scheme. A key concern was that many personnel raised questions about the competencies that were to be assessed. Since many could not tie these to actual police targets there was a tendency to award a grade 'C', an average grade, or in fact leave them blank because 'you can't define what the police really do by ticking a few boxes' (Chief Inspector Personnel). A significant stand against the output controls of the PRS was the decision by CID ranks across the force to opt out of the scheme altogether. They felt it 'distracted them from their policing priorities' (Detective Inspector City), and that it was a 'form to fill in for personnel' (Detective Sergeant City). This stand was not challenged by police management and is reflective of the CID police culture, which stresses autonomy and task control (Reiner, 2000). Similarly, in the Rural Division four out of the six Shift Inspectors stated that the PRS did little to monitor and help improve individual performance. There was thus strong cultural resistance to PRS at all hierarchical ranks. So while it has been shown that the disciplinary logic of the PRS scheme constituted a commitment to 'hard performance', and this is institutionalised through external accountability mechanisms as well; internally, the 'colonizing power' (Jary, 2002) of audit is resisted and renegotiated by individual officers. It is the interconnections between police accountability and assessing police performance, and the implications that this has for critiques of *new police management* that I will address in the conclusion.

Policing Performance and Accountability

The aim of this chapter has been to consider how discourses of performance have colonised police governance and accountability. By presenting case data on the design and implementation of a disciplinary technology, namely a performance management system in a large shire police force, I have sought to show how this disciplinary technology has reconstituted police management and organisation. While it is evident that 'policing force performance' is being increasingly monitored by central government, this is not necessarily the case for the management of individual police officers. Perhaps more than any other public agency performance evaluation and accountability in the police are more intertwined: as Sheehy comments: 'police are ordinary citizens with extraordinary powers' (1993: 3), and so marketisation pressures to make them accountable for what they do will remain a long term government agenda.

While this chapter has presented only tentative findings from a far broader study, the preceding arguments reinforce the complex interconnections and debates surrounding police roles and identities, police accountability and judging police performance. While some aspects of police work may lend itself to precise assessment in terms of an end product, or 'output controls' (Pollitt, 1993; Sanderson, 2001; Bruijn, 2002), the move towards community policing styles emphasises the need to evaluate the *processes* involved in police work. Reiner has convincingly argued that many forces are concerned with monitoring and controlling 'hard' measurement indicators but: 'for much police work ... it is the *process* not the *product,* that is crucial' (1998: 71, *italics* my insertion). Reiner believes that assessment of individual police performance is 'desirable' as a process of democratic accountability. He also indicates that it is 'inevitable' (1992, 1994, 1999, 2000). The lack of coherence and ambiguity in policing roles and associated governance controls suggests that the Home Office and individual forces must be clear about what they want to assess and measure, and this may mean coming to firm conclusions about the nature of 'policing style' in Britain.

Resistance to the new accountability technologies perhaps suggests that forces are successful at presenting a 'symbolic rather than real commitment to performance values' (Loveday, 1999: 375; see also Sanderson, 2001; Bruijn, 2002). New accountability attempts to move away from deterrence to a compliance mode of regulation, which aims at improving performance through individual evaluation, force inspection and audit. Yet, information from performance reviews, routine surveillance, and police complaints show that there is little transparency of high-risk officers and situations. Police performance indicators are notoriously difficult to identify, especially at the individual level and the use of systematically collected data for risk management is not widespread amongst police watchdogs and police agencies as the case analysis of the PRS demonstrates. Yet, the new accountability may have already succeeded in penetrating the culture of resistance since officers are increasingly being subject to managerial surveillance, through extensive crime reporting obligations and systematic audits (See also Waters, 2000), as well as performance controls emphasised in the PRS. The social texts of senior officers presented in this paper reveal that *new police management* is to some extent embedded in social and managerial practices, and it is likely that this managerialist ideology will grow stronger as the Home Office, as part of ongoing police restructuring, continue to strategically position those who support their philosophy (see Leishman et al, 1995). The new accountability technologies work in subtle ways, they have the capacity to create new knowledges and institutions, structure officers' conceptual frames, and create new cultures in organisations. Although critics of the new accountability generally distrust its managerialist approach and challenge its market orientation of accountability it may not necessarily be counterproductive. It could be argued that the new accountability is no more than a rational response to the failure of a deterrence based, individualistic approach to police accountability. Yet given that new accountability technologies have been defined more at the constabulary level, and resisted at the individual levels, there does appear to be a certain level of ambivalence about 'let the police managers manage'. This should not be surprising given that within Western economies it is certainly the case that the modern state is deeply ambivalent about the way in which police performance should be evaluated and held accountable (Reiner, 2000; Loveday, 2000). This ambivalence perhaps also suggests a reluctance to challenge police powers. As highlighted in this chapter current accountability structures allow senior police officers in individual forces strong administrative and managerial control over external force inspection and audit (Loveday, 2000; Waters, 2000), in addition to the long standing autonomy of police personnel decision makers. And, if police accountability cannot be assisted via performance appraisal techniques guided by the broader managerialist controls of NPM, can we therefore meaningfully state that *new police management* has successfully transformed police organisations? This chapter has suggested to some extent yes, since the 'colonizing power of audit' (Jary, 2002) has certainly reconstituted managerial roles and identities. However, existing police policy networks and police powers, as well as the police occupational culture show that the colonisation of performance will continue to be resisted.

Notes

1 *Helping with Enquires* (Audit Commission 1993) and *Streetwise, Effective Police Patrol* (Audit Commission 1996) were influential studies that indicated that policing resources needed to be more stringently managed.

2 The HMIC was until recently (i.e. within the last 2 years) something like a 'House of Lords' for the police (Reiner, 2000: 191) where distinguished Chief Constables could retire. However, it now recruits relatively young police Chief Constables in the prime of their careers with the prospect of operational command still ahead of them.

3 I do not have space to discuss this in detail here but am mindful of Power's (1997: 144) observation that 'self-organisation' and 'responsible regulation' require a mix of external and internal audits, and that 'regulatory sensitivity' should pick up on 'the side effects of the instruments of knowledge'. This is not necessarily the case with the current police auditing structures.

4 The original intention was to link pay increases with individual officer performance. The Police Federation and ACPO successfully resisted the implementation of the policy and as yet police pay is not in any way tied to either individual performance or force performance. Perhaps there has been one advancement and that is the majority of Chief Officers are now employed on a performance contract basis (usually 5 or 7 years).

5 Note that Sheehy 'instructed' forces to implement a performance and development review system, although the 'detail' was to be left to individual forces. It is perhaps symbolic that *ForceCo* chose to call the system Performance Review rather than Performance and Development Review.

References

Audit Commission (1993), *Helping With Enquiries: Tackling Crime Effectively*, HMSO: London.

Audit Commission, (1996), *Streetwise: Effective Police Patrol*, HMSO: London.

Audit Commission (1998), *Local Authority Performance Indicators, Police Services*, HMSO: London.

Armstrong, M. and Baron, A. (1998), *Performance Management, The New Realities*, IPD: London.

Bennett, T.H., (1998), 'Police and Public Involvement in the Delivery of Community Policing', in P. Brodeur (ed) *How to Recognise Good Policing*, Police Executive Research Forum, Sage, Thousand Oaks California.

Bevan, S. and Thompson, M. (1992), 'An Overview of Policy and Practice', in S. Bevan and M. Thompson (eds), *Performance Management in the UK: An Analysis of the Issues*, IPD: London.

Brodeur, P. (1998), 'The Assessment of Police Performance', in P. Brodeur (eds), *How to Recognise Good Policing*, Police Executive Research Forum, Sage: Thousand Oaks California.

Bruijn, H. (2002), 'Performance Measurement in the Public Sector: Strategies to Cope with the Risks of Performance Measurement', *International Journal of Public Sector Management*, 15(7): 578-94.

Chan, J. (1999), 'Governing Police Practice: Limits of the New Accountability', *British Journal of Sociology*, 50(2): 251-70.

Collier, P. (2001), Police Performance Measurement and Human Rights, *Public Money and Management*, 21(3): 35-9.

Cope, S., Leishman, F. and Starie, P. (1997), 'Globalisation, New Public Management, and the Enabling State Futures of Police Management', *International Journal of Public Sector Management*, 10(6): 444-60.

Correia, M.E. (1999), 'The Conceptual Ambiguity in Community Policing: Filtering The Muddy Waters', *Policing: International Journal of Police Strategies and Management*, 23(2): 218-33.

Exworthy, M. and Halford, S. (1999), *Professionals and the New Managerialism in the Public Sector*, Open University Press: Milton Keynes.

Flynn, R. (1999), 'Managerialism, Professionalism, and Quasi Markets', in M. Exworthy and S. Halford (1999), *Professionals and the New Managerialism in the Public Sector*, Open University Press: Milton Keynes.

Flynn, R. (2001), *Public Sector Management*, Prentice Hall, Harvester Wheatsheaf: London.

Guest, D. (1987), 'Human Resource Management and Industrial Relations', *Journal of Management Studies*, 24(5): 503-21.

Guest, D. (1998), 'Beyond HRM; Commitment and the Contract Culture', in P. Sparrow and M. Marchington (eds), *Human Resource Management: The New Agenda*, FT Pitman Publishing: London.

Her Majesty's Inspectorate of Constabulary (HMIC) (1998), *Greater Manchester Police Primary Inspection Report*, Home Office: London.

HMIC (2000), *Greater Manchester Police Primary Inspection Report*, Home Office: London.

HMIC (1998), *Kent County Constabulary Inspection*, London: Home Office.

Home Office (1996), *Staff Appraisal: The Performance and Development Review System*, No. 43/96.

Hood, C. (1991), 'A Public Management For All Seasons', *Public Administration*, 69: 3-19.

Jary, D. (2002), 'Aspects of the Audit Society: Issues Arising From the Colonization of Professional Academic Identities by a Portable Management Tool', in M. Dent and S. Whitehead (eds), *Managing Professional Identities, Knowledge, Performativity and the New Professional*, Routledge: London.

Jones, T. and Newburn, T. (2002), 'The Transformation of Policing: Understanding Current Trends in Policing Systems', *British Journal of Criminology*, 42: 129-46.

Leigh, A., Reid, T., Tilley, N. (1998), *Brit POP II: Problem Oriented Policing in Practice*, Police Research Series Paper 93, Reducing Crime Unit, Home Office: London.

Leishman, F., Loveday, B. and Savage, S. (1996), *Core Issues in Policing*, Pte Publishers: London.

Leishman, F., Cope, S. and Starie, P. (1995), Reforming the Police in Britain, New Public Management, Policy Networks and the Tough 'Old Bill' *International Journal of Public Sector Management*, 8(4): 27-37.

Loveday, B. (1999), The Impact of Performance Cultures on Criminal Justice Agencies in England and Wales, *International Journal of the Sociology of Law*, 27: 351-77.

Loveday, B. (2000), 'New Directions in Accountability', in F. Leishman, B. Loveday, and S. Savage (eds), *Core issues in Policing*, Pearson Education: Harlow.

Metcalfe, B. (2001), 'The Strategic Integration of Performance Management and Problem Oriented Policing: A Viable Partnership?', *Policing and Society*, 11: 209-34.

Metcalfe, B. and Dick, G (2002), 'Is The Force Still With Her? Gender and Commitment in the Police', *Women in Management Review*, 17(8): 392-403.

Osborne, D. and Plastrik, P. (2000), *The Reinventors Field Book: Tools for Transforming Your Government*, Jossey Bass: San Francisco.

Pollitt, C. (1993), *Managerialism and the Public Services: Cuts or Cultural Change in 1990s*, Blackwell: Oxford.

Power, M (1997), *The Audit Society: Rituals of Verification*, Oxford University Press: Oxford.

Redshaw, I., Mawby, and R.,I., Bunt, P. (1998), 'Evaluating Core Police in Britain: The Views of Police and Consumers', *International Journal of the Sociology of Law*, 25: 283-301.

Reiner, R. (1992), 'Policing a Post-Modern Society', *Modern Law Review*, 55(6): 761-81

Reiner, R. (1994), 'What Should The Police Be Doing?' *Policing*, 10(2): 151-57.

Reiner, R. (1998), 'Problems of Assessing Police Performance', in P. Brodeur (eds), *How to Recognise Good Policing*, Police Executive Research Forum, Sage: Thousand Oaks California.

Reiner, R. (2000), *The Politics of the Police*, Oxford, Oxford University Press.

Rogerson, P. (1995), 'Performance Measurement and Policing: Police Service or Law Enforcement Agency?' in *Public Money and Management*, October-December: 25-35.

Rosenbaum, D.P. (1998), 'The Changing Role of The Police: Assessing the Current Transition to Community Policing', in P. Brodeur (ed), *How to Recognise Good Policing*, Police Executive Research Forum, Sage: Thousand Oaks California.

Sanderson, I. (2001), 'Performance Management, Evaluation and Learning in Modern Local Government', *Public Administration*, 79 (2): 297-314.

Sheehy, Sir P. (1993), *Report of Inquiry into Police Responsibilities and Rewards*, HMSO London.

Stiles, P. (1997), 'Performance Management and the Psychological Contract', *Human Resource Management*, 7 (1): 57-63.

Storey, J. (1992), *Developments in the Management of Human Resources*, Routledge: London.

Storey, J. (ed), (1995), *HRM: A Critical Text*, Routledge: London.

Townley, B. (1994), *Reframing Human Resource Management: Power, Ethics and the Subject at Work*, Sage: London.

Waters, I. (2000), 'Quality and Performance Monitoring', in F. Leishman, B. Loveday and S. Savage (eds), *Core issues in Policing*, Pearson Education: Harlow.

Winstanley, D. and Stuart-Smith, K. (1996), Policing Performance: The Ethics Of Performance Management, *Personnel Review*, 25 (6): 66-84.

PART III

HYDRA-HEADED
NEW PUBLIC MANAGEMENT:
THE CASE OF THE
NATIONAL HEALTH SERVICE

Chapter 7

Dilemmas Beyond the Glass Ceiling...: The Performances of Senior Women Managers in the National Health Service

Alison Linstead and Geraldine Catlow

[T]he chaos of identities, and of strategies, in the world today is the effect of real, and highly structured, forces that are constantly felt in the lives of those trying to get from one day to the next

(Friedman, 1992: 363).

It's still tougher at the top for women

(*Financial Times*, 21 May 2003: 15).

Introduction

In 1995 the Department of Health launched *Opportunity 2000 – NHS achievements and New Goals*. Ken Jarrod, Director of Human Resources wrote on the employment of women in the NHS: 'The overall goal for the NHS remains: "to take full advantage of the potential of women in the NHS so that we can provide the best health care for all members of the population"'. The relevant objectives for the progression of senior women in the NHS included the following: to increase the number of women in general management posts; to raise the number of qualified women accountants, women Directors of Finance and women consultants; to enhance the representation of women as members of authorities and trusts; to raise the percentage of 'women *Chairmen*' [our emphasis]; the provision of systematic programmes allowing women aspiring to management positions to go through a career development centre with a view to establishing their own personal development needs; the development of initiatives on recruitment and retention to ensure that the numbers of staff leaving, in particular those from professions allied to medicine, nursing and midwifery, did not rise; the monitoring of appointments, career progression and access to training, to ensure that women and men have equal access to clinical and management leadership positions.

Recognising the under-presentation of women in the senior echelons of the NHS, *Opportunity 2000* outlined the above strategy to promote women in the NHS from lower positions into senior management. However, since this report institutional changes in the NHS and the subsequent organisational restructurings have created barriers to this agenda. In this chapter we analyse the gendered nature of senior women's identity work from a critical feminist perspective and an interpretative, life history, methodology to explore the micro processes of how and more importantly *why* these female managers *perform* their identities. We present the narratives of three senior women who sat on an NHS Trust Board in the Midlands of the United Kingdom. The focus on the NHS is particularly interesting since the introduction of the internal market and New Public Management (NPM) (Hood, 1995; Newman and Clarke, 1994; Exworthy and Halford, 1999) into the NHS, which was intended to break down the pre-existing bureau-professional organisation through entrepreneurial management practices (du Gay, 1996). The focus on effective *management* practice resulted in the growth of managerial positions, and the adoption of new managerial roles by clinicians. More recently, the move away from the internal market, towards an environment of co-operation and the creation of 'super' Trusts through the merger process, entails mounting pressures and continual change for managers.

We have been concerned to contribute to existing studies on women in management by taking a critical feminist persuasion to give voice to women that are often under-represented and under-acknowledged in their field and the literature, whilst at the same time investigating our theoretical interest of how senior women in an NHS context actively construct and reconstruct their identities beyond the hypothesised 'glass ceiling'. Rather than focusing on how women disrupt, penetrate and eventually break through the glass ceiling as other well established studies in the women in management have long done (Ledwith and Colgan, 1996; Wyatt and Langridge, 1996; Maddock, 1999), we explore women's experiences of their career histories, the barriers they encounter, and the coping strategies they employ in sustaining their positions in top posts, and more importantly as minority figures in senior management, in a female dominated industry.

Critical studies on NPM in the public sector have documented the radical changes to the sector (Newman, 1995; Brewis, 1999; Maile, 1999; Whitehead and Moodley, 1999; Thomas and Davies, 2002) and have explored how social and organisational change influence individual subjectivity. At the time of its implementation NPM had been seen as an opportunity to feminise the NHS (see Fondas, 1997 for an exploration of feminisation of management), but as authors researching NPM in different sectors argue the masculinist discourses of NPM threaten women's identities as the feminine is rendered abject (see Thomas and Davies, 2002 for an exploration of NPM and women academics). In this chapter we are interested in how senior women in the NHS through their everyday interactions *perform* their gendered identities. Gender for the women we have studied here is a paradox, a paradox that they manage as a woman, doctor, mother, nursing manager etc. Supporting Butler's position (1999) that selves are reflexively constantly changing, performed and enacted, our analysis reveals how femininity must be, on the one hand, challenged and contested whilst simultaneously defended and legitimised. The management of performance and the performance of management is a gendered project in which the women in this study invested on their professional journeys. However, we will see that sitting on Trust Boards is also a site for identity work that is on the one hand a sporting challenge which is rewarding when barriers are overcome, and at the same time a source of discomfort and humiliation as these women are sexualised in attempts to manipulate and render them other.

The three women analysed here performed modernist projects of the self (Giddens, 1991) in which they constructed their present positions consistently with that of past episodes. As such Lena, Selina and Martha all had different career routes and these paths influenced the ways in which they constructed their current gendered identities. For example, Lena, having worked in a masculinist environment as a medic draws on masculinity as a resource in her self-project. Our analysis also reveals how women legitimise 'self' as other in their career projects (Grey, 1994) by focusing on *significant events* in their life histories which we would argue is partly dealing with the ontological insecurity of becoming successful women and more importantly legitimising themselves as women, as 'good' female professionals within an increasingly performance driven environment. To conclude we suggest that rather than emphasise strategies of 'shattering the glass ceiling' (Davidson and Cooper, 1992), which relies on discontinuity of the dominant social order, the narratives of *continuity* of the senior, and extremely successful, women studied here suggest that women who perform their present identities consistently with their retrospective career routes find the glass ceiling *permeable*.

This chapter is structured as follows. First, we highlight the critical issues in the women in management and gender literature from three perspectives characteristic of modernist management – hierarchy, accountability and achievement. Second, we discuss the interpretative perspective and life history research methodology adopted for this study. Third, fragments of Lena, Selina and Martha's narratives are analysed. Finally, we offer our conclusions and directions for future research in the area.

Identity Themes of Women in the NHS: Hierarchy, Accountability and Achievement

Historically the NHS has been extremely hierarchical (Walby and Greenwell, 1994; Kowalczyk, 2002) in that it differentiates and discriminates between medics and nurses, specialists and general practitioners and managers and clinicians. The hegemonic structures of the NHS pose rigid structures and barriers for women. Women are predominantly employed at lower levels and in nursing and represent the minority within the echelons of senior management. The implications for women's careers in making the transition from jobs dominated by women to senior management where men prevail are vast. The women in management literature (Davidson and Cooper, 1992; Fagenson, 1993; Vinnicombe and Colwill, 1995; Marshall, 1995; Ledwith and Colgan, 1996) has long recalled the toils of women who frequently face the 'glass ceiling' with many women remaining at middle or lower level management positions (Reskin and Roos, 1992). However, in this women in management literature the increasing entry of women into traditionally male occupations (Crompton and Sanderson, 1990) is being acknowledged and we have a plethora of research that suggests that female managers experience their working lives differently from their male counterparts (Watson and Harris, 1999; Roper, 1994) which in turn influences their career choices and patterns. Indeed there is a growing awareness that the gender of managers does matter (Wajcman, 1999).

Adopting a gendered perspective (Acker, 1990; Calás and Smircich, 1992a, 1992b) this study contributes to existing theoretical debates on how senior women, who have in one way or another passed to the 'other side of the glass ceiling', construct their professional identities. Although there is a great deal of literature on women in management in general organisational contexts (Marshall, 1984, 1995; Rosener, 1990; Fondas, 1997), there has been an overall neglect of empirical research on women in the NHS, particularly within the echelons of senior management. Existing research on gender and careers such as by Halford, Savage and Witz (1997), focuses on nursing, banking and local government, and investigates women working in female dominated environments. In contrast, this critical feminist research focuses on the individual experiences of senior women managers in their careers and the barriers that women encounter in an NHS environment where gender segregation and cultural stereotypes prevail.

In the section that follows we review the management and organisation literature to consider women's positions in the NHS from three perspectives – hierarchy, achievement and accountability (Gowler and Legge, 1996).[1] Firstly, at the level of *hierarchy* organisations have often been viewed as gender neutral (Wilson, 1996) or gender blind (Linstead, 2000). Feminist writings, especially the feminisation of management argument (see Casey, 1995), illustrate women's stunted entry into and slow progression through the management ranks and the vertical and horizontal *gender segregation* and discrimination that prevails even though the changing nature of women's roles and work in the labour market have been acknowledged (Reskin and Roos, 1990; Wajcman, 1998). This inroad into management can be seen as an attempt to implement the feminine in management and this has partially been achieved by recognising the importance of feminine skills and behaviours (Rosener, 1990; Fondas, 1997). Therefore the hierarchical structures and controls in modern organisations are based on structures, roles and controls that are inherently masculinist and pose problems for women progressing through management, especially at senior management levels (Wajcman, 1998). However, the lack of recognition of the feminine at a structural level privileges masculinist systems of order and control. The NPM discourse infers that restructuring and the associated flexibility and delegation of traditional managerial controls throughout the hierarchy have been seen to offer increasing opportunities for women. With flatter, and perhaps more fluid, organisational structures upward mobility is seen to enable women's career progression with structural barriers dispersed. Additionally, the emphasis on feminine leadership styles and skills in contemporary organisations enhances the opportunities presented for women. However, one can argue that feminist politics further subordinate the feminine by firmly setting up the feminine as the other, which sustains gender demarcation and subordination of the feminine, thus failing to destabilise the hierarchical structures, roles and controls.

At the level of *accountability* the moral and technical reckoning that enforces the hierarchy suppresses the feminine by endorsing accounting practices based on objectivity and standardised accounting practices, Gowler and Legge's analysis, for instance, highlights task and financial accounting practices. However, NPM discourses recognise that there have been changing forms of accountability based more on performativity. These *gendered discourses of performance* are fashioned around and support feminine ways of managing, which may offer increasing opportunities for women. That said, we argue here that the potential of feminine management practices to reconfigure masculinist organisational practices are outweighed by the increasingly masculinist nature of the discourses of management that seduce members. Individuals are therefore engaged in legitimising their roles in keeping with increasingly heightened performance measures and cultural controls (Barker, 1993; Kunda, 1992). A growing body of research suggests that managers are required to display increasing levels of commitment to their organisations and this is itself gendered (Davidson and Cooper, 1992; Scase and Goffee, 1993; Dickens, 1998). If we take Wajcman's argument (1998) that men and women offer the same leadership qualities although women have to manage their femininity and adopt masculine traits such as objectivity, drive, authoritativeness and rationality to manage their performance, then performing the feminine implies that 'men will be advantaged by adding new qualities to those they are already deemed to have, women will continue to be seen as offering feminine dualities' (Wajcman, 1998: 77). Overall then feminisms that strive for sameness by minimising difference within and between subjects and subject positioning do not create change because the feminine is perpetually reinforced as other and this poses further problems for theorising women's gendered identities.

The theme of *achievement* reinforces hierarchy and accountability and governs by inserting individuals into a rational natural order (Gowler and Legge, 1996). Achievement for women therefore is based on masculinist systems of achievement that many women, and men, find difficult to achieve or maintain. Achievement in the 'feminisation of management' thesis is seen as the ability to adopt feminine skills to manage the new public organisation. These feminine attributes that women may naturally possess not only create opportunities for women in management but also are now considered to be essential assets for men. Women's performance may be measured on the ability to adopt masculine skills and capabilities that prevent those women unable to 'manage like a man' (Wajcman, 1998: 8) from achieving, performing and competing. Thus whilst feminism has gone a long way to raise the concerns of women in management, focusing on the ways 'women are disadvantaged by the fact that they are not men' and the outcomes of having to 'manage like a man' (Wacjman, 1998: 8), it has done very little to destabilise the systems of control that reinforce masculinist practices of management. Furthermore, such feminism not only denies difference between women, it classifies all men as benefiting from hegemony. Homogenising sameness between and within men and women reinforces woman as other, endlessly subordinated.

Equally new forms of masculinity are emerging that don't benefit all men and may benefit some women (Pateman, 1989 cited in Wajcman, 1998: 30).

Our analysis shows that issues surrounding the themes of hierarchy, accountability and achievement present women with barriers to be overcome in the NHS. Taking a feminist perspective challenges the dominance of masculinist practices but fails to embrace and initiate change. Recent feminist critiques of NPM (see for example, Thomas and Davies, 2002) have argued that even though NPM aimed to challenge masculinist organizational practices they are indeed sustained which threaten increased opportunities for women in the workplace. Our interest here is how women who have succeeded *beyond* the glass ceiling in environments which make it difficult for them to thrive, recognise the dilemmas they face as they construct their identities within a NPM environment.

Doing Identity: An Interpretive Approach

> *[T]he masks used by managers in their performance of the self may actually enable the managers to be and say what they would fear to otherwise* (Linstead, 2003: 84).

This chapter is concerned with providing a gendered perspective on women's identity construction from an increasingly fluid and relational construction of femininity and masculinity, as many other studies before have done (Calás and Smircich, 1993; Collinson and Hearn, 1996; Fondas, 1997; Alvesson and Billing, 1997; Kerfoot and Knights, 1998; Whitehead, 2001; Linstead and Thomas, 2002). Our interest is in researching women's identities as changing but relatively stable, towards the recognition of identity construction as a form of first order accounting (Garfinkel, 1967) that is characterised by paradox, fluidity, inconsistency and emergence. Identities are constructed reflexively from past and anticipated future experiences and is used, manipulated and promoted by these managers as a form of first order accounting in their *persuasive* accounts (Silverman, 1975). Additionally any reading and representation of these accounts are persuasive since the processes of selecting and filtering operate throughout our analysis and writing. Silverman (1975: 42) states:

> writing and reading are always acts of production – of societies, of selves. And that production is both mine and not mine alone. Mine because in my acts of production I re-member my-self. Not mine because 'I' exist in and through a dialogue with a tradition that always already precedes me, and with an emerging social order that will be the readings of my text.

The paradoxical nature of identity that emerges reveals how the women in our research sought to establish and draw on relatively stable, coherent and fixed features of their identity construction whilst at the same time highlighting fluidity, inconsistency and emergence. This tension between the stable and the fluid flows through the women's retrospective-prospective processes. The critical feminist position[2] adopted here denies the presence of an essential, fixed self on which feminist standpoint research is theorised (Oakley, 1981), the self is constructed through discourses of social relations (Weedon, 1999; Grosz, 1994; Foucault, 1980) and within specific interactions with the other (Potter and Wetherall, 1987). We 'analyse how texts address the problems of presence, lived experience, the real and its representations, and the issues of the subjects, authors and their intentionalities' (Denzin, 1992: 151 cited in Schwandt, 1998: 235) to uncover the fluid production and organisation of difference within women's subjectivities. We must note that as female researchers studying women we are aware that at times we may privilege fragments of text from the women studied over others and therefore reflexive of the authority of the researcher to inscribe the meaning of the text. As such we present women's narratives, but these narratives must be placed within the context of other narratives of their lives and from our research, which we cannot present here. As such we view the interview text obtained as fragments of an ongoing episode in which women perform their identity work. Appreciating the intertexuality of the narratives produced and recognising that interviews *interrupt* narrative, a life history methodology (Plummer, 1996; Musson, 1998) was adopted to examine how women undergo identity construction in the light of their own life and biography. This approach moves beyond collecting interview data that more often than not is a superficial performance that masks rich, insightful and personal revelations. We suggest that the life history methodology facilitates the surfacing of Scott's (1992) 'hidden text', which is absent in many other studies of women in the public sector management. However, as Musson rightly notes, this methodology places demands on the researcher for they 'must [be] prepare[d] to be as flexible and fluid as the situation demands, allowing the lead to be taken by the storyteller, rather than trying to impose some rigid predetermined framework on to the interview situation' (in Cassell and Symon, 1998: 18). Investigating individuals' subjectivities by focusing on naturally occurring 'talk' therefore recognises that these texts are the product of both the researcher and research participant's negotiation of their subjectivities; subjectivities that are continually in flux, multiple, competing and gendered. These texts are already to be regarded as an account that was partially produced collectively. Although the individuals we spoke to formed part of a larger sample, this has little epistemological significance for this research. We analyse and present fragments-in-process from women's narratives rather than unified accounts, to recognise the ontological condition of the individuals providing those fragments where identities are fragments and constantly in process. This perspective promotes the multiplicity, fragmentation, fractured nature and plurality of experience that many studies of women in management have not.

The individual narratives from three women discussed in this chapter were selected to illustrate how they formulated, performed and justified self as other. These data were collected from individual face-to-face, semi-structured interviews with the individuals over an eighteen-month period. This sample was part of a larger study that interviewed 30 women in the NHS. Employing a longitudinal method enabled the researchers to reflect back the emerging issues to the participants and to monitor changes in how they interpreted their lives. The interviewees discussed their day-to-day experiences within the organisation and their life outside the work place. The basic objective for our analysis is the process of individual identity construction and although there are different ways that this could be approached, and even though we challenge the unitary conceptions of the subject, the choice of individual cases of identity construction as a basic unit of analysis offers a number of advantages.

The benefits of using the individual subject as a source of information for investigating identity construction is that it provides the justification for our adoption of one to one interviews which enabled us to listen to the individuals' stories. The interviews produced in-depth accounts of individual's working experiences, the tensions between personal and public aspects of their lives and we were particularly concerned with analysing the tensions and contradictions within individual accounts. The blurring of public and private boundaries of individual managers' lives shapes the construction and reconstruction of individual subjectivities. A key aspect of this socially constructed identity is that it is created in conditions of asymmetry – people are not all equally positioned in the organisation and within the discourses that shape meaning, so it makes a difference whether they are male or female; black or white; old or young.

The *fragments* of accounts selected here have been chosen from a larger mosaic because these fragments appeared significant to the participants; they resonated with each other across their accounts, and they dealt with issues widely acknowledged in the data set we obtained. These data are representative of this set in so far as they are drawn from it and reproduce elements found elsewhere in the set, without being isomorphic or microcosmic. In the sections that follow we present fragments of Lena, Selina and Martha's interview texts and analyse the gendered identity work within discourses of performativity and new managerialism.

Narratives of the Self

In the analysis that follows we see how the women studied constructed their identities by drawing on gendered discourses to legitimise self as other, as woman. Within the masculine discourses of management and organisation theory, woman becomes presented as the other, necessary to the constitution of (masculine) identity but always threatening to it (Cixous and Clément, 1986). 'Woman' is the site of the fluid and relational, those elements of human experience and consciousness, which evade definition, measurement, formal construction and explicit expression – which both sustain and subvert rational modes of organisation, presenting new creative opportunities but also a destabilising threat. Our analysis shows how they justified their commitment to work and home to resolve some of the tension between being a competent professional and managing their private lives, which for these women were issues of being a wife and mother. As the women talked about their life histories and their career projects, they all focused on significant events, episodes that were particularly pertinent for them and past events as justification for their current and future performances. This retrospective-prospective identity construction was both consistent and continuous and as such their career backgrounds and experiences of gender bias and discrimination determined how they developed their careers in the senior ranks of the NHS. Such continuity in identity work suggests that women do not break through the glass ceiling by doing something different, such as adopting masculine styles of leadership, managing their womanhood, or 'managing like a man', but by consistently and continuously doing what they have been socialised and indoctrinated into, just sometimes putting their own stamp on it. This finding contradicts women in management literature that offers strategies for successfully travelling in a male world (Marshall, 1995) and suggests that more discreet, manipulative and carefully articulated performances of self – whether the negation of the feminine other or the overemphasis of self as other, as feminine, enables women to permeate barriers such as the glass ceiling that women in management have long argued stand in opposition to them.

Lena

Lena is in her late forties and is a senior GP in an inner city practice where she has held this position for the last 10 years. She has a very high profile nationally within the NHS and is involved in a wide range of community activities, including the chairmanship of a company promoting the city where her practice is situated. During her interviews she suggested that her entrepreneurial father, whom she described as having very Victorian attitudes, had been her role model. She expressed a wish to work in the family business after 'A' levels but this was not considered appropriate for a daughter and at his suggestion she applied to study medicine. Lena trained at Kings College Medical School, which was an extremely male dominated environment at that time.

> We were many, many times told that we were the *tokenism* and we had to have a few women in, but it was a waste of time, particularly in surgery; a waste of time because you're not going to be serious doctors... I always grew up with this idea.... don't take time off, plan everything and not going to ever be seen as a *weak* woman who was needing time away... I left hospital medicine as soon as I became pregnant, some nine years after my marriage, because I had this view that I couldn't mix being a mother, being pregnant and being taken seriously.

> My day here starts at seven. Don't forget I'm not a typical GP I've got all those other jobs. I'm often not home until about 10 at night, or, if I am home, it's only to start working at home. So my days are very, very long, but that's self imposed because I'm very motivated to do what I do.

> I just wasn't around and I just didn't do those things that a mother does and they seem very well adjusted, they seem good kids, we have a very good relationship, but it's not the same as being around and being a mother... I would never take time off because of family commitments. I would always

have people to sort those out. I have a very supportive husband and an extended family that I depend on enormously. Without them, well... [long pause]

To *achieve* I had to be like them [male doctors] and I was always told that the men never have these *excuses*, and therefore you shouldn't... certainly a lot of the men I'm working with continually let me down by domestic situations... I would like to argue that the whole thing's wrong. We need to change that back to say that everyone deserves a bit of a life and maybe it should be seen as quite normal, that all of us were to take time off in certain situations. I actually make sure my staff work flexibly and they fit it around their families... you know I trust you, you know what your workload is, you've got all your computer bits at home, why are you running in when you could do exactly that at home? Now I'm not going to ring her up to check she's at the computer, I know she will do her work... and I need loyalty... so I need them to feel that they've got my confidence.

I don't see myself as a woman... If that's old boys, I'm a boy... So I hope they don't see me as a woman, I don't want them to... I see myself as a man and I'm a very happy married woman and therefore I've never considered my gender has made a difference... I'm a 'one man band'... a 'jack of all trades'... an honorary man.

In the opening fragments, Lena's referral to women as 'we were the tokenism' highlights how as a woman in medicine she was always cast as other – but marginal rather than oppositional. Following her father's stereotyping of what was acceptable work for women, Lena entered medicine, but very openly 'confesses' that even as a career orientated individual with high professional autonomy who has sacrificed personal and family commitments for the sake of her career, she gave up hospital medicine when she became pregnant because in those days she 'couldn't mix hospital medicine [a male role] with being a mother' and she wanted 'to be taken seriously' and she wouldn't be as a mother. This opting out is a significant event for Lena, and in her encounters with us she focuses on this pertinent moment a great deal – opting out of the hyper competitive hierarchical environment – saw her then becoming more competitive in less structured settings and holding herself hostage for the sake of her career project. Being a high performer for Lena has two consequences – negating her identity as a mother where we see her openly admitting to neglecting her family life and secondly being *totally* committed to her work. Recall Lena's comments: 'I couldn't mix being a mother, being pregnant and being taken seriously' – to be a good doctor, a good professional is equated with hard work, not being weak and not being a mother. Casting out the maternal at the level of identity is consistent with Höpfl and Kostera's (2002) analysis of the negation of the maternal in organisation *per se*. The tension for Lena was balancing a family with her professional roles so she took up General Practice at that point as a compromise: this illustrates how general practice was historically subordinated to medicine. Since those days Lena has become tremendously successful in the community within which she has her practice where she lectures and researches and is also involved in numerous outreach projects. Lena talks of the past, her family background and medical training, to legitimise her job and career decisions, which can be seen as aggressive, especially when she explicitly negates being a woman. Lena's training as a doctor in a male, competitive and aggressive climate became the platform upon which she assessed her future competence and commitment. As a minority female medical student she faced many barriers during her early career that shaped her values; one of these is to not be 'a weak woman'. Weakness was closely associated with the stereotypes of feminine styles and characteristics.

Although at moments in our encounters with Lena she showed some resentment towards this environment, she was unapologetic that this masculinist standard became the platform against which she held herself *accountable*. We may wish to argue that Lena's past consumed her present – she was literally mortified by it. As an independent practitioner Lena sets herself unreasonable targets and standards to deliver, and is her own worst enemy in terms of work/life balance (Hochschild, 1997). Nonetheless, she has set performance targets and career targets for herself and wants also to make a difference for others in her community work, for which she is already recognised nationally. However, there is a tension between her masculinist performance measures and her management of her staff with children. Her management style is consistent with more feminised styles of managing and management practice. That said, we see Lena showing no compassion for family men who let her down and she holds them accountable in the way that she holds herself accountable. Achievement, for Lena, is set against a masculine norm despite her history of having been disadvantaged by such practices. Womanhood is something to be overcome for Lena: it has caused her enough pain and she thrives on being constantly better. What is most fascinating in Lena's fragments is how she refers to being a woman at the same time as drawing on the language of boys/lads.

Lena's suppression of her femaleness, an issue to manage and in some sense to overcome, this sets achievement standards against which others are held accountable. Although there are tensions for Lena as she goes about her identity work, we suggest that overall she adopts a position of hyper-masculinity which we would argue is a coping strategy developed in order to succeed in a male dominated environment. As such then we could continue to maintain that she accounts for herself in the present in a way that is continuous with the past. Her rational and unidirectional retrospective accounting practices suggest that the only way for Lena cope beyond the glass ceiling was to perform her present to be consistent with her perceived career route. This continuity is also evident in Lena's prospective accounting as masculinity seems to be the only path she will consider to be open for her in her career, to continue to be better than the men (see Linstead and Thomas, 2002), to be a different woman in some instances and not to be a woman at all in others. Lena's dilemma was one of being reflexive on why she downplayed her identity as woman, mother and wife – it was not something she did without thinking, as many masculine roles performed by men might be. This echoes Braidotti's (1994) comments on how 'women cannot afford to abandon attention to the embodied nature of the feminine in favour of an idea of "postgender" in a world where gender difference is material and often the basis for inequality' (cited in Weedon, 1999:115). Without 'womanhood', Braidotti argues, processes of femininity become lost in 'asexual', 'postgender' and 'androgynous' spheres. This negation of the feminine is Lena's coping strategy and professional autonomy for her has been about finding a niche where she is not exposed to the tokenism that she had experienced in her early career. Kerfoot (1999: 197) continues to reveal how masculine subjects strive for control which we argue contributes to the demise of self:

> Masculine subjects thereby deny the possibility for 'play' within social relations – of shifting between subject positions – for masculinity and management necessitate that the other is subordinated to self. Masculine subjectivity is equally unreflexive and unreflective in its unwillingness, or sheer inability, to challenge the conditions of its own perpetuation, however self-destructive or impoverishing the consequences.

In the final fragment, Lena comments 'I've never considered my gender has made a difference', but ironically it has indeed made *all* the difference to Lena – her career project has been all about reconciling difference.

Selina

Selina holds a regional post as a Nursing Director and Director of Education, having achieved very rapid promotion throughout her nursing career. She had worked at Board level in the hospital sector for fifteen years prior to moving to a regional post. During her career Selina has encountered and overcome many barriers, perhaps best indicated by the following account of her experience in applying for promotion some years ago.

> On the first occasion I went to enquire about a director of nursing post... I didn't get an application form. The then district nursing officer...who was male, had been asked about me, and he'd said, yes, good, all the rest of it, but you know you don't know what happens to women when they have babies. I can't vouch for what she'll be like when she's had the baby. So consequently I didn't get an application form. Undaunted I tried again [pause] I'm the sort of person that you only have to tell me I can't do something and it's a challenge. I was short listed and interviewed, and the interview panel, was six people strong ...one woman who was the chair... she asked me, 'what does your husband think about you applying for this job? It's going to mean unsociable hours for your husband and child' and I was just horrified! This was coming from a woman! ... now I would have said I think that's irrelevant.

> I remember that I got home that night [the day she heard the news that she was successful] and the district nursing officer, this man, phoned at about 6 o'clock at night. He said to me 'Are you sitting down?' and I said: 'Well, I will do'. He said: 'Well you've got the job' and he said it was a 'unanimous opinion' and

that 'the new general manager just wants to get his hands in your knickers, I think there's a real issue with the selection process, particularly for nursing, which is possibly because it's predominantly female, and commonly I think, although it's becoming less, the nurses have had to jump through more hoops than the males have to get the jobs.

Well, I normally work on a Sunday afternoon anyway [Selina was interviewed at her home on a Sunday afternoon because of a very full diary]... I've always done that for the last 15 years or so, I guess. Since I was working at director level... I don't have time through the average working week to sit and read documents or to prepare papers, so I do that at weekends... but I do not expect the same level of commitment from my subordinates... no, I don't. Within reason I suppose I would, and have been completely supportive of anybody else with family needs and in fact I'm probably the one that says get home you've got children to go to.

Thomas [Selina's son] was four, he'd only been at school about 2 months and I said something to him about his school and he said to me 'Mummy, do you know where my school is?'...What if one of them is ill? They very rarely are – touch wood – but that comes first, absolutely, no question.

I've always done the job that is there in front of me. If it's taken long hours then I've done the long hours but I don't feel bad about walking away in the middle of an afternoon if I suddenly find I've got half a meeting cancelled or something. I don't feel bad about that.

I think particularly to the medical workforce as a nurse and woman I think you have to prove yourself in some way or another to gain their respect and it's different things for different people... I spent a lot of time getting to know them as individuals and then positioning myself appropriately so that I pressed the right buttons.

As a member of the Board I have been faced with difficult situations... he [boss] saw that there was a male station in life and a female station in life.... I was told before I took up post that the chairman there was male chauvinist and did not think that women should be in senior business positions. I knew I as a woman had to prove myself to him; that I was as good as anybody else at being a director. So, I spent a lot of time going to him and seeking his counsel and his advice and telling him about what we were doing and bouncing the ideas off him, so that he was inclusive with what I was doing.

Always, my whole life, as I see it, is a learning process. I learn best from mistakes if you like or from experience, that's where my learning comes from... You need to have had that experience to have built that level of confidence. Your confidence comes from the learning, your life long learning and having that trust in yourself.

Perhaps not surprisingly, Selina feels that women face significant barriers in reaching senior positions in the NHS. As a woman who climbed through female dominated nursing ranks she was determined and driven by ambition that she would succeed, eventually. Selina's story reminds us of Kowalczyk's research (2002) on the subordination of nursing to medicine and Selina's perception was that there were barriers to reaching senior management as a nurse. The career route for Selina was highly gendered and she recalled on many encounters with us the stories of her appointment as the best candidate for the job, she was still sexualised as a nurse. The humour that her male colleagues drew on as they worked with her on the Trusts centred around her role as a nurse rather than as a senior manager, constantly referring to the nurse's uniform. Selina found this humiliating and at times this showed in her lack of confidence on the Trust Board. But she remained driven and sees the job as something of a battle at times, constantly justifying and legitimising herself as manager over nurse, as Trust Board member over tea lady. She confirms her identities overtly when she states 'as a nurse and woman' and this is subordinate to medicine and then she comments 'as a member of the board' – she constantly has to legitimise herself in one way or another to address the difference and to reposition herself in her roles. Indeed she comments that she has to be 'positioning myself appropriately' so that she 'pressed the right buttons' which shows how as a female nurse moving through the management ranks she had to manage her political and emotional performance at the right level at the right time – and more importantly she had consciously to *work* at it, especially in her experiences with her boss. Note how she comments 'I was as good as anybody else' but 'I had to prove myself to *him*' (our emphasis) and do more for what we could argue was identity work, as a woman.

Unlike what we saw with Lena, however, Selina evidenced a sense of balance in her attitude to work. Selina had family responsibilities that she handled alongside work commitments and, although this might at times have meant compromises, she was very clear about her priorities. Although clearly very committed in terms of the hours and effort she puts into her job, work does not consume her even though her male colleagues try to commodify her as nurse. Selina as a nurse manager, in contrast to Lena, was working within a female dominated environment until she reached Board level; and how she made sense of her identity in the present is consistent with her background. She was not marginalised as an individual, or as a token, as was Lena, but was a member of a devalued group and carries a sense of collective identity into her self-project. Selina believes that her confidence and experience, developed within the female dominated environment, enable her to resist the negation of the feminine in her current role. We see Selina actively promoting the feminine, the other, in her leadership styles and she genuinely feels that she has a lot of much needed skills to offer as a senior female in the NHS.

We see her drawing on a specific encounter at a selection panel and other specific encounters with her new boss when she became a director of nursing as significant events in legitimising herself as a competent professional and, more importantly, as a competent woman. In this incident it is significant that the selectors, and her future boss, also cast doubt on whether she could become a mother; keeping the two roles going has been a struggle for her in her identity work. Selina's text also suggests that when she became a director the pressures for balancing work and home became more pronounced as she had to work longer hours. However, paradoxically, she also notes that she works more flexibly than she used to. The need to balance her commitments and put her job into perspective came as she recalled another significant event – when her son asked about whether she knew where his school was. This moment was extremely important for Selina in establishing her sense of self and in maintaining her feminine style, as she calls it, throughout her career journey. This continuity of style from a female dominated environment through to senior management has been successful for her and the maintenance of her femininity does not support existing studies that women always have to alternative strategies to travel through a male world.

Martha

Martha is in her late thirties and is a hospital director, having previously held posts as Director of Strategy/Strategic Development. As a younger, non-medical professional manager in the NHS she worked in a mixed gender environment until reaching Board level. Martha felt she faced many instances of gender bias.

> I knew it was going to be a tough meeting [tough meeting] because I wanted something and this Chief Executive did not want to give it to me. He said to me: 'You're getting very upset about this, aren't you?' And it started going into the emotional, get upset, get irrational and they are the things that... I guess women need to be very sensitive to, because it's very important that I deal with those sorts of messages quite early on. That can be difficult. I'm not getting upset, I'm being assertive about how I'm feeling or what I want. Because I don't like my wants to be labelled as irrational or emotional... That moment *validated* me as a woman on the Board... I can't explain to you what it felt like – it was the most amazing relief.

> People feel they can take the liberty to call my comments 'silly'. I'm confident that a man would not call another man's comments silly... Some of them given the opportunity will do it and this is about women working at strategies, having to work out strategies all of the time to manage this sort of behaviour. In years gone by the way that I would have coped with it is to become more male-like, is to sort of hit back, or be aggressive back, wear very masculine cold clothes, keep a very closed body language. But over the years, I've learned more and more to be myself.

> The preconceptions are, well Martha's a woman, so everything she does is going to be a bit soft and a bit woolly. There's a danger that if she does the empowerment bit too much, that we're not going to drive the performance in the organisation and hone that enough. That sort of style doesn't get results. It's all well and good but it's not gonna get results at the end of the day. So I'm doing that, but I'm driving it at the other end as well. I am pretty tough; that's

about credibility because I think the clinicians will think that they can get one over on me and that I won't be tough with them and I've worked hard on that as well. So there's an extra effort that I'm having to put in.

I have developed a style that I'm comfortable with and I genuinely have a very collaborative and participative style. I don't think that I know it all. I don't believe that human beings naturally want to be led like the Pied Piper. I often think that listening and being led is part of being a good leader.

Martha's text is interesting in that as a younger, successful manager, is reflexive on how her coping strategies have changed and the gendered ways in which she conducted her identity work. Martha draws on a particular Trust Board meeting as a significant event to explain the barriers that she has faced as a woman and a non-medical manager. The barriers and pressures she felt until 'that moment validated me as a woman on the board' and the relief with which she expressed this statement indicates the struggles that she endured throughout her career. Much of Martha's text exposes the gendered behaviours of men and women and her management of the tension between masculine and feminine styles. Note how she felt threatened by being seen as 'irrational and emotional' and 'soft and a bit woolly' and how she felt that she had to 'become more male-like' in the past. For Martha being a woman was being different and she coped with this by being the *same*, at least on the surface. As her confidence developed, Martha felt that she could be herself. Her career project was one of also managing the difference between clinicians and her being a non-clinician, which meant that Martha had to put more effort into managing being a woman, non-clinician. Even though she espoused more feminised styles of leadership in keeping with new ways of working, she was nevertheless performance driven and we note how she drew on masculine language to legitimise this – tough and driven, yes, but this needs to be balanced by being a good leader too. The desire for stability and security, involves Martha in 'fixing' her identity project. This fixing has masculinist underpinnings and, as Kerfoot (1999: 185) contends, reveals how *masks* are used to *validate* achievement and performance:

those for whom masculinity resonates most loudly appear to be so preoccupied with *'fixing'* the world around them and others in it as to detract from the possibilities of other forms of engagement. As a result, in its concerns to achieve a fixity in social relations and quash the 'uncontrollable' elements of everyday existence, masculinity expends considerable energy in the drive for success, and overlooks the possibilities for other forms of interaction. Yet even this success in conquering the insecurity that is itself both a condition and consequence of 'the social' and of masculinity, can only ever be so momentary and superficial, such that its achievement requires constant *validation*

(*emphasis* added).

Conclusion

Drawing on the discourses of new managerial work to position themselves for future episodes in their identity projects, together with using identity work as a present resource, protects and shelters these women from their experience of lack and/or loss. The emphasis they placed on significant events, often many years later, may suggest that these retrospective formative episodes still matter, because these women have considered it necessary to perform their selves in specific ways as a result. From the fragments of the stories of the women we have studied we can see them, using Kerfoot's term, 'fixing' moments of their identity projects on significant events in their past to cope, manage and perform their present roles as senior women in the NHS. We have been exposed to some of the barriers each woman faced and the ways in which they have attempted to manage and address them. The findings of the study suggest that the coping strategies adopted by women are influenced by their career experience in passing through the glass ceiling.

Women who have been exposed to a predominantly male environment before passing through the ceiling are more likely to adopt a strategy of hyper masculinity (Lena) than those who have experienced a female dominated (Selina) or mixed sex (Martha) environment during their career. Managing identity is crucial. Our analysis based on these women's narratives suggests that each of them, albeit in different ways, have been consumed to some extent by their gender in that their careers have been commodified by traditional stereotypes of women. As such much of their identity work has been about managing, and in the case of Lena eliminating, difference. To be seen as a competent professional, each of the women drew on gendered discourses of what a good manager is. In their own ways, each woman managed the tension between professional expectations and differences from the male norm and the perceived sex differences within the NHS. However, if we accept that within the masculine discourses of management and organisation, woman becomes presented as the other, necessary to the constitution of identity but always threatening to it (Cixous and Clément, 1986) and that 'woman' is the dangerous site of the fluid and relational, those elements of human experience and consciousness which evade definition, measurement, formal construction and explicit expression – which both sustains and subverts rational modes of organisation, presenting new creative opportunities but also a destabilising threat. Our study suggests that the need and motivation for these women to 'fix' and validate themselves on the masculine, suppressed the opportunities and potential of the fluid feminine as Baudrillard (1990: 7) contends:

> The strength of the feminine is that of seduction... A universe that can no longer be interpreted in terms of structures and diacritical oppositions, but implies a seductive reversibility – a universe where the feminine is not what opposes the masculine, but what seduces the masculine.

And:

seduction and femininity are confounded, indeed confused. Masculinity has always been haunted by this sudden reversibility within the feminine. Seduction and femininity are ineluctable as the reverse side of sex, meaning and power

(1990: 2).

In Baudrillard, the abstract 'feminine' is understood as that which, quite simply, cannot be fixed positively by any label, which eludes control, which itself is subliminal, and is beyond the borders of inscription (Brewis and Linstead, 2000). The power of the feminine to seduce the masculine, and we may argue destabilise the dialectical structure (man/woman) that dominates the formation of subjectivity, cannot be underestimated. As such we may wish to conclude that if women are choosing to fix and validate their identities by drawing on masculinist discourses this will threaten the ability of NPM to challenge masculinist representations of new managerial work. But both Selina – in 'pressing the buttons' – and Martha – in her awareness and acceptance of change and learning – are not without feminine strengths which they do, however covertly, finds ways to deploy.

To conclude we suggest that rather than emphasise strategies of 'shattering the glass ceiling' (Davidson and Cooper, 1992) which rely on achieving a discontinuity in the dominant social order, the narratives of *continuity* of the senior, and extremely successful women studied here suggests that women who perform their present identities consistently with their retrospective career routes find the glass ceiling *permeable*. In terms of performing beyond the glass ceiling in the light of our findings we can question whether it needs to be broken through because if women need to do this then discontinuity must be said to have occurred. The women in our research all find themselves beyond the glass ceiling and adopt retrospective strategies of continuity, but vary in the degree to which their prospective strategies allow for further *becoming*. These women found themselves in senior positions in the NHS and have all to some extent challenged the dominant practices in their involvement with the NHS Trust Boards. From this study, we suggest that women need not focus on breaking through the hypothesised 'glass ceiling' because it is already porous. For the women included in this account their identity projects and career routes are on-going and in which case offer the possibility that the more continuous women are in their identity projects and career routes the more permeable and plastic becomes the glass ceiling for them. Women's performances have been presented consistently with their retrospective career routes, offering continuity in an environment that expects discontinuity. Finally, to retreat from the unknown, the insecure, discrimination and challenge the women studied – though not without compromise and improvisation and not uniformly – employ modernist projects of self-identity (Giddens, 1991). This involves fixing and stabilising, which is inconsistent with the claimed feminisation of NPM, which requires increased fluidity to offer increased opportunities for women. NPM has a long way to go to challenge the masculinist practices, yet it cannot be argued, from consideration of the prospective dimension of these women's identity accounts and the potential for learning and change we find there, that it is a lost cause.

Notes

1   Gowler and Legge's (1983) work on rhetoric in 'The Meaning of Management and the Management of Meaning' (reprinted in S. Linstead et al, 1996), is one of the earliest discussions of management – rather than managers – that investigates the socially constructed and hence *fluid* nature of management. Gowler and Legge identify the themes of hierarchy, accountability and achievement and while the model is need of extension (see Linstead, 2003) the three organising themes have proven useful for the organisation of the present account.

2   The critical feminist approach adopted in this chapter is influenced by post-structuralism (see Linstead and Thomas 2002) which enables us to theorise the multiplicities of identity although we have not explored the ontological and epistemological fluidity necessary to adopt a poststructuralist feminism approach in this research.

References

Acker, J. (1990), 'Hierarchies, Jobs, Bodies: A Theory of Gendered Organizations', *Gender and Society*, 4(2): 139-58.

Alvesson, M. and Due Billing, Y. (1997), *Understanding Gender and Organizations*, Sage: London.

Barker, J. (1993), 'Tightening the Iron Cage', *Administrative Science Quarterly*, 38(3): 408-37.

Baudrillard, J. (1990), *Seduction*, St Martin's Press: New York.

Brewis, J. (1999), 'How Does it Feel? Women Managers, Embodiment and Public-Sector Cultures', in S. Whitehead R. and Moodley (eds), *Transforming Managers: Gendering Change in the Public Sector*, UCL Press: London.

Brewis, J. and Linstead, S. (2001), *Sex, Work and Sex Work*, Routledge: London.

Butler, J. (1999), *Gender Trouble: Feminism and the Subversion of Identity*, Routledge: New York.

Calás, M.B. and Smircich, L. (1992a), Re-writing Gender into Organizational Theorizing: Directions from Feminist Perspectives, in M. Reed and M. (eds), *Rethinking Organization*, Sage: London.

Calás, M.B. and Smircich, L. (1992b), 'Using the "F" Word: Feminist Theories and the Social Consequences of Organisational Research', in A. Mills and P. Tancred (eds), *Gendering Organisational Analysis*, Sage: London.

Calás, M.B. and Smircich, L. (1993), 'Dangerous Liaisons: The "Feminisation-in Management" Meets "Globalisation"', *Business Horizons*, March-April: 73-83.

Cassell, G. and Symon, C. (1998), *Qualitative Methods and Analysis in Organizational Research: a Practical Guide*, Sage: London.

Cixous, H. and Clement, C. (1986), *The Newly Born Woman*, University of Minnesota Press: Minneapolis.

Collinson, D. and Hearn, J. (1996), *Men as Managers, Managers as Men*, Sage: London.

Crompton, R. and Sanderson, K. (1990), *Gendered Jobs and Social Change*, Hyman: London.

Davidson, M.J. and Cooper, C.L. (1992), *Shattering the Glass Ceiling: The Woman Manager*, Paul Chapman: London.

Dickens, L. (1998), 'What HRM Means for Gender Equality', *Human Resource Management Journal*, 8(1): 23-40.

du Gay, P. (1996), *Consumption and Identity at Work*, London: Sage.

Exworthy, M. and Halford, S. (1999), *Professionals and the New Managerialism in the Public Sector*, Open University Press: Buckingham.

Fagenson, E. (1993), *Women in Management: Trends, Issues and Challenges in Managerial Diversity*, Sage: Newbury Park.

Fondas, N. (1997), 'Feminisation Unveiled: Management Qualities in Contemporary Writings', *Academy of Management Review*, 22(1): 257-82

Foucault, M. (1980), *Power/Knowledge*, Harvester Wheatsheaf: Brighton.

Friedman, J. (1992), 'Narcissism, Roots and Postmodernity: the Construction of Selfhood in the Global Crisis', in S. Lash and J. Friedman (eds), *Modernity and Identity*, Blackwell: Oxford.

Garfinkel, H. (1967), *Studies in Ethnomethodology*, Prentice-Hall: Englewood Cliffs, NJ.

Giddens, A. (1991), *Modernity and Self-Identity*, Polity Press: Cambridge.

Gowler, D. and Legge, K. (1996), 'The Meaning of Management and The Management of Meaning', in S. Linstead, R. Grafton-Small and P. Jeffcutt (eds), *Understanding Management*, Sage: London.

Grey, C. (1994), 'Career as a Project of the Self and Labour Process Discipline', *Sociology* 28(2): 479-97.

Grosz, E. (1994), *Volatile Bodies: Towards a Corporeal Feminism*, Indiana University Press: Bloomington and Indianapolis.

Halford, S., Savage, M. and Witz, A. (1997), *Gender, Careers and Organisations*, Macmillan: London.

Hochschild, A. (1997), *The Managed Heart*, Berkeley, CA: University of California Press.

Hood, C. (1995), 'The New Public Management in the 1980s: Variations on a Theme', *Accounting, Organisation and Society*, 20(2/3): 93-109.

Höpfl, H. and Kostera, M. (eds), (2002), *Interpreting the Maternal Organization*, Routledge: London.

Kerfoot, D. (1999), 'The Organization of Intimacy: Managerialism, Masculinity and the Masculine Subject', in S. Whitehead and R. Moodley (eds), *Transforming Managers: Gendering Change in the Public Sector*, UCL Press: London.

Kowalczyk, R. (2002), 'The Effect of New Public Management on Intensive Care Unit Staff', *International Journal of Public Sector Management*, 15(2): 118-28.

Kunda, G. (1992), *Engineered Culture: Control and Commitment in a High Tech Corporation*, Temple University Press: Philadelphia.

Kerfoot, D. and Knights, D. (1998), 'Managing Masculinity in Contemporary Organizational Life: A "Man"agerial Project', *Organization*. 5(1): 7-26.

Ledwith, S. and Colgan, F. (1996), *Women in Organizations: Challenging Gender Politics*, Macmillan: Basingstoke.

Linstead, A. (2003), *No Particular Place to Go: a Poststructuralist Reading of Middle Managers' Subjectivities*, Unpublished PhD thesis: Sheffield Hallam University.

Linstead, A. and Thomas, R. (2002), 'What Do You Want From Me? A Poststructuralist Feminist Reading of Middle Managers' Identities', *Culture and Organization*, 8(1): 1-20.

Linstead, S.A. (2000), 'Gender Blindness or Gender Suppression? A Comment on Fiona Wilson's Research Note', *Organization Studies*, 21(1): 297-303.

Maddock, S. (1999), *Challenging Women: Gender, Culture and Organization*, Sage: London.

Maile, S. (1999), 'Inter-managerial Rivalries, Organizational Restructuring and the Transformation of Management Masculinities', in S. Whitehead and R. Moodley, (eds), *Transforming Managers: Gendering Change in the Public Sector*, UCL Press: London.

Marshall, J. (1984), *Women Managers: Travellers in a Male World*, Chichester: John Wiley.

Marshall, J. (1995), *Women Managers Moving On: Exploring Career and Life Choices*, Routledge: London.

Musson, G. (1998), 'Life Histories', in G. Cassell and C. Symon (eds), (1998), *Qualitative Methods and Analysis in Organizational Research: a Practical Guide*, Sage: London.

Newman, J. (1995), 'Gender and Cultural Change', in C. Itzin and J. Newman (eds), *Gender, Culture and Organizational Change*, Routledge: London.

Newman, J. and Clarke, J. (1994), 'Going About Our Business? The Managerialization of Public Services', in J. Clarke, A, Cochrane and E. McLaughlin (eds), *Managing Social Policy*, Sage: London.

Oakley, A. (1981), 'Interviewing Women: A Contradiction in Terms?' In H. Roberts (ed), *Doing Feminist Research*, Routledge: London.

Plummer, K. (1996), 'Life Story Research', in J.A. Smith, R. Harre and L. Van Langenhove (eds), *Rethinking Methods in Psychology*, Sage: London.

Potter, J. and Wetherell, M. (1987), *Discourse and Social Psychology: Beyond Attitudes and Behaviour*, London: Sage.

Reskin, B. and Roos, P. (1990), *Job Queues, Gender Queues: Explaining Women's Inroads into Male Occupations*, Temple University Press: Philadelphia.

Reskin, B. and Roos, P. (1992), 'Jobs, Authority and Earnings Among Managers: The Continuing Significance of Sex', *Work and Occupations*, 19(4), 342-65.

Roper, M. (1994), *Masculinity and the British Organization Man Since 1945*, Oxford: Oxford University Press.

Rosener, J. (1990), 'Ways Women Lead', *Harvard Business Review*, November-December: 119-25.

Scase, R. and Goffee, R. (1989), *Reluctant Managers*, Unwin Hyman: London.

Schwandt, T.A. (1998), 'Constructivist, Interpretivist Approaches to Human Inquiry', in N.K. Denzin and Y.S. Lincoln (eds), *The Landscape of Qualitative Research: Theories and Issues*, Sage: Thousand Oaks, CA.

Scott, J. (1992), *Domination and The Arts of Resistance: Hidden Transcripts*, Yale University Press: New Haven.

Silverman, D. (1975), *Reading Castaneda*, Routledge: London.

Thomas, R. and Davies, A. (2002), 'Gender and New Public Management: Reconstituting Academic Subjectivities', *Gender, Work and Organization*, 9(4): 372-97.

Vinnicombe, S. and Colwill, N.L. (1995), *The Essence of Women in Management*, London: Prentice-Hall.

Wajcman, J. (1998), *Managing Like a Man: Women and Men in Corporate Management*, Polity Press: Oxford.

Walby, S. and Greenwell, J. (1994), 'Managing the National Health Service', in J. Clarke, A. Cochrane and E. McLaughlin (eds), *Managing Social Policy*, Sage: London.

Watson, T. and Harris, P. (1999), *The Emergent Manager*, London: Sage.

Weedon, C. (1999), *Feminism, Theory and the Politics of Difference*, Blackwell: Oxford.

Whitehead, S. (1998), 'Disrupted Selves: Resistance and Identity Work in the Managerial Arena', *Gender and Education*, 10(2): 199-215.

Whitehead, S. and Moodley, R. (eds), (1999), *Transforming Managers: Gendering Change in the Public Sector*, UCL Press: London.

Wilson, F. (1996), 'Organizational Theory: Blind and Deaf to Gender?', *Organization Studies*, 17(5): 825-42.

Wyatt, S. and Langridge, C. (1996), 'Getting to the Top in the National Health Service', in S. Ledwith and F. Colgan, (eds), *Women in Organizations: Challenging Gender Politics*, Macmillan: Basingstoke.

Chapter 8

Can the Public Sector *Learn*? The Importation of 'Patient-Focused Care' in an NHS Hospital Trust

Chris Howorth, Frank Mueller and Charles Harvey

Introduction

This chapter deals with the diffusion and adoption of an organisational innovation, 'Patient Focused Care' (PFC), at a British Hospital Trust. We will be discussing how PFC emerged in the US context, was propagated by policy-makers, and judged worth adopting by organisational decision-makers. In providing an analysis of the case, we are attempting to show how actors within an organisational field, the National Health Service (NHS), were confronted by a 'problem', for which no solutions seemed available within the boundaries of the organisational field.[1] Under such conditions, actors will search outside their organisational field boundaries.

The chapter is structured as follows: firstly there is a discussion of the global/U.S. context of the emergence of PFC; this is followed by a section on methodology and research methods. Finally, there is a section dealing with the appropriation process at organisational level – we have integrated our discussion of the literature within the case material. Finally, there is a summary and conclusion.

The Emergence of an Organisational Innovation in the US Social Policy Context

In discussing managerial knowledge between globalisation and local contexts, the health sector is an interesting case as it has not played a significant role in the literature on cross-border diffusion of innovation. Partly because diffusion agencies increasingly operate across national borders, as in the case of multinational consulting companies, partly because of increasing willingness to learn from other countries, there has been increasing diffusion of templates or sectoral recipes *across* national borders – 'privatisation' and 'contracting out' are only the most publicised and visible examples (Mossialos and Le Grand, 1999). Health care provision provides us with an activity which is typified by an extraordinary degree of national convergence in clinical practice, financial management problems faced and, in the developed world at least, by a growing and emergent culture of 'managerialism' (Pollitt, 1993). This is beginning to co-exist – sometimes more successfully than at other times – with the ethos of traditional health professions. The cross-border nature of learning in this context is illustrated by the number of publications, which purport to help health care system designers learn from each other in terms of management, finance and clinical practice (Mossialos and Le Grand, 1999; Yach and Bettcher, 1998a,b; Weil, 1997; Busse and Schwartz, 1997; Lenaghan, 1997). The extent to which there is political involvement in the development of these strategies varies from country to country, both in the level of openness to other systems, and in the degree to which 'recipes' from other organisational fields is appropriate. Some models are widely copied with diagnosis-related groups (DRGs) in costing health care interventions being one particularly good example (Kerres and Lohmann, 2000; Mossialos and Le Grand, 1999). Market reforms have also been common features of health care reform during the last decade (Mossialos and Le Grand, 1999).

Whilst the market has had a greater impact on the US health care system, due to its large private sector, Yach and Bettcher's (1998a) argument for cross-fertilisation of experiences regarding health system reform has extended far beyond the American system, as governments have adopted market (and quasi-market) solutions to encourage a greater level of efficiency and transparency in health care delivery. *Sectoral Recipes* in health care may be influenced, not only through learning from other sectors, or from the leaders within the national sector, but also from providers in other countries. There have been some major catalysts in the NHS driving the search for new practices from abroad. Policy statements thus link the national arena with the trans-national arena (Mueller, 1994) and extend the boundaries of the organisational field.

Data Collection and Methodology

This research follows a qualitative, grounded theory methodology (Strauss and Corbin, 1994). The project was initiated through a series of (ten) interviews with the board team (including both executive and non-executive directors), of West London Hospital, carried out between November 1996 and January 1997. These interviews were followed up by both participant observation (one of the researchers was a member of the board team), and non-participant observation (another of the researchers was a frequent observer of board meetings and discussions between various board members). During this period a number of informal discussions were held with board members, and a full set of public and non-public board papers was collected. At the end of the study period, a further series of (twelve) interviews was held with the board team, during February and March 1999. The final twelve interviews were carried out with the (eight) members of the board team who remained in place throughout the research period, together with (four) other members of the board who were not interviewed in the initial interviews.

The British NHS as a National Organisational Field

The study is based on the West London Hospital Trust (hereafter West London Hospital) a medium sized District General Hospital in London. The hospital serves an ethnically and socially diverse population, with conditions such as sickle cell anaemia and HIV at above average prevalence. The hospital has been at the forefront of some innovative clinical practices. These may be seen in particular around the hospital's pioneering of the ambulatory and diagnostic care concept in the UK, and the collaborative care concept, in conjunction with a community health trust and local social services. In common with other NHS acute hospital trusts, West London Hospital has a number of different stakeholder groups which must be consulted, persuaded, and/or informed about the activities and strategies of the trust. Prime amongst these are the Health Authorities and GP fundholders/Primary Care Groups – Trusts, CHCs, Department of Health, and staff groups.

The political influence of these various stakeholder groups has developed during the constant reorganisation experienced over the fifty years that the UK NHS has existed. The growth of management (as opposed to administration), in the NHS has been a drawn out process, always long on rhetoric but often short on real change, and has often been a case of 'shuffling the boxes'. The 1974 reform of the NHS, whilst beginning a debate on managerialism within the NHS, and intended to improve the efficiency of the NHS, contained a number of flaws which made achieving this aim difficult (Klein, 1995; Dopson, 1997). The so-called consensus era in the NHS was ended by the 1983 report of the NHS Management Inquiry (Griffiths Report), which introduced general management (rather than administration), into the NHS. (Klein, 1995). This was, however, also the decade in which comparison with templates from foreign health care systems and with other organisational fields began to take place in NHS planning. Criticisms had led the Central Policy Review Staff to suggest private health insurance for some sectors of the population in keeping with the more free market US model (Riddell, 1991; Klein, 1995; Timmins, 1995; West, 1998). However political sensitivities and the potential transaction costs involved in private health insurance led to such a radical solution being rapidly rejected.

Despite these reservations US ideas still had a major impact on the reform of the NHS, and in 1985 the American academic Alain Enthoven put forward the idea of an internal market based on the US Health Maintenance Organisation (HMO) model, with budgetary autonomy devolved to District Health Authorities (similar to ideas presented by the Institute of Economic Affairs over twenty-five years). Diffusion agents like Enthoven operate at the level of applying models to a new national, sometimes organisational context. According to Dent (1993:266) 'Enthoven's intervention and advocacy of the HMO model was therefore crucial in permitting the introduction of market principles within the NHS without privatisation'.

Scrutiny of the NHS throughout the 1980s culminated in the review started in 1988, and ending in the Government White Paper 'Working for Patients', which created an internal market, with hospitals being permitted self governing Trust status, and larger GP practices gaining control over a portion of their own budgets to use in purchasing services from hospitals. The introduction of 'Trustification' into the British NHS during the early 1990s resulted in an acceleration of the pace of change within the organisations providing the majority of health care in the UK. Chief Executive Officers (CEOs) and Finance Directors, in particular, were taking on much broader managerial roles in the newly established Trusts than in the old-style NHS. The emergence of the internal market in the UK NHS was then, at least in part, the result of the incorporation of influences, both from abroad, and from other sectors.

Extending the Cognitive Boundaries of the Organisational Field: The Case Of West London Hospital Trust

The changes outlined above can be explained as evidence of ideologically (market liberalism) driven restructuring, and an attempt by government to break a professional stranglehold on the NHS (Klein, 1995: 203). This amounted to a radical change of the environment within which health care providers in the UK operated. Although there are obvious political dangers in allowing hospitals to fail within a public sector market, the financial performance of business units became more transparent with the publication of individual annual reports, and unit closures together with forced mergers began to emerge.

West London's position made it uniquely suited to its development as a potential exemplar of global learning in health care organisation. The reforms of the 1980s and 1990s in the UK NHS resulted in a spate of hospital closures and mergers by the end of the 1990s. West London (which was a 'first wave' Trust) was threatened with closure during the early 1990s and faced organisational threats, which placed great pressure on management to consider innovating to ensure survival. Organisational change in response to a financial crisis is a common pattern in the history of the NHS (Ham and Hunter, 1988).

The local situation in which West London Hospital was operating meant that the organisation was faced with a very clearly defined threat against which to *Set an Agenda* of innovation. Indeed Hurst (undated), showing West London as an early adopter of patient focussed care highlights the need for innovation in terms of survival. In a strategic planning document the West London Board faced the prospect that:

> Any potential organisational change must seek to anticipate and meet these pressures and opportunities. Simple administrative, bureaucratic and organisational changes, which do not recognise these trends will be short-sighted and relatively fruitless
>
> (Hurst, undated: 13).

Faced with an uncertain future, West London was then forced first to carefully consider and then *select* strategies that could ensure its survival and future success. In attempting to ensure this survival West London Hospital chose to follow a radical innovative change programme rather than relying on doing 'business as usual' better.

The central idea that West London 'imported' into the UK health arena was *Patient Focused Care*. The concept of patient focused care was first introduced into the UK in 1988 by the UK arm of the American based Consulting firm Booz Allen and Hamilton (Morgan, 1993). This concept was epitomised through two main projects in the hospital during the 1990s, the *Protocolisation of Medical Care* and the *Ambulatory Care and Diagnostic Centre (ACAD)*.

The first of these ideas to be adopted was that of protocolisation:

> In November 1991, West London Hospital NHS Trust began implementing patient focused care (PFC) principles in two pilot areas (with the view of eventually extending this philosophy of care throughout the entire hospital). As the focus for the programme, West London Hospital adopted [the following key elements]:
> - Care organised according to clinical protocols
> - A unitary patient record
> - Care delivered by teams of multi-skilled staff members
> - A simplified process
>
> (Hurst, undated: 51ff).

These are the core principles of Booz Allen Hamilton's (1988) model. Indeed, both Morgan and Layton (1996:1) and Hurst (undated) identify the US as being the template for patient focused care and the protocolisation required to implement it, while Hurst identifies Booz Allen Hamilton as the conduit of transmission:

> According to Pitt (1993:27) patient focused care evolved from the San-Francisco Planetree healthcare programme in 1985. Two years later patient focused care was introduced to the United Kingdom health care professionals by Booz Allen and Hamilton management consultants...
>
> (Hurst, undated: 1).

The diffusion of organisational innovations from the US to the UK (Kogut, 1990; Kogut and Parkinson, 1993) or Japan to the UK (Elger and Smith, 1994) has been dealt with before in the literature, although not especially for public sector organisations. Here we can begin to identify both the uncertainty surrounding the implementation of the *national* change process in the planning of West London Hospital's future, and the emergence of search processes in response to this uncertainty. Faced with structural changes beyond their own control, the management of West London Hospital began to search for a model that would create a more stable future. As the national model was developing along market lines it was logical to adopt a model taken from successful organisations in the same field that had already been successful. The model had to be, however, adaptable to the local setting, meaning, both local to the UK NHS, and local in terms of West London Hospital's immediate regional catchment. In adopting a suggestion from the innovation management literature we could call this process 'appropriation' (Kamoche and Mueller, 1998): implementing an innovation which looks good 'in theory' or looks good somewhere else requires 'articulation' in specific new settings and this includes the following:

1. adapting it;
2. selling it to the main stakeholders;
3. carrying along the main principally interested parties;
4. negotiating the politics involved.

West London Hospital shows aspects of both mimicry and innovative leadership. The hospital is innovative in introducing the patient focused care concept into the UK setting. At the same time the organisation has, in the face of uncertainty, rather than developing a bespoke solution, copied a model, which has been proven in a different national setting: 'The North American pilot (so-called pioneer) sites are a few years ahead of the United Kingdom' (Hurst, undated: 1).

The Director of Nursing and Quality at West London Hospital and others at West London Hospital were well aware of the global context of PFC, and make a point of stressing the proven nature of the innovation:

> Clinical protocols and medical guidelines have long been used by individual professional groups. This is particularly so in the United States, where the use of pathways [Protocols] of care is well established
>
> (November 1998).

The ability to point out that the model being adopted is not untried within the professional organisational field legitimised its introduction into a new 'spatial' area. West London Hospital benefited from being innovative, and was able at the same time, to argue that it was following a 'tried and tested' route. *This allowed the organisation to manage professional conservatism, and strategic organisational risk simultaneously* – cross-border innovation is thus advantageous as it allows the organisation to 'have the cake and eat it'. Significant reputational benefits can be expected without incurring significant risks.

This use of globally tested models was especially evident in the case of the move towards accelerated discharges from hospital, with the creation of the *Collaborative Care* team concept out of the previous *Hospital at Home* and *Bridging* team concepts:

> The concept of hospital at home originated with 'Hospitalisation a Domicile' in France in 1961 and has been implemented in a number of other countries, including the United States, Canada, and the Netherlands...
>
> (Shepperd and Iliffe, 1998: 344).

The use of this model did not rely merely on the proven nature of the concept outside the UK NHS environment, but also on the fact that it represented incremental change in the way in which cases were handled. The *Collaborative*

Care concept may be 'marketed' either as a step development of the *Hospital at Home* and *Bridging Team* concepts, or as a new (to the UK), concept imported after international comparison.

The appropriation process means that seemingly attractive global ideas will not automatically be embraced, however, unless they address agendas, which have formed in the local context. In this sense, innovations are 'embedded'. In the West London Hospital case, the local situation has facilitated the embrace of new ideas. First of all, protocols allowed West London Hospital to manage its patient throughput more effectively (improved care quality), more efficiently (reduced costs), and more speedily. All of these addressed items on West London Hospital's agenda. More specifically,

> The impetus for change was saving money but the idea of the collaborative care team fitted in to the longer term strategy of the trust which was to re-engineer care and as part of that process to look at a reduction in patient beds... The setting up of the team met the strategic objectives of the trust, and at the same time reduced costs by closing almost two wards
> (Director of Nursing and Quality, West London Hospital – November 1998).

This 'double payoff' is echoed in the literature (Parkes and Shepperd, 1998; Cochrane Stroke Group, 1998; Evans, 1993 and Kollef *et al.*, 1997), both from the UK and from North America. Hurst (undated) identifies better care as the number one reason for adoption of PFC in the US (88 per cent), with lower costs as most important (55 per cent), and [organisational] survival as fifth most important (37 per cent). It is instructive to consider discussion of 'length of stay' in hospitals in the global context: reforms throughout the European Union and America have centred on changing funding criteria, away from *per diem* payments for hospital stay towards DRG based case fees, which give an incentive to reduce length of stay faster than would otherwise be the case (Mossialos and Le Grand, 1999; Arnold and Paffrath, 1998). In the UK the focus on length of stay has included quality in terms of patient satisfaction and hospital acquired infections (Struelens, 1998). Adoption of global models into NHS organisations is, potentially, made particularly difficult in that the NHS is an organisation in which the collision of clinical and managerial agendas provides the ground for conflict (Lorbiecki, 1995). Such conflicts are especially likely where change is substantial and where the drivers for change are not purely clinical:

> conflict *will* occur (as indeed has been the case) when managers press professionals to behave in ways which the latter do not want
> (Harrison and Pollitt, 1994: 2).

The need for co-operation in implementing the change process was acknowledged in the development of protocol based nursing and collaborative care at West London Hospital and it was indicated that acceptance of protocols for PFC at West London Hospital was achieved in part through the:

appointment of a facilitator with a clinical background and with credibility among the clinical professionals within the organisation

(Morgan and Layton, 1996: 3).

Benchmarking of 'best practices' in the NHS is potentially problematic. Any drive to improve efficiency may well lead to a loss in effectiveness as clinical professionals withdraw their goodwill. Crucially, clinicians did not object to the introduction of new innovative practices, as they were perceived as potentially addressing two *professional* objectives: firstly, to serve the local community (patients); secondly, to employ the re-engineering project in order to modernise and provide a much improved service to patients through cutting waiting lists, smoother passage through the system, and the more systematic delivery of treatments (protocols). Similar to our case, Ackroyd and Bolton (1999: 377) found a 'natural alliance emerging between doctors and managers' in implementing a new pattern of service provision on a gynaecological ward.

The need for such acceptance is demonstrated in the experience of developing the ACAD project within the West London Hospital Trust. A new state-of-the-art hospital was to be constructed in two stages: the UK's first purpose-built ambulatory care and diagnostic centre (ACAD) and the Brent emergency care development (BECAD). The ACAD centre received Treasury approval in 1995. The ACAD project, which separates elective patients from emergency admissions was politically controversial in the UK, although it had already been proven successful in Austria, Switzerland and the USA (Mayo Clinic). In order to drive change forward there was a perceived need to sideline those interests whose identity is reproduced along national, historical lines. These lines of conflict are forcefully expressed by the 'pro-innovation' chairman:

We should not run the project and plan on the basis of reactionary and negative tendencies of consultants and nurses... The consultants will do as they're told – it's a process of re-education – they're all young

(Chairman [and Director of Contracting], West London Hospital, ACAD project pre-meeting notes, 30 July 1996).

That the ACAD project was a 'transformation of the old West London Hospital service... [intending] to separate elective and emergency care' and was a concept accepted in some way by all at West London Hospital. That it would 'provide reduced cost and improved elective care to the NHS and other purchasers' or that it would 'offer clinicians the opportunity to extend the range of care which can be accomplished in the ambulatory mode' was, perhaps, more contentious. The message that:

ACAD presents an important NHS opportunity to realise the benefits of complete reorganisation of clinical care protocols and staffing arrangements from a zero base

(ACAD Full Business Case, 1996)

was not read as a positive one by all the actors involved and it was the micro-political constellations that would decide the fate of this particular 'global template'.

Within the ACAD business plan specification there were a number of key features designed to improve patient flow, thus improving efficiency, reducing waiting lists and increasing patient satisfaction, whilst providing medical care at a 'cutting edge standard'. The ACAD project leader was a non-medically trained hospital management board member, who also had lead responsibility for the Clinical Policies Group. The medical staff focus groups, on the other hand, were not fully integrated into the project implementation structure. Almost inevitably, tensions grew which threatened the ACAD concept. The ACAD project included many radical changes to the routine of medical management, affecting the way in which referrals to the facility are dealt with:

> At present there are a number of factors, which adversely affect waiting list and theatre list management [including]:
> - GP [referral] to specific consultants resulting in persistent over and underloading by consultant, thereby affecting the Hospital's overall activity levels;...
> The ACAD project will be responsible for reviewing the management of waiting lists... ACAD based 'scheduling staff' will be responsible for elective care waiting list management... The ACAD project will review and optimise the following:
> - Scheduling pre-assessment;
> - Pre-assessment;
> - Assigning a 'To Come In' (TCI) date;
> - Scheduling tests and investigations associated with elective care;
> - Cancellation and re-book ...
> (ACAD Business Specification documentation).

Given that the project documentation was drafted by the (non-medically qualified), project leader it was unsurprising that tensions arose around this project. The project was designed to enable West London Hospital to perform well in a political climate, which was demanding reductions in the waiting times for elective procedures, at the same time as setting stricter guidelines over the processing of emergency admissions. In order to ensure that both admission groups could be handled effectively they were to be separated and managed. Whilst this response to uncertainty had been employed elsewhere, West London Hospital was at the forefront of innovation in the UK. This 'lead' role was gradually turning into a favourable reputation and praise from prominent corners and ACAD was opened by Prime Minister Tony Blair in September 1999. In his preliminary remarks the Prime Minister acknowledged the reputation West London Hospital had won for innovation:

> I have just been so excited by what I have seen here. This is the future for the National Health Service... I have heard about those people working in breast

cancer surgery who are able to get people in within two weeks and then on the same day tell whether they are clear or if they need more work. And this is what the future of the health service needs to be...

> (Tony Blair, ACAD launch, September 1999).

The ACAD centre was also favourably discussed in a *Financial Times* article dated 8 April 2000, which emphasised the pioneering status of ACAD in the UK. The use of an ambulatory care and diagnostic centre also required a radical change in the way in which treatment was administered and scheduled:

> To optimise the use of theatre facilities it will be necessary to schedule surgical interventions based [on] the availability of resources and expected patient recovery times. This approach will require radical changes to the existing theatre and recovery management process, where currently theatre lists are controlled by consultants and held manually by medical secretaries. The ACAD project will be responsible for reviewing and optimising the following:
> - Scheduling theatre usage (based on theatre availability, patient recovery times and availability of recovery 'bed slots');
> - Scheduling patients and staff;
> - Multi-disciplinary working.
>
> (ACAD Business Specification documentation).

Ackroyd and Bolton (1999: 376-7) discuss how organisational changes initiated by management led to significant increases in patient throughput within a gynaecological ward. They, however, focused on the implications for working practices of nurses. What in the ACAD documentation is couched here in 'technospeak' and neutral management language has wide ranging implications in terms of changes in professional autonomy, work practices and roles of clinical staff (cf. Harrison, 1999). Improved scheduling management and facilitation of cross-disciplinary/cross-functional working are core elements of private sector 'best practices'. The ACAD project reduced clinical autonomy, embedded the use of protocols and shifted control of patient throughput from individual medical consultants to the scheduling team.

Improvements were also sought in theatre management and clinical audit. Changes were not restricted to scheduling and protocols but also encompassed clinical practice:

> [General anaesthetic will] be induced on the table, as *all* preparation is done. Therefore, anaesthetic rooms are not needed for all theatres, one only to be provided and to serve two theatres
>
> (ACAD project documentation).

Management sought to avoid risk to themselves and to their organisation through the adoption of models, which have already been proved in the same field albeit in another national setting. At the same time members of the medical profession engaged in 'normative isomorphism' (DiMaggio and Powell 1983), using the norms and codes of their profession (education, specialist knowledge veto – both legally mandated, and informal but effective), to oppose those parts of change, which they did not like. Professional concerns about 'unsafe' changes in working practices could act as a powerful obstacle to change which threatened the planned innovations in throughput management, the more efficient usage of expensive equipment and room facilities. We know from the literature that where managerialism touches on questions of professional control and established working practices, a contest will ensue. This may even include attempts to invoke the power of professional status gradients, in order to maintain existing professional control. Not surprisingly, therefore, on October 3rd 1996 consultants from the department of urology and lithotripsy wrote:

> It is important that we do not regard the ACAD centre as being a facility that would revolutionise clinical practice. The investigations and treatment that patients require will not change overnight... The way in which the facilities are used must be orchestrated around the requirements of those surgical disciplines which will be using the facility most.

> Service departments, e.g., Radiology and Anaesthetics, cannot be the prime movers in the way in which the organisation works. The illnesses that patients have and the management thereof will not change fundamentally because of ACAD...

This letter indicates an attempt by an existing powerful professional subgroup to protect its boundaries, and to do this by appealing to existing professional values. The letter represented the very real possibility of the ACAD project becoming unstable or failing because of the lack of ownership of its aims, objectives and processes by the main body of the medical profession within the Trust. Here was the beginning of a period where management, in implementing the 'global' model had failed to adequately address the 'local' issues and had therefore failed to build consensus within the wider organisation and the crucial professional groups. This episode also shows that the actual implementation of an (organisational) innovation will depend on the specific context into which it is introduced:

> A large group of sixty staff, including thirty consultants, met with the steering group on 31st October in order to voice their worries about ACAD...

Another consultant expressed his concern very strongly in an interview:

> This is a ludicrous concept to have operating theatres without anaesthetics. Even before a clinician can scrub hands after a patient is operated on, the next patient comes
>
> (Consultant, West London Hospital).

Professional concerns (i.e. normative isomorphic processes) emerged as in contradiction to mimetic learning processes. Put differently: mimetically-based learning faces normatively-based resistance. Indeed Denis et al, (1996) identify some actors within a Canadian hospital change situation defining financial pressure as:

> an opportunity rather than a threat…: *'the current period is fantastic for me, because it's during budget constraints that you invent things that hang together'*
>
> (*emphases* in the original).

At West London Hospital the threats to organisational change are similar to the ones discussed by Denis et al, (1996) and the outcome is also comparable. The consultant body was to be integrated into the process:

> [CEO] reported on the Consultant ACAD Evening on Thursday 31st October. [The Non-Executive Director, Project Director, and CEO] updated the attendees and concluded that a Medical Staff Focus Group should be created. It was agreed that [Project Director and Medical Director] would report back to the next [steering group]. Design issues on anaesthetic rooms would be addressed. [The Project Director] to report back to the next SG
>
> (Minutes of Steering Group Meeting, 5th November 1996).

This quote demonstrates not only the strength of feeling being aroused among clinical professionals, but also their ability to modify management agendas. The exact outcome of this micro-political contest, however, is the subject of another paper (see Mueller et al, 2000).

Summary, Conclusion and Implications

Global innovative practices – such as Patient Focused Care and Collaborative Care Teams – were embraced and relatively successfully implemented as a result of the specific local situation at West London Hospital which, originally, was characterised by threat of closure and a specific population mix, the latter putting premium urgency on speeding hospital patient throughput.

We looked at the importance of the 'local' context in shaping the adoption of a 'global' organisational innovation. Most importantly, we attempted to show that the cognitive boundaries of the organisational field have started to breach national borders, even though resource dependencies and legitimation are still largely national. Defining the new boundaries of the organisational field becomes, therefore, ambiguous and problematic: whilst the NHS is still basically a national field, cognitive learning is taking on a more global orientation. In this sense, the *local connects directly with the global*, and the global organisational innovation will be appropriated in *locally*-specific, rather than *nationally*-specific ways:

1. The absence of anaesthetic rooms was problematised by some clinical professionals demonstrating that the adoption process at local level was not unproblematic.
2. The 'foreign' origin of the innovation played out advantageously: the innovation, whilst already been tested, can still provide the kudos of being a pioneering organisation.
3. Public policy-makers influence the appropriation process: their role is not restricted to coercive legislation.

As far as (1) and (2) are concerned, management's role is important here: as coercive, normative and mimetic pressures and processes conflict, executives need to mediate between these demands. In many ways, therefore, organisations' executives will need to mediate the claims emerging from mimetic isomorphic *pressures* rather than simply implementing such isomorphic *processes*.

In their 1999 paper Mizruchi and Fein describe the way in which *mimetic* isomorphism has eclipsed *coercive* and *normative* isomorphism in the literature, since the publication of DiMaggio and Powell's (1983) work. The third point is, perhaps, crucial in explaining these findings. Attempts by government at coercive processes for change, and subsequent organisational homogeneity are evident in the NHS reform process, but the direct success of these have been limited by the health professions' (especially medicine's) ability to resist structural change, and once that change is imposed, to reduce its impact (Mueller *et al.*, 2000). In our case, public policy-makers have attempted to promote mimetic learning by encouraging organisations to seek out 'best practices'. This particular aspect has not been discussed in the existing literature where primarily government's *coercive* role is described. In some way then the impact of normative isomorphic processes plays out as a foil to coercive isomorphic processes, so that although both are to be seen, they take on a subservient role to the mimetic processes. The main impact of both may in fact be argued to be the creation of the instability and uncertainty required as a catalyst for public sector organisations, first to seek innovations, and then for these innovations to be spread rapidly through the field.

Acknowledgements

Funding from Reed Charity supported the research reported in this chapter and the authors would like to acknowledge their thanks for this assistance. This chapter is adapted from an earlier version (Howorth et al. 2002).

Note

1. DiMaggio and Powell (1983: 148) define an organisational field as encompassing 'those organizations that, in the aggregate, constitute a recognized area of institutional life'. In the case of an NHS Trust this will include other Trusts, pharmaceutical companies and other suppliers, professional bodies and government agencies as well as patients.

References

Ackroyd, S. and Bolton, S. (1999), 'It is Not Taylorism: Mechanisms of Work Intensification in the Provision of Gynaecology Services in a NHS Hospital', *Work, Employment and Society*, 13, 367-85.
Arnold, M. and Paffrath, D. (eds) (1998), *Krankenhausreport '98: Schwerpunkt: Überkapazitäten im Krankenhaus*, Gustav Fischer: Stuttgart.
Booz, Allen and Hamilton (1988), *Operational Restructuring – A Recipe for Success*, Booz Allen and Hamilton: London.
Busse, R. and Schwartz, F-W. (1997), 'The Philippines' National Health Insurance Act: a German Perspective', *International Journal of Health Planning and Management*, 12, 131-48.
Cochrane Stroke Group (1998), 'Organised Inpatient (Stroke Unit) Care After Stroke', *The Cochrane Database of Systematic Reviews*, 3.
Denis, J-L., Langley, A. and Cazale, L. (1996), 'Leadership and Strategic Change Under Ambiguity', *Organisation Studies*, 17, 673-99.
Dent, M. (1993), 'Professionalism, Educated Labour and the State: Hospital Medicine and the New Managerialism', *Sociological Review*, 41, 244-73.
DiMaggio, P.J. and Powell, W.W. (1983), 'The Iron Cage Revisited: Institutional Isomorphism and Collective Rationality in Organizational Fields', *American Sociological Review*, 48 (April), 147-60.
Dopson, S. (1997), *Managing Ambiguity and Change*, Macmillan: Basingstoke.
Elger, T. and Smith, C. (1994), 'Global Japanisation? Convergence and Competition in the Organisation of the Labour Process' in T. Elger and C. Smith, (eds), *Global Japanisation? The Transnational Transformation of the Labour Process*, Routledge: London.
Evans, R.L. (1993), 'Hospital Discharge Planning for High Risk Patients', *Medical Care*, 31, 358-70.
Ham, C. and Hunter, D.J. (1988), *Managing Clinical Activity in the NHS*, King's Fund Institute: London.
Harrison, S. (1999), 'Clinical Autonomy and Health Policy: Past and Futures', in M. Exworthy, and S. Halford, (eds), *Professionals and the New Managerialism in the Public Sector*, Open University Press: Buckingham.
Harrison, S. and Pollitt, C. (1994), *Controlling Health Professionals: the Future of Work and Organization in the National Health Service*, Open University Press: Buckingham.
Howorth, C., Mueller, F. and Harvey, C (2002), 'The Diffusion of an Organisational Innovation: Adopting 'Patient-Focused Care' in an NHS Hospital Trust', *Competition and Change*, 6, 213-32.
Hurst, K. (undated), *Progress with Patient Focused Care in the United Kingdom*, Nuffield Institute for Health: Leeds.
Kamoche, K. and Mueller, F. (1998), Human Resource Management: an Appropriation-Learning Perspective', *Human Relations*, 51, 1033-60.

Kerres, M. and Lohmann, H. (2000), *Der Gesundheitssektor: Chance zur Erneuerung: Vom regulierten Krankenhaus zum wettbewerb erbsfähigen*, Ueberreuter Wirtschaft: Frankfurt.

Klein, R. (1995), *The New Politics of the NHS* (Third Edition), Addison Wesley Longman: Harlow.

Kogut, B. (1990), 'The Permeability of Borders and the Speed of Learning Among Countries', in J.H. Dunning, B. Kogut and M. Blomström, (eds), *Globalization of Firms and the Competitiveness of Nations*, Lund University Press: Lund.

Kogut, B. and Parkinson, D. (1993), The Diffusion of American Organizing Principles to Europe, in Kogut, B, (ed), *Country Competitiveness: Technology and the Organizing of Work*, Oxford University Press: New York.

Kollef, M.H., Shapiro, S.D., Silver, P., et al, (1997), 'A Randomized, Controlled Trial of Protocol-Directed Versus Physician-Directed Weaning from Medical Ventilation', *Critical Care Medicine*, 25, 567-74.

Lenaghan, J. (1997), *Hard Choices in Health Care*, British Medical Journal Publishing: London.

Lorbiecki, A. (1995), 'Clinicians as Managers: Convergence or Collusion?', in Soothill, K., Mackay, L. and Webb, C. (eds), *Interprofessional Relations in Health Care*, Arnold: London.

Meyer, J.W. and Rowan, B. (1977), 'Institutionalized Organizations: Formal Structure as Myth and Ceremony', *American Sociological Review*, 83, 340-63.

Mizruchi, M.S. and Fein, L.C. (1999), 'The Social Construction of Organisational Knowledge: a Study of the Uses of Coercive, Mimetic, and Normative Isomorphism', *Administrative Science Quarterly*, 44, 653-83.

Morgan, G. (1993), 'The Implications of Patient Focused Care', *Nursing Standard*, 7(52), 37-39.

Morgan, G. and Layton, A. (1996), *Clinical Protocols: The Clinical Record*, Council of International Hospitals Advisory Board Company: London.

Mossialos, E. and Le Grand, J. (1999), *Health Care and Cost Containment in the European Union*, Ashgate: Aldershot.

Mueller, F., Howorth, C. and Harvey, C. (2000), *Managers and Clinical Professionals in a Hospital Trust Board: Negotiating 'Finance' and Innovation*, EGOS Conference, Helsinki, 2-4 July.

Mueller, F. (1994), 'Societal Effect, Organizational Effect and Globalisation', *Organization Studies*, 15, 407-28.

Parkes, J. and Shepperd, S. (1998), Discharge Planning from Hospital to Home, *The Cochrane Database of Systematic Reviews*, 3.

Pollitt, C. (1993), *Managerialism and the Public Services* (Second Edition), Blackwell: Oxford.

Pitt, C. (1993), 'Quality Health Care: Identifying and Meeting Customer Needs', *International Journal of Health Care Quality Assurance*, 6, 25-28.

Riddell, P. (1991), *The Thatcher Era: and Its Legacy*, Blackwell: Oxford.

Shepperd, S. and Iliffe, S. (1998), 'Effectiveness of Hospital at Home Compared to In-Patient Hospital Care: a Systematic Review', *Journal of Public Health Medicine*, 20, 344-50.

Strauss, A. and Corbin, J. (1994), 'Grounded Theory Methodology: An Overview', in Denzin, N.K. and Lincoln, Y.S. (eds), *Handbook of Qualitative Research*, Sage Publications: Thousand Oaks, CA.

Struelens, M.J. (1998), 'The Epidemiology of Antimicrobial Resistance in Hospital Aquired Infections: Problems and Possible Solutions', *British Medical Journal*, 317, 652-54.

Timmins, N. (1995), *Five Giants: Biography of the Welfare State*, Harper Collins, London.

Weil, T.P. (1997), 'Merging Managed Care with the German Model', *International Journal of Health Planning and Management*, 12, 115-30.

West, P. (1998), *Managed Care: a Model for the UK?* Office of Health Economics: London.

Whitley, R.D. (1992), 'The Comparative Study of Business Systems in Europe: Issues and Choices', in Whitley, R. (ed), *European Business Systems: Firms and Markets in their National Contexts*, Sage: London.

Whitley, R.D. (1994a), 'Dominant Forms of Economic Organization in Market Economies', *Organization Studies*, 15, 153-82.

Whitley, R.D. (1994b), 'The Internationalization of Firms and Markets: Its Significance and Institutional Structuring', *Organization*, 1, 101-24.

Yach, D. and Bettcher, D. (1998a), 'The Globalization of Public Health, I: Threats and Opportunities', *American Journal of Public Health*, 88, 735-38.

Yach, D. and Bettcher, D. (1998b), The Globalization of Public Health, II: The Convergence of Self-Interest and Altruism, *American Journal of Public Health*, 88, 738-41.

Chapter 9

'It's a Leap of Faith, Isn't It?' Managers' Perceptions of PFI in the NHS

Sally Ruane

Introduction

The Private Finance Initiative (PFI) was introduced in November 1992 by the then Chancellor to make private capital available for the development of 'public' infrastructure and facilities. Revised arrangements in 1994 required that the PFI option be explored by any public body seeking capital investment. Progress in the health sector lagged under the Conservative administration and attempts to negotiate large-scale new build acute hospital schemes have proved complex, protracted and controversial. From the late 1990s, under New Labour, these large schemes have fared better, legislation was enacted which first, clarified the legal powers of NHS bodies to enter into PFI contractual agreements and second, provided a guarantee in law that PFI payments by NHS bodies would be 'ring-fenced' to protect them from any future pressure on NHS budgets. In addition to this legal groundwork, the government's strategy was to prioritise a handful of schemes and to establish a centre of expertise within the Treasury, the Treasury Taskforce, which could address and help resolve problems through the regular issuing of policy statements and technical guidance and which could supplement expertise within the Department of Health until such time as it became no longer necessary. The first 'wave' of thirteen PFI new build acute hospital schemes was announced in July 1997 and it is with these that this paper is concerned.

The 'private finance initiative' is a misnomer since it entails bringing into the public arena not merely private finance but also managerial, commercial and creative skills. The NHS Trust determines a detailed 'specification of outputs' and invites private sector consortia to submit bids, in these instances, to design, finance and build a new hospital and to operate a range of services in relation to it. These services include the running, maintenance and upkeep of the hospital itself (known as hard facilities management - 'hard FM'), a variety of a 'soft FM' services (e.g. portering, cleaning, catering) and possibly other services such as IT, equipment maintenance, or sterile supplies. Despite, the flow of information, policy clarification and technical guidance which contributed in a piecemeal fashion, to establishing 'tramlines' along which subsequent schemes were to proceed, problems remained for the parties engaged in these first wave developments. It was in this context that I wished to gain some understanding of the experiences and perceptions of Trust managers.

New Labour's embracing of PFI, which was after all a Conservative policy, should be seen against the backdrop of their broader acceptance of many of the public sector reforms executed by Thatcher and Major (Massey, 2001). The new managerialism within the public sector, known as new public management (NPM), sought to identify more clearly the objectives of an *institution* or service and to measure the attainment (or otherwise) of these more explicitly; to promote greater efficiency, economy and effectiveness and value for money; to make use of market mechanisms and competitive environments in the pursuit of these objectives, including a consideration of private organisations as alternative providers of services; to identify more clearly the objectives and responsibilities of *individual employees* and to measure individual performance against objectives more explicitly; and to restructure from hierarchical centralised bureaucracies to flattened, flexible and devolved management structures in which decisions were taken much closer to the point of delivery and managers were given the tools they needed to manage (Horton and Farnham, 1999; Massey, 2001).

This radical restructuring of the state and the procedures by which it conducts its affairs has involved a refashioning of the relationship between state and capital (Leys, 2001; Whitfield, 2001a). Carter and Fairbrother (1995) and Kerr (1998) believe this refashioning entails a re-articulation of class relations within the state and between business and the state through changes in the labour process, changes in dominant modes of control and relations of authority and control, and through the emergence of a managerial elite enjoying the privileges of enhanced powers of control and comparatively high levels of remuneration. Relations between the state and business have been widened. State sectors have always purchased some goods and services from commercial suppliers (e.g. drugs and equipment within the NHS) but now relations are more multi-faceted. Public bodies purchase a broader range of goods and services from the private sector and some now include those relating to 'core' state sector business; commercial management practices and styles have been adopted and adapted; perhaps most far-reaching, commercial expertise is used in the planning of state services and the defining of public sector needs and interests (Ruane, 2001). This chapter explores the experiences of those who are directly engaged in this restructuring and speculates upon the longer-term consequences for their NPM-related roles.

The role of PFI within the new public management agenda can be seen in official documentation. A handbook produced by the Department of Health (DoH) prior to the general election in 1997 claims that PFI helps to secure more effective achievement of service objectives, more efficient use of public money and improved value for money and quality through the use of competition (DoH, 1997). There is little between this and New Labour's early guide: 'PFI is about creating a structure in which improved value for money is achieved through private sector innovation and management skills delivering significant performance improvement and efficiency savings' (Treasury Taskforce, 1997: 8). Such savings might arise from appropriate risk allocation, better materials and materials management as well as a 'integration and synergies between design, build and operat[ion]' (ibid).

Following a brief sectioning describing the research methods, the remainder of the paper is organised to consider first, what benefits managers speak about in relation to PFI; second, the difficulties and concerns they have experienced with it; and finally, the relationship of PFI to the new public management agenda.

Method of Investigation

The material presented in this paper draws upon interview data, collected between 1998 and 2000 from eleven Trust managers in seven 'first PFI wave' schemes. All the managers were centrally involved with the schemes albeit in different capacities, such as project director, director of finance or capital planning manager. This sample of managers has been arrived at for various reasons, including geographical feasibility and willingness to be interviewed. It is not possible to claim that their views are representative of those of all Trust managers engaged with PFI, even within a single scheme. Instead of claiming some overarching representativeness, it is more useful to regard this material as indicative of a range of substantive issues pertinent to the PFI process.

There are a number of reasons why we might expect Trust managers to present accounts that are justificatory in character. PFI has been a controversial policy development, involving 'big business' in the NHS. Schemes have been dogged with difficulty relating to complexity and affordability and managers have sometimes felt that they have been 'inventing the wheel' or that it has been a case of 'the blind leading the blind'. On top of this, most workers likely to be transferred in PFI deals into the private sector are members of Unison, whose national stance has been vigorously hostile to PFI. Several managers had experience of critical press coverage and hostile press releases. Managers then might be reluctant to become embroiled in political discussion and to be concerned to ensure that, even if they themselves have misgivings about PFI, their own efforts to complete a deal are not ridiculed and misrepresented.

Some Advantages of the PFI Schemes

Although managers varied in their fundamental stances towards PFI, they all spoke well of certain aspects of their schemes. They were in no doubt as to the superiority of the new hospital over existing arrangements. The new hospitals offered a rational approach to service delivery, free from 'historical hang-overs' and the 'hugger-mugger' of piecemeal development. Dilapidated buildings, which put patients' safety at risk, would be replaced. In some instances, the PFI scheme entailed rationalisation onto one site and this was also believed to improve the patient environment and patient care and to facilitate improved management of the Trust. Furthermore, savings would flow from eliminating the duplication of services. Many perceived attractions centred upon design, which reflected the functional relationships of the various departments. These 'improved adjacencies' combined with the compact nature of the new developments were expected to cut down on 'leg work' which, in turn, would effect savings in clinical and ancillary staff budgets as well as speeding up services for patients. Arguably, these benefits could have arisen from any publicly funded new scheme and some managers suggested this. However, under PFI more cash could be raised than would have been available from the Treasury, making possible a new rather than refurbished hospital, completed in a single phase. Two managers claimed one advantage of PFI was that it got the job done: under the former public system, it had taken years to bring a capital development plan to fruition. Two other managers shared a belief that, in certain respects, PFI could improve the overall management of health services, either because it required a more thoughtful approach to strategic planning, or because it would make the organisation more 'commercial' or 'professional' in its approach. For example, the first of these vigorously defended the notion of a thirty years contract:

> The private finance process makes you think harder about it. It's been too easy to waste public money...We have had to think out our strategy more than we would have done. It's made people think further into the future: what should health care be? what should the NHS be about?

Some managers believed another benefit of PFI lay in the transfer of risks to the private consortium, for example in relation to 'life-cycle' costs: where a company has to maintain a building over a thirty year period, it will seek to ensure the initial build minimises the cost of subsequent maintenance. Were maintenance to be undertaken by the public sector, no such incentive to high quality building standards would apply. These managers admitted to no ideological reservations about PFI, they were engaged in a process of reshaping the relationship of business to the health sector and although they demonstrated a keen grasp of the profit imperative driving the consortia, they gave no indication that they saw PFI as a mechanism for furthering the interest of capital more abstractly. These Managers believed that PFI did not mark a privatising of health services because clinical and non-clinical services where clearly separated, as one of them argued:

> The clinical aspects are all - which is the core work of the Trust - under the Trust. PFI is just a fancy word for leasing, isn't it? Yes, they're employing hundreds of people but it's support services - they're not really core. The clinical staff is entirely within the Trust. I can't see it being privatised at all. If BUPA was, say, part of the consortium and the Health Authority were hiring a hospital, I would see that as very much privatised but not this kind of arrangement. There is no danger at all.

So these managers identified a number of positive features in their schemes or in PFI itself. Even so, most of them spent more time in interviews discussing the difficulties they had faced with PFI and to these we now turn.

Difficulties Experienced with the Private Finance Initiative

Negotiating a Deal

All managers admitted to daunting problems encountered in the lengthy procurement and negotiation process. The sheer scale and complexity of the deals contributed to this. The more services to be transferred, the more parties there were involved and the more there was to agree and to resolve. Beside these companies, the banks had their own interests to protect. Each party had its own or bought in legal advice and many clauses in the contract required advice from specialists in different spheres of the law (e.g. labour law; contract law; commercial law). Other experts were also required from time to time, for instance: project managers, architects, engineers, cost consultants and facilities management advisors. Much of this consultancy expertise was duplicated across the parties. Estimates of 'enabling costs' varied from £2.5 to £4m, although this might include the costs of work in the earliest stages when public funding was expected or hoped for. In particular, lawyers' fees contributed a significant slice of the costs with a figure of £300 per hour being mentioned and one manager estimated that on one scheme lawyers' fees alone totalled some £1m. Some managers resented paying these fees, one observing that lawyers still couched advice in a language which protected them from subsequent liability should advice prove mistaken. Generally, the consortium recouped its own costs through the fees paid by the Trust.

One source of significant difficulty in negotiation was risk analysis. Trusts found themselves having to speculate and negotiate around a wide range of potential risks, some more far-fetched and obscure than others. Some managers found these discussions baffling and awesome. Each risk identified had to be distributed among the parties and assigned a financial value on the basis of the likelihood of its realisation and the extent of its effect. What action would need to be taken in certain envisaged scenarios and the life cycle costs and future services needs had to be thought through, planned for and monetarised.

Perhaps the most significant factor was for first wave schemes that everyone was new to the process. No-one was sure what PFI was about; what was permissible and what not. One manager suggested:

There are no templates for what is required in certain circumstances... I think to myself there must be a better way of doing things but I wonder how much my experience over the last months is because it's a new system and people are feeling their way through.

Moreover, the publication of new guidelines by the Labour government sometimes required items already agreed to be revisited and as one manager commented: 'there is a price for going back to negotiate'. Some specific problems in the PFI process were highlighted and it is to these we now turn.

Affordability Problems

Some managers were prepared to talk about or, at least, allude to the 'affordability problems' they had had to address in negotiating the PFI deal. There are a number of reasons why we might expect PFI to be more expensive than traditional public sector procurement. Capital is more expensive to borrow in the private sector. There has been a tendency for schemes to grow metamorphosing from refurbishment or part refurbishment schemes to new builds (Gaffney and Pollock, 1997). One manager even spoke openly of the generally weak financial position of the Trust when it first embarked on the PFI negotiations. He was particularly concerned about the affordability of PFI given that the Trust had a pre-existing annual operating gap of several million pounds; on top of this the original scheme included an annual fee, of several million more pounds per year. A number of strategies did emerge as responses to these financial problems. One manager juggled the monies available to him to pay for temporary works 'up front' out of public money rather than incorporating those works into the overall cost of the deal:

> This is how you massage things. What I'm doing is all sorts of manoeuvres.

Affordability problems resulted in some instances in a scaling down of the project by reducing bed numbers or the scope of the private sector's participation. Overall, though, managers were fairly defensive about the reduction in bed numbers consequent upon the new development. They were aware that this issue had been the subject of considerable criticism, some of it in the popular press. None of the managers said they had too few beds. Two managers claimed that the private nature of the scheme had not in itself had an appreciable impact upon bed numbers. One insisted:

> It's not a question of PFI. All new schemes must demonstrate that they can make savings and part of that is looking at bed utilisation. There has been no reduction in our beds whatsoever since we started looking at PFI.

The second suggested that PFI had simply brought forward what would have happened in publicly funded capital development anyway, for reasons of 'pure economics'. However, if these particular managers approached the matter of downsizing with apparent equanimity, two other managers conveyed more concern about bed numbers. One suggested that the bed modelling, by assuming a given level of activity, might have understated the impact of the local ageing population. He admitted that the move to fewer beds was already the subject of some dispute within the Trust since transition arrangements were to be guided by a business plan which insisted upon bed reductions long before the new development was to be operational and in the context of rising emergency admissions as well as waiting list pressures in surgery:

Obviously, it's a more flexible design: but it depends upon whether you can convert that into fewer beds. It's a leap of faith, isn't it? A lot of clinical staff say it can't be done. The Chief Executive and the Nursing Director think we do need to open up more beds and we've had discussions on that in the management team.... We've got a big debate to win internally.

Losing Control

Some managers forecast future difficulties in terms of pressure on resources. One manager rejected the idea that PFI itself could lead to resource pressures, but another warned that the loss of control incurred in PFI schemes would dramatically constrain future attempts to manage pressures, leaving little option but to cut clinical services:

When you look at our financial structure after the PFI deal, so much of it is a fixed cost. It's out of the door and we have no influence over that. And if we've got financial pressures, we're immediately focusing upon the main clinical services.

The complex and convoluted concession agreement wedged between the Trust and the services it depended upon ensured that any future attempt to make savings in 'operational services' would prove both costly and arduous:

It's still there if we want to say to the consortium to reduce the specification. They'll reduce the level of service and we'll pay less. We can sit around the table but that will be a lot more complicated than going to your catering manager and saying: 'I'm sorry but we'll have to do this'.

One manager took this line of thought much further claiming that, with PFI, *all* future change became problematic. Any development in technology which had implications for the location or the way in which clinical work was carried out rendered aspects of the concession agreement potentially redundant or at best in need of re-write with the inevitable lengthy negotiations. This echoes the objections raised by Best (1996): 'PFI will lock us into historic patterns of care instead of freeing us for innovation'.

Contracts contained agreements to benchmarking every few years with the possibility of market testing where service fees seemed discrepant with those charged in other comparable organisations. One manager said the Trust had negotiated hard over this so as 'not to get stuffed' should the consortium provider become the sole bidder. Another manager echoed this concern in greater detail:

In theory, they can escalate by higher than indexation and you can imagine being in a room with them for a long period of time negotiating. I think there is going to be a tendency for them to maximise, isn't there? And we're gonna have to argue and fight with them presumably every five years to minimise it.

We'll have to collect our own evidence to put to them so I can envisage a lot of management effort will go to addressing this and bidding them down.

The anticipated loss of control over services transferred out had actually persuaded managers in some instances to withdraw certain services from the original tender. Loss of control, for instance, in sterile services, consequent upon transferring out could in no way be compensated for through a system of financial penalties since any failure on the part of the sterile supplies service operator would result in problems running operating theatres. Since downsizing would have to be compensated for by speeded-up throughput, any delays surrounding theatres would be disproportionately problematic for the Trust.

These issues of affordability and loss of financial control suggest that PFI schemes may not have been successful in achieving savings. One manager believed that rationalising onto one site rather than PFI *per se* had created savings, which were to be used in investing in complementary community services. Where one manager admitted PFI cost more but insisted his scheme represented better value for money, another manager laughed and retorted:

Value for money? Of course it's not value for money!

The Elusive Benefits of Private Sector Involvement

Of course it is possible that these disadvantages might be outweighed by the benefits of PFI. Advantages believed to accrue from the involvement of private sector investment concern not merely the availability of cash but include also a range of design innovation and business skills. Not all of these proclaimed benefits were experienced by trusts, sometimes for reasons to do with PFI itself. The benefits of design flexibility, for instance, allowing designated areas to be used in future for different purposes depending upon changing Trust needs, seemed to have been exaggerated. One manager pointed out that the engineering services, which accompany different hospital areas, vary enormously and that there were limits to the uses to which a specified area could be put. One manager was quite adamant that no design innovation whatsoever had resulted from the PFI approach. On the contrary, he insisted that although there were laudable aspects to the design, these would have featured in any *publicly* procured hospital. Three trust managers were scornful of the notion that the hospital had been designed with long term maintenance, energy efficiency or use considerations in mind - the supposed 'synergies of design, build and operate'. They had found little evidence of any communication between those responsible for building and those who would undertake long term maintenance - in fact, they were fairly certain the two organisations had worked entirely separately: 'The way these people work, it's all done out of different offices in different areas'. Several managers believed that weaknesses within the consortium accounted for some of the failure of anticipated benefits to be realised:

The whole thrust of PFI was that there was supposed to be innovation brought in from the private sector. And *we* had to tell *them* what to do. Our support staff had to spend hours with them. They didn't fill us with confidence.

Two managers suggested the comparative neglect of design approaches to reducing ongoing maintenance and life-cycle costs resulted from two obstacles – the cost of capital and reluctance of the private sector to take risks.

Risk transfer is heralded as one of the great benefits of PFI and a central criterion in assessing the financial acceptability of a scheme. In the full business cases which Trusts produce, a financial value is attached to the amount of risk deemed to be transferred to the private partner in the scheme. This value is usually decisive in 'demonstrating' the superiority of the PFI route over the public sector comparator. In interview though, most managers stressed the reluctance of private sector institutions to accept risk. There is no 'true' measure of the value of a risk. The extent and probability of something turning out sub-optimal were both matters for persuasion and negotiation and the distribution and value attached to various risks thus the outcome of power and leverage. One manager expressed serious doubts as to the manner in which risk was valued. This formed part of a broader critique of the accounting treatment of PFI which, he believed, resulted in sub-optimal outcomes. Like some other managers, he insisted that cost and time overruns would have been transferred to the private sector even if the scheme had been publicly funded. He observed that the PFI and the public sector options had compared very closely on paper, with the PFI option only taking a slight advantage after risk transfer. The financial value of transferred risk had been arrived at through following all the relevant accounting guidance, which effectively exaggerated it.

In terms of the risk analysis, you say: Well, it's a public scheme so that'll slip and that'll cost us money; it's a public capital scheme and it'll overspend and if you look at the historical data it will overspend by a lot and you build that in. And then you say inflation could be higher and you build that in. And then you build in assumptions that there will be operational cost pressures. Although we followed all the guidance and did all the work - I'm not saying for one minute that the analysis was faulty - when you sit back and say: How likely is it that the public sector route will actually generate that much more risk in net present value terms over that period?... Well, actually, no. I can't believe it.

The effect of this statement is to undermine much of the financial rationale of PFI.

Discussion

It is clear from the experiences of these managers, as well as from the growing body of literature on PFI in health care, that these schemes have significant implications for the new public management. An obvious starting point is the attention given under NPM to the promotion of efficiency, economy, effectiveness and value for money. Clearly these are not economical schemes in the sense that they are not cheap; they have been criticised (e.g. Whitfield, 2001b) for their very high start-up or enabling costs and for the high rates of return private investors have succeeded in securing. However, all schemes must demonstrate value for money if they are to receive the go-ahead from the Department of Health. In fact, the accounting treatment prescribed for PFI has been strongly criticised not only by academic observers (e.g. Gaffney et al, 1999) but also explicitly by two of the managers here. These criticisms suggest that the financial value assigned to the risk transferred is exaggerated, thereby conferring an accounting advantage upon the PFI (vis-à-vis the public) option which it does not deserve and that, in any event, the fact that the public body will always 'carry the can' implies risk is ultimately left with the hospital. Containing costs and working to budget are important features of NPM and yet in these schemes we see the seeds of potential future financial difficulties for hospitals which face 'ring-fenced' costs for the use of the building and a range of services. Although flexibility is so highly valued under NPM, negotiating changes to the specification will be costly and time-consuming. This points to potential control problems for these managers and it is worth reflecting on their position and responsibilities in relation to managing finance, controlling the workforce and dealing with commercial operators, in the light of Kerr's (1998) comments on PFI as a mechanism for the re-articulation of class relations in the public sector. Senior managers have control over organisational income and, in the context of cuts and efficiency savings, they become forced into a position where they must intensify the extraction of surplus labour. This can occur through an impoverishment in contractual conditions, as with Compulsory Competitive Tendering (CCT). Under CCT, managers lost direct control over the labour process in those tendered out services. However, specifications were complex and contracts were short-term (typically one to three years). Under PFI, services are transferred long-term – and it is not always clear to whom, since the private partner might sub-contract or even sell on. Trust managers now seek control not through direct surveillance or the threat of terminating the individual worker's contract but remotely via a complex concession agreement not with the individual worker or even (typically) with the individual company but with the 'special purpose vehicle' set up to negotiate on behalf of the consortium and with whom the Trust contracts. This will take Trust managers into relationships of control with private sector managers through the practice of contract management[1] (monitoring quality, ensuring compliance). Here, effective control could be compromised not only by the reduced staffing levels and information at the Trust's disposal but also, arguably, by the ideology of 'partnership', in which the emphasis is on good working relationships and 'light touch' monitoring (Ruane, 2002). Two managers linked this loss of control over the labour process with reduced control over Trust finances. Managers retain responsibility for managing the budget but now within different constraints and parameters, which serve to reduce manoeuvrability, thereby threatening the funding of clinical areas. This suggests institutional objectives may be jeopardised. The Trust wants an efficient, safe and functional building built on time, suited to health care in the twenty first century and capable of meeting anticipated need and it wants good quality and appropriate services. Although hopes for design-build-operate synergies and design innovation have not always been realised (Headley, 2001), managers do expect hospital facilities far superior to those they already manage and these are being completed on time. However, the 'downsizing' (Gaffney and Pollock, 1998) of the first wave hospital schemes is already reaping the whirlwind (*Evening Chronicle*, 2002). Despite the optimism of the two managers quoted here, under PFI, planning is finance-led rather than needs-led (Price and Green, 2000), and further strategic decisions may well be reactive with finance-driven reconfigurations of services (e.g. *Journal*, 2002).

There are respects in which the pro-competitive, pro-market stance of NPM seems to be at odds with the attainment of other objectives. Building a hospital is a complex undertaking at the best of times; under PFI, public sector managers are attempting this often without the benefit of in-house experience and in-house expertise in finance, the law, quantity surveying and so forth. The pro-private bias and focus on 'core' activities require them increasingly to obtain this expertise on the market. Moreover, they are entering negotiations with companies whose priority is profit maximisation and whose skill and experience in negotiation (if not in hospitals) cannot be matched. In this respect, managers have not had the 'tools' necessary to do the job. In some respects, the PFI approach is not pro-competition in that, particularly in first wave schemes, choice of preferred bidder was made quite early in the process. The consortium itself decides what its component parts are: Trusts cannot pick and choose. Dropping a 'preferred bidder' midway through negotiations is highly costly to both parties. Moreover, despite the emphasis within NPM on decentralisation of decision-making and local responsibility, even where managers have had serious doubt about the value for money aspect of the deals they are developing, they have been unable to act accordingly. The public sector 'option' is so in name alone: managers believe no money can be obtained from the Treasury. In short, it appears the constituent parts of the NPM may conflict with each other in the PFI context and that it is the pro-private element, which new Labour have prioritised.

Note

1. This does not substantially change under the Retention of Employment agreement secured by Unison.

References

Best, G. (1996), *PFI: Back to the Future?* Unpublished paper presented at *Unison Conference on PFI in the NHS*, (June) London.

Carter, B. and Fairbrother, P. (1995), 'The Remaking of the State Middle Class', in T. Butler and M. Savage (eds), *Social Change and the Middle Classes*, UCL Press: London.

Department of Health (1997), *The Purpose, Organisation, Management, Funding of the National Health Service*, Department of Health: London.

The Evening Chronicle (2002), 'Beds Crisis is Hitting Hospital Target Plans', 10th February, Newcastle.

Gaffney, D. and Pollock, A. (1997), *Can the NHS Afford the Private Finance Initiative?* BMA: London.

Gaffney, D. and Pollock, A. (1998), *Downsizing for the 21st Century*, School of Public Policy, University College London/Unison: London.

Gaffney, D. Pollock, A. Price, D. and Shaoul, J. (1999), 'PFI in the NHS – Is There An Economic Case?', *British Medical Journal*, 319: 116-19.

Horton, D. and Farnham, S. (1999), *Public Management in Britain*, Macmillan: Basingstoke.

Headley, B. (2001), 'Design in PFI', presentation to *The Private Finance Initiative and the NHS Conference*, (April): London.

Journal, The (2002), 'Consultants Angry Over Trusts' Merger', 13th September, Newcastle: 1.

Kerr, D. (1998), 'The PFI Miracle', in *Capital and Class,* 64 (Spring): 17-27.

Leys, C. (2001), *Market-Driven Politics*, Verso: London.

Massey, A. (2001), 'Policy, Management and Implementation', in S. Savage and R. Atkinson (eds), *Public Policy Under Blair*, Basingstoke: Palgrave.

Price, D. and Green, J. (2000), 'Capital Planning and the Private Finance Initiative: Cost Minimization or Health Care Planning?', in *Critical Public Health*, 10 (1): 71-80.

Ruane, S. (2001), 'A Clear Public Mission? Public-Private Partnerships and the Recommodification of the NHS', in *Capital and Class*, No. 73 (Spring): 1-6.

Ruane, S. (2002), 'PPPs - The Case of PFI', in C. Glendinning, M. Powell and K. Rummery (eds), *Partnerships, New Labour and the Governance of Welfare*, Policy Press: Bristol.

Treasury Taskforce (1997), *Partnerships for Prosperity: The Private Finance Initiative*, HM Treasury: London.

Whitfield, D. (2001a), *Public Services or Corporate Welfare*, Pluto Press: London.

Whitfield, D. (2001b), *Private Finance Initiative and Public Private Partnerships: What Future for the Public Services?* <www.centre.public.org.uk/briefings>.

Chapter 10

New Forms of 'Out-of-Hours' Care: From Collaboration to Competitive Entrepreneurialism

Catrina Alferoff and Mike Dent

Introduction

This chapter provides a localised analysis of the division of labour between hospital-based emergency services and those provided by general practitioners over the contested terrain of 'out-of-hours' services. Research for the chapter was undertaken in three District Health Authority (DHA) areas in the Midlands. Interviews with key informants revealed a relationship that was simultaneously symbiotic and competitive as both GPs and Accident and Emergency (A&E) departments attempted to rationalise the services they provided to the public. We explore the methods exercised by these interdependent networks of healthcare organisations as each attempted to dictate the terms by which the traffic between them.

Background

During the 1990s the National Health Service (NHS) in the United Kingdom (UK) underwent significant restructuring as the Conservative Government of the time introduced radical changes in the ways in which services were delivered. The ideas that shaped these changes reflected the widely held beliefs that the best way to improve efficiency was to change the incentives to providers through some form of market-like competition while, at the same time, purporting to retain all that was seen to be best in the NHS (Klein, 1995).

The 1991 reforms to the NHS not only radically altered the mechanisms by which health care was delivered, but also created a new set of relationships between purchasers and providers of such services. 'Out-of-hours' cover was a particularly interesting case, amongst many others, which demonstrated the limitations of the internal market.

Neo-institutionalist commentators on changes to the healthcare system have argued that the gains from what amounted to a 'quasi-market' were likely to be offset by the substantial transaction costs generally associated with the operation of markets (see Bartlett, 1991; Le Grand and Bartlett, 1993; Mark and Brennan, 1995). Relationships based on trust would give way to opportunistic behaviour as both purchasers and providers attempted to maximise their control over resources. As a consequence of these changes, legitimacy *qua* categorical rules inevitably would come into conflict with the logic of efficiency. This new ethos of competition was expected to force organisational actors into a position where they would be confronted with the problem involved in maintaining the myth and so the legitimacy of the institution whilst also devising strategies to minimise the costs of the organisation's activities in the pursuit of efficiency.

In contrast to static institutional arguments that offered little insight as to how the link is made between structure and action the argument set forward by the neo-institutionalist commentators Meyer and Rowan (1991) was based on their concept of 'decoupling'. This is a process in which a distance is created between the formal structure and some of its activities and also some activities from each other. The notion of 'decoupling' gives a dynamic quality to the analysis providing a way of accounting for the role of discretion and autonomy within organisations and avoids the dangers of determinism in accounting for organisational adaptation to environmental change. For organisations 'in the same line of business' (DiMaggio and Powell, 1991: 61), in this case healthcare, the power to influence or resist policy concerns the relative power of different professional groups who may attempt to adapt, or modify, the behaviour of others in a network of organisations in ways that are beneficial to their own purposes.

As our research demonstrates, growing public demand for easy access 'out-of-hours' care drains the resources of both A&E departments and General Practices. Professionals in both the primary and secondary sectors, in many cases, fail to agree on a unified strategy and may erect thresholds, thus selectively 'de-marketing' their services to certain groups of users to prevent further incursions (Mark and Brennan, 1995).

Within a configuration of networked organisations engaged in a symbiotic but not necessarily symmetric relationship local influence also plays an important role in shaping the repertoire of accounts available to actors to justify action (Davis and Greve 1997). In the micro-politics of local level action the three A&E departments that were the subject of this study had attempted to impose thresholds to limit access (Sixxma and Debakker, 1996), by selectively 'de-marketing' their services to particular groups (Mark and Brennan, 1995) they deemed to be more suitably treated by general practitioners. According to Sixxma and De Bakker, A&E departments may invoke one of two strategies to manage over-demand depending upon the local situation. Where demand is high and provision over-stretched, departments may impose thresholds to access. In the case of manageable demand and alternatively available provision, departments may need to compete for patients to retain their legitimacy. We found departments of both types in this study. Even so, A&E continues to be seen by many of the users we interviewed as providing a more accessible, convenient and better quality service than that provided by general practitioners.

Methodology

Light (1997), in a recent analysis of the British health system, construes the recent transformation of the health service as a move from 'managed competition' to 'managed collaboration' an adaptive capacity inherent in the new model NHS which, according to Klein, makes it difficult to evaluate (1995: 300). Despite similarities at the general level of the organisational field of health services in that they are 'in the same line of business' (Dimaggio and Powell, 1991: 65), as Pfeffer and Salancik (1978: 63) argue, the environment of organisations 'consists of the entire system of interconnected individuals who are related to one another and to the focal organisation through the organisation's transactions'. For the purposes of this inquiry the parties to the transactions comprised, firstly, purchasers of 'out-of-hours' care: District Health Authorities (DHAs) and fund-holding General Practitioners (GPs), and, secondly, providers of both 'out-of-hours' care and emergency services: secondary sector A&E departments; GPs (both fund-holding and non-fund-holding); doctors co-operatives; commercial deputising services.

In an earlier phase of this research the objective was to establish the reasons why self-referred attenders chose to come to the A&E department rather than contact their own general practitioners (Alferoff and Dent, 1996). Patient interviews took place at times when family practices were closed (8pm to 8am on a typical Friday night to Saturday morning and over a Bank Holiday weekend). The research found that nearly three out of four of the target group had not contacted their GP and later analysis by clinicians in the department revealed that of these 26 per cent could be classified as 'inappropriate', or primary care attenders as defined by Dale et al (1995:424):

Self referred patients with symptoms likely to be caused by conditions not in need of immediate resuscitation or urgent care, and unlikely to require hospital admission. Or, self-referred patients with non-urgent complications of chronic conditions.

Two of the three A&E departments were located in hospital trusts in urban areas, one in a major conurbation with a high ethnic minority population suffering relative deprivation. The catchment area of the other was an urban/rural mix. Primary sector 'out-of-hours' cover was provided mainly by two commercial deputising services in the conurbation (at four centres). This area was distinctive in that majority of GPs were single-handed fund-holders. There was an equal split between fund-holding and non fund-holding in the other urban catchment area where 'out-of-hours' cover was provided either by a large doctors' co-operative or a long established commercial deputising service (two and one primary care 'out-of-hours' centres respectively). Group practices predominated in this area as they did in the third area where the majority of GPs were members of a county-wide doctors' co-operative. The co-operative provided 'out-of-hours' covered at four centres. Few GPs in this last area were fund-holders.

The earlier phase of this research focused on the view expressed by consultants in A&E departments. At this phase of the research we were seeking information on 'out-of-hours' healthcare in general, rather than that solely provided by A&E Departments. We therefore used a structured interview as well as a postal survey tool to collect the opinions and 'out-of-hours' practices of 41 GPs in all. As the surveyed GPs were quite free in expressing their views, the open-ended questions provided very rich data. We also administered a questionnaire to 203 self-referred attenders to the three A&E departments at times when their family practitioner's surgery were closed.

Existing Forms of Emergency Provision: Redtown, Goldington and Greenshire

Brief details of the 'out-of-hours' cover provision within the three areas of Redtown, Goldington and Greenshire are summarised in Table 10.1 :

Table 10.1 'Out-of-Hours' Cover Provision

Area	DHA Catchment Area	Main A&E Department(s)	DHA Alternative Provision	GP Out-of-Hours Cover
Green-shire	Mainly rural	2 departments 18 miles apart	3 GP-staffed MIUs 2 'out-of-hours' centres	Countywide GP co-op
Redtown	Mixed urban /rural	2 departments 17 miles apart	2 GP/staffed MIUs 1 'out-of-hours' centre	50/50 GP co-op & deputising service
Golding-ton	Urban conurbation	3 departments	4 'out-of-hours' centres	GP deputising service

Two of the areas studied – Redtown and Goldington – were largely urban, though the Redtown District Health Authority catchment area also included a semi-rural marginal area. Greenshire, as its pseudonym suggests, was largely rural, with two major towns situated to the north and south of the county. Goldington DHA provides services for a socially deprived inner-city mixed community, Redtown DHA provides services for an urban population which has relied, until very recently, on a traditional industrial base (which generated characteristic health problems). The rural fringe, although part of the District, had developed a pattern of emergency services at variance with much of the rest of the area.

Four A&E departments served the population of Goldington. The majority of GPs within that borough at the time of the research worked in small, or single-handed practices (as fund-holders). Nearly all 'out-of-hours' cover – telephone advice, appointments at the primary care emergency centres, and home visits – were provided by commercial deputising services of which there were four that provided emergency centres and two of which where located in the grounds of local hospital trusts. Redtown had only one A&E department and had no one distinctive pattern of out-hours provision, or type of practice but group practices predominating slightly over single-handed ones. One doctors' co-operative provided 'out-of-hours' cover for most of the city whilst a commercial deputising service covered much of the rural fringe. The co-operative had an emergency centre near to the city centre and there was a commercial deputising service in the outer suburbs. There was also a minor injuries unit (MIU) staffed by nurses with commercial deputising service doctors on call in a small town on the rural margin. Greenshire was different again and nearly all of its GPs were organised into a single countywide doctors' co-operative that provided Out-of-Hours for the area. The co-operative had two emergency centres located in each of the major towns, one of which was located in the grounds of a hospital trust. On call duties at minor injuries units were located within community hospitals

'Out-of-Hours' Services: The Problem of Overuse

Inappropriate users were a particular problem and cost for A&E departments. Since these patients were more likely to seek hospital care at times when their GP's surgery was closed it was not surprising that, in common with other studies (see Latimer et al, 1996), this enquiry found that general practitioners were reluctant to accommodate patients requiring attention outside office hours without the accompanying extra resources. This had led to varying degrees of conflict in negotiations between professionals in the three Midlands areas analysed here.

The ways in which the various actors dealt with the problem demonstrated that in order to understand organisational action one must indeed study the micro-level of attention and perception as active processes that must be present for events to occur (Pfeffer and Salancik, 1978: 63). Over time, distinct ideologies had shaped the forms of 'out-of-hours' provision by both General Practitioners and the A&E departments studied and the arrangements had become, in effect, culturally embedded as a result of processes similar to those identified by Davis and Greve (1997:2) who argue that this also leads to particular consequences:

over time the configuration of a network of organisations becomes culturally embedded affecting the 'repertoire' of accounts available to the organisation's decision-makers to justify actions and shape individual actions.

It was evident that each of the three local healthcare networks had approached the problem of 'out-of-hours' cover in ways that reflected not only societal influences, but also the reciprocal patterns of influence – at the micro-level – of key individuals within a set of interacting organisations (Bloor and Dawson, 1994). There was a complexity of relations within the three case studies that varied from competitive entrepreneurialism through to collaboration. In part this was a function of the dominant organisational arrangements (e.g. single-handed vs group practices) and environment (e.g. urban or rural) but it also reflected the cultural-embeddedness of the pre-existing interactions between individuals and the organisations comprising the networks.

The problem of overuse of A&E services has been the topic of an ongoing debate in the medical press (see for examples: Dale et al, 1995, Campbell 1996, Hallam 1994, Wass and Zoltie, 1996). It has not been an exclusively British problem – there were similarities in the attempts by A&E departments to come up with a solution internationally (Dale et al, 1995) and the explanatory model developed by Dutch researchers Sixxma and Debakker (1996) will be explored later in this paper. From the perspective of the A&E department, treating patients who could have been treated in the primary care sector not only contributed to inappropriate utilisation of hospital resources and expertise, but also to prolonged waiting time and staff stress.

Given their propensity for inappropriate attendance, it would be easy to blame individual patients for abusing the service although proponents of the market economy approach believe that medical services should be treated just like any other 'commodity' with patients encouraged to shop around, to actively evaluate doctors' services and go elsewhere if the 'commodity' was unsatisfactory (Lupton 1997: 373). Dissatisfaction with the appointment system correlated significantly with list size in Campbell's study (1996) of self-referrals to A&E departments. Our research demonstrated that over 70 per cent of self-referring attenders had not contacted their GP before going to the A&E department. In line with other studies (see Hallam 1994) we found attenders also citing a number of reasons for their behaviour with delays in receiving help from GP deputising services: geographical proximity, anticipation of referral by a GP and perceived seriousness of the symptoms.

All three A&E departments covered in this further study were experiencing the problem of rising attendances. In part this was caused by 'inappropriate' use of the service. Under the then prevailing system of block contracts independent providers bore a high share of the risk associated with cost uncertainty since the fee was fixed but the delivery was variable (Bartlett 1991). In the absence of some mechanism to share the burden of any unforeseen excess costs with the purchaser, providers were more at risk for any losses arising from it (Bartlett and Harrison, 1993). The source of purchaser difficulties in this case would seem to have arisen from contracts that, while fixed, were exposed to an uncertain and unpredictable environment (Bartlett, 1991). Hospital trusts were, however, embedded in an environment comprised of other organisations: purchasers in the form of District Health Authorities, fund-holding GPs and, more recently, groups of GPs banded together as 'multi-funds' and commissioning groups, on whom they depend for the resources that they require (Pfeffer and Salancik, 1978), and with whom future planning decisions were made.

The A&E consultants would – from time to time – censure patients for misusing the service but the local practitioners also received blame for their failure to provide a sufficiently comprehensive and accessible service (Dale et al, 1995: 423). One respondent, an A&E consultant, argued:

> People use A&E as a drop-in centre. It all comes down to cost – GPs have no incentive to drain their resources.

This comment suggests that some A&E staff saw GPs as acting opportunistically. Against this accusation it must be noted that night visits for GPs have increased fivefold over the last 25 years at a cost in 1992/93 of £70 million (Latimer et al, 1996: 352). It is not surprising, therefore, that many GPs wish to replace their 24-hour responsibility for patients with a more limited commitment (Hallam, 1994) and rely on other agencies to provide the 'out-of-hours' cover.

In addition to the possibility of 'opportunism' a further complication for the A&E departments was that the internal market was not a 'perfect' one – to borrow the terminology of the economists – for hospital trusts transacted with relatively small numbers of organisations and could not easily change partners since there were few buyers and sellers and barriers to entry and exit were high. As Light (1997: 299) argues these are: 'hardly the base requirements for ensuring competitive benefits for society at large' (1997: 299).

Managing Demand: Hard-wired Approaches to Chronic Over-popularity

A&E departments have reviewed their strategies to cope with the problem of increasing use of services. Two of the three A&E departments studied here had introduced tough systems of triage to be applied at times when they had a great number of patients with major trauma. Using the Mark and Brennan model (1995: 20) this could be seen as 'selective de-marketing' – discouraging demand coming from certain customer classes. A recently opened A&E department in the Netherlands where 'thresholds' limited accessibility to the department adopted such an approach. The department was not open to self-referrals who were sent back to their GPs. Although agreed with GPs and hospital staff the policy proved so unpopular with the public that the board of governors decided to cancel the rule (Sixxma and Debakker, 1996). The Report of the Royal Commission on the NHS appears to support that view, stating that:

> Where the tradition of using [A&E departments for primary care] is strong, it may be preferable for hospitals to accept this role and make specific arrangements for fulfilling it, rather than to try and resist established local preferences
>
> (cited in Dale et al, 1995: 423).

While two of the A&E departments in this study, Redtown and Goldington, had introduced some elements of the 'threshold' model, Greenshire had attempted, unsuccessfully, to introduce such a system but was unable to in the face of hostility from representatives of local GPs. In Redtown the A&E department adopted a 'continuous' system of triage and returned primary care type attenders to their own GP at times when the department was up to capacity with major trauma. Goldington the A&E department used an information system incorporating nationally agreed protocols to grade patients into five groups. The lowest group could, in principle, be returned to the care of their GP, should the need arise, but three factors worked against this occurring in reality:

1. three alternative A&E departments were available within reasonably easy travelling distance of the focal department;
2. the department over-performed on its budget and met its required quality targets so did not feel it was under particular pressure to change;
3. The belief of the senior consultant, who – despite the use of an expletive to describe some of the cases referred to the department by local GPs – felt that judgements based on whether the attender was appropriate for A&E care could only be made retrospectively.

This resembles Sixxma and Debakker's 'competitive model', in which the focal A&E department made little effort to discourage attenders of all types since it was competing with other hospital and primary care units for patients in order to retain funding and stay open.

The senior consultant in the third A&E department, Greenshire, had attempted to negotiate an agreed protocol with representatives from the DHA, the district – wide doctors' co-operative and the Local Medical Committee. Yet, whilst representatives from all constituencies were not against the idea, they, nevertheless, later rejected it. Since the consultant and representatives from the doctors' co-operative had collaborated successfully on other ventures this, as the representative from the DHA intimated to us, represented a serious breakdown in relations.

The threshold model can be fairly closely applied to Redtown and to a slightly lesser degree by Goldington, Greenshire's attempt at imposing a threshold failed even through pursued with determination by the A&E consultant. Redtown A&E department was the sole provider of 'out-of-hours' services in the locality and Greenshire A&E department provided cover for patients living within a seventeen mile radius. In terms of competing primary care emergency provision, there was a difference, Greenshire and Goldington hospitals had primary care GP-staffed centres on site. These services were provided by a commercial deputising service on site in Goldington and a doctors' co-operative in the Greenshire (both also operated 'out-of-hours' centres at other locations within the catchment area of the A&E departments). Access to these centres was independent of the A&E departments, although the consultant from the Greenshire A&E department was negotiating with the doctors' co-operative for the installation of a telephone from which primary care attenders could contact the co-operative's 'out-of-hours' number. Goldington, however, also competed with three other A&E departments for patients.

These on-site arrangements for 'out-of-hours' cover have had very different impacts on attendance rates at these Goldington and Greenshire A&E departments. In Goldington it had increased primary care attendance at the A&E department, but in the case of Greenshire with its 'attempted threshold' model (with no agreed protocols) it had decreased inappropriate attendance by 46 per cent. There may be a number of contributory factors for this unexpected finding. Firstly there may be demographic reasons in that the Goldington hospital was located in an inner-city area with a high ethnic minority and relatively deprived population, whereas the Greenshire hospital was located in a largely rural area. Secondly there was variability in the services provided by the commercial deputising agency in Goldington and by the co-operative in Greenshire, where communication systems were better organised. There may, however, be a third factor, as yet relatively unexplored: the web of values, norms, beliefs and taken-for-granted assumptions in which individuals are suspended, and which have a cultural influence on decision-making (Barley and Tolbert, 1997).

Relations between GPs representatives and A&E staff and discussions on emergency provision were well established in the Greenshire case, whereas no such cooperation was reported between GPs and A&E staff in Goldington competitive model. In Redtown threshold case a recently set up A&E working group have, as yet, failed to reach agreement on changes in A&E provision, although it has been suggested that a partial solution could be realised through recruiting a primary care consultant to the A&E department, funded through the doctors' co-operative. This area was already quite advanced in plans for cover provided through the primary sector. The dimensions to which the A&E department was (a) active in imposing a threshold and, (b) collaborating with GPs is represented by Figure 10.1 below. The research that informs this chapter took place at the crux point of further changes in the Health Services, but our respondents had not yet considered the impact these changes might have in terms of the provision of 'out-of-hours' care. Discussions on a more integrated approach to managing demand had taken place between hospital-based and primary care professionals, but limited progress had been made, excepting in the case of Goldington where a small group of GPs were instrumental in the planning of a new 'softer' approach to 'out-of-hours' provision.

'Softer' approaches to the problem of managing demand include incorporating GPs into the staff of A&E, greater use of nurse practitioners and creating a new role of primary care consultant within A&E departments. This accommodation accords with Moore's view that power has shifted from consultants to other health professionals (1995:25). Further changes in primary care commissioning may erode the power of consultants even further, requiring new strategies to maintain the status of A&E departments. Accommodating primary care within the department or outreach A&E were both possible ways to maintain the role and status of secondary sector emergency care. Wass and Zoltie (1996) argued that District Health Authorities as purchasers had to be aware of the increase in demand and make rational decisions to provide extra primary care under the current system, or provide adequate facilities by alternative means. Health Authorities acting in concert with general practitioners and, in some cases A&E department representatives have come up with a variety arrangements for 'out-of-hours' cover, both as providers and purchasers of services.

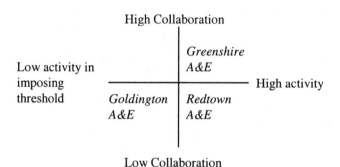

High Collaboration

Low activity in imposing threshold

Greenshire A&E   High activity

Goldington A&E   *Redtown A&E*

Low Collaboration

Figure 10.1 Imposing Threshold on 'Out-of-Hours' Services

Primary Sector 'Out-of-Hours' Service: Existing Arrangements

In the Latimer et al's (1996) study of two GP research networks respondents opted for primary care emergency centres as a first choice for 'out-of-hours' cover, followed by co-operatives and, lastly telephone triage. Out-of hours cover by telephone is well established in Canada, the US and Scandinavia. There are some in The UK in the form of nurse-led primary care helplines later introduced as NHS Direct (ibid). Homerton hospital in Hackney has opened a primary care unit run by nurse practitioners in an A&E department (Beales, 1997). Emergency centres had been opened by both co-operatives and commercial deputising services in one or the other of the districts studied. In line with the new ethos of integrating provision, 'out-of-hours' cover from a commissioning perspective, looks not only at the role of A&E departments but also GPs and nurse practitioners, working with them to develop a mini-emergency service (Singer, 1996). Given the diversity of provision that presently exists in the three areas of study it was expected that the process of negotiation amongst decision-makers and opinion formers (consultants, district health authority representatives and general practitioners) would vary considerably. As Klein (1995: 300) acknowledges:

(A)ny attempt to compare developments in different parts of the UK would have...added an extra dimension of complexity to what is already a many threaded story.

In part this was because the de-coupling strategies adopted (Meyer and Rowan, 1991) will vary considerably from place to place depending on a whole range of local conditions and contingencies, including the pattern of general practice provision.

Integrating Emergency Provision

This complex story embraces a societal sector of organisations operating at the median level of district, but as Scott and Meyer assert: 'organisational sectors in modern society are likely to stretch from local to national actors' (1991: 117). Certainly this appears to be so regarding the push for reform of 'out-of-hours' provision that was eventually adopted as policy, advocated as it was by the association of general practitioners. That such initiatives were already well established at local level in the areas under study demonstrates that trends in national professional opinion constrain the influence at the centre (Rhodes: 1991). In Greenshire fund-holding was minimal. Key individuals in both the health service and general practice acted to discourage its adoption. General practitioner fund-holding (introduced in the NHS and Community Care Act, 1990) has always been controversial; whilst it has forced health service planners to recognise primary care, and placed it at the centre of the health service, it can also be seen as the GP-end of the competitive, internal market. Fund-holding at the time covered only about 38 per cent of the population and many GPs were 'reluctant fund-holders' (Singer 1996:6). The diffusion of negative ideas on the values underlying fund-holding initiated by the key actors in the DHA and an influential radical GP was very successful in dissuading a majority of GPs from adopting the practice in Greenshire, shaping individual action and the process of aggregation (Davis and Greve, 1997). This area was well ahead of present Government policy on GP commissioning with two established groups. One large doctors' co-operative provided emergency cover for much of the county. In Goldington a spirit of competitive entrepreneurialism characterised the district. Most GPs were single-handed fund-holders. According to our informant in the DHA, group practices, when initiated, tended to fall apart due to disagreements among the partners. Although eager to embrace the DHA's ideas on fund-holding GPs in this area resisted attempts to persuade them to form co-operatives, preferring to use the commercial deputising services for 'out-of-hours' cover. The GPs did, however, get together to request that the DHA's agreement to commercially provided emergency centres. Links between the A&E department and GPs (as regards future plans) would appear to be minimal as far as we were able to determine at this time. Redtown, with a mix of fund-holding and commissioning groups, co-operatives and commercial deputising services did not display a clearpattern.

In two of the areas – the urban mixed-economy (Goldington) and the urban/rural (Redtown) – predominately co-operative, working groups were established to resolve the problem of over-loaded A&E departments and future provision of care. The groups included members from both primary and secondary care, GP representatives, A&E consultants and DHA contractors. In neither case had consensus been reached on the problems of A&E departments, although some movement on this issue had been made. In the Greenshire case maintenance of existing relations had been fostered in part by moving the responsibility to potential users (attenders) of the A&E department. A publicity campaign designed to promote appropriate behaviour involved circulating information through the press, GP practices and A&E departments.

For a core of the public, A&E departments were their routine, 24-hour, access points to health services. This has been their traditional role. Major trauma, may be a small part of their actual workload:

> Trauma is probably less than one percent of the major workload up there. Therefore, it is not acceptable to say that Accident and Emergency are only there for trauma and will not want to deal with anything else, which is what they are saying
>
> (Chair of a GP Commissioning Forum).

Losing a percentage of their attendees would threaten their arguments for keeping departments open. Although none of the A&E departments we studied were under threat of closure, others within their District would, inevitably close fairly soon. This was true of two hospitals in Goldington, and a possibility for the A&E department at one of the hospitals in Greenshire.

Retaining a foothold in the primary care market may seem to be a farsighted strategy, with Government policy on rationalisation threatening the professional role of GPs and Consultants. Collaborating to maintain a presence in as many situations as possible might seem to be shrewd. The possibility of increasing the primary care role by recruiting GPs into A&E departments was cited as the solution to over-attendance in both sectors. Indeed it has been a common practice until the advent of advanced technologies made it difficult for a generalist to keep up to date, according to one of our GP survey respondents.

GPs, District Health Authorities and Senior A&E consultants had attempted to bring the other parties to the table to resolve the problems of 'out-of-hours' care. One of the Hospital Trusts we were researching, 'wrote to GPs asking about their views' before appointing a new consultant in the A&E department. GPs expressed a wish that 'whoever was appointed should have a strong background in primary care'. The A&E department went some way towards meeting this requirement, but some GPs were not content with the appointment. The individual in question had some past experience in general practice, but local GPs felt that:

> Their main concern in the appointment was to have somebody who was going to take part in major trauma
>
> (GP).

General Practitioners were seen to have a role in the Goldington A&E, where two were on the staff of the department. Local GPs felt that 'better decisions are being made and fewer people admitted'.

GP 'Out-of-Hours' Provision

At an earlier stage in this research we noted that the web of relationships between health care professionals had a particular local identity that appeared to shape the way they inter-related with other health care professionals. Goldington with its many single-handed practitioners, had a preference for commercially provided out-of-hours provision, antipathy to forming a GP co-operative and little contact between GPs and A&E personnel, appeared to be quite entrepreneurial in character. Greenshire GPs on the other hand exhibited a strong trend towards solidarity, the countywide doctors' co-operative being a case in point. Redtown, was different again, it exhibited no single identity – city practices tended to use the co-operative to cover 'out-of-hours' while the small and homogeneous rural community depended on its nurse-led, local minor injuries unit and commercial deputising agency cover. Although within one DHA area geographical distance seemed to have forced two separate forms to emerge.

Whilst Goldington GPs seemed, in the main, to act independently, GPs in two practices to the north of the borough were uncharacteristic of the prevailing ethos in that they had, unsuccessfully, attempted to generate interest in forming a co-operative. More recently they showed their entrepreneurial skills in initiating a new venture, backed by 'City Challenge' funding, they attempted to develop the first multi-agency polyclinic in the UK. The commercial deputising agency would still provide the 'out-of-hours' care – at least to begin with – and a nurse staffed minor injuries unit would provide daytime care according to strict protocols. The local District General Hospital would develop on-site outreach outpatient clinics and it was hoped that a nearby A&E Department would also move some of its activities to the site. From this joint venture a new type of health professional could emerge, the community consultant, a role that would blur the boundary between the primary and secondary sectors of health care. This can be explained in new institutionalist terms as a process of 'isomorphism':

> Once disparate organisations in the same line of business are structured into an actual field by competition, the state, or the professions, powerful forces emerge that lead them to become more similar to one another
>
> (DiMaggio and Powell, 1991:65).

A consequence, following Barley and Tolbert (1997: 93), of the actors:

> Becom[ing] suspended in a web of values, norms, rules, beliefs and taken for granted assumptions that come to define the way the world is and should be.

Conclusion

Salter argues that the introduction of the division between purchaser and provider brought into sharp focus the key political problem of the NHS that is the demand for health care would always exceed supply. Changing the NHS from a provider-driven to a purchaser-led system in which money and power would no longer be allocated in response to further increases in the practice of service delivery resulted in an internal market in which '(t)he unbridled pluralism of the game function and the absence of accepted rules and procedures' (1993: 171) has altered the distribution of power. In this case between hospital A&E consultants who claim that they are as weak in relation to local GPs.

A&E services were not included in the GP fund-holder contracts with secondary care providers. These services were generally funded by the DHA on a block contract based on the number of attendances in prior years. This is where, at the local and decoupled level of A&E departments and GP practices, generalisation comes into conflict with varying 'specific unstandardized and possibly unique conditions' (Meyer and Rowan, 1991:56). In the face of rising demand A&E; departments were constantly running to stay in the same place. When it comes to inappropriate use of A&E services, the initial question is whether there is a clear understanding about what criteria being used to judge the type of health care being purchased, for whom, by what means of need assessment and funding formula? (Salter 1993:175).

A&E consultants in our research laid the blame for rising attendances on both GPs and inappropriate users of the service. Fairly vitriolic comments were made about GPs and their perceived practice of off-loading of the costs of providing an emergency service:

> It has everything to do with the GP's pocket. For the GP, the fund-holder, there is a cost attached, so there is no incentive to provide emergency cover. It drains their resources
>
> (A&E Consultant, Redtown).

According to Moore (1995) the internal market, GP fund-holders, rising consumer demand and the control purchasers have over resources were all perceived as factors weakening the power of consultants *vis-à-vis* other health service groups. GP respondents to this survey were cognisant of the ways in which weakening of the funding route to A&E departments by moving from the existing DHA block contract would shift the balance of power towards the primary care sector. The following remarks from GPs reflect this view:

> The consultant at (Greenshire A&E) feels that he is seeing cases for which he is not being paid, and we should be seeing them...

> If we are going to take up to two thirds of the A&E cases, you're talking about tens of thousands of cases. There's no way that the GP could cope with that, no way at all, without a transfer of funding...

> The money has to come to GPs and not to hospital A&E. GPs know what they want. A&E referrals will go down if we can manage this way...

In the absence of a transfer of funding, this member of a working group attempting to reach some consensus on the solution to the local A&E department's problems expressed a view that we encountered in all the three areas:

There was a clear message from the primary sector that referrals considered to be inappropriate should not, on any account, be redirected to the primary care emergency sector. It was pointed out us that A&E was not the only department with an increasing workload. It was equally true of primary care nationally

(GP).

The GPs that we studied, were, as a professional group, quite enthusiastic about Primary Care Groups, seeing them as a way forward for health care decisions, which would actually meet the needs of their local populations. This policy may also be seen another way for the DHA to draw back the power lost as a result of the internal market. At the time of this research it would still be some years before Primary Care groups could act (under the direction of the HA) as Trusts in their own right, however.

These, then, were the conditions which confront those about to introduce a further re-configuration of the health service in which: 'GP representatives working together with their health authorities and local hospitals, with their practice colleagues and the wider primary care team' bring about the change to primary care commissioning groups (Singer 1996), change which will undoubtedly have an impact on the future form of emergency 'out-of-hours' care.

Research for this paper took place at a time when the NHS was on the cusp of yet another change with the shift to an even more primary-care led system of healthcare provision. How the provision of an 'out-of-hours' service will be affected by the move to a primary led health service can only be conjectured at this time. Pre-existing inter-organisational relationships will, undoubtedly, shape the process by which changes are negotiated between those involved: purchasers and providers of service, GPs, hospital consultants and the wider care team.

It was in the context of developments to meet the demands for out-of-hour's healthcare that this research was planned. This phase expands on an earlier study of the issue of over-attendance at a specific A&E department. This research was carried out at an early stage in the recent changes to Primary Care Groups and Trusts, so it was not possible to draw any fixed conclusions on the emerging forms of out-of-hours provision of emergency care which will arise as a result of imminent reconfiguration of the NHS.

As Klein (1995) argues, attempting to evaluate the health service is problematic. This brief overview of existing and emerging forms of 'out-of-hours' provision demonstrates the variety of arrangements that have evolved in distinctive situations. With further changes imminent the process of negotiation on this issue will, no doubt reflect the both the structural and cultural contexts informing the process by which decisions are reached on new forms of emergency cover, whether provided by the primary or secondary sector.

References

Alferoff, C. and Dent, M. (1996), *A & E Patient Survey* (unpublished report), Staffordshire University: Stoke-on-Trent.

Barley, S.R. and Tolbert, P.S. (1997), 'Institutionalization and Structuration: Studying the Links between Action and Institution', *Organization Studies*, 18 (1): 93-197.

Bartlett, W. (1991), 'Quasi-Markets and Contracts: A Markets and Hierarchies Perspective on NHS Reform', *Public Money and Management*, 11(3): 53-61.

Bartlett, W. and Harrison, L. (1993), 'Quasi-Markets and the National Health Service Reforms', in J. Le Grand and W. Bartlett (eds) (1993), *Quasi-Markets and Social Policy*, Macmillan: Basingstoke.

Beales, J. (1997), 'A Godsend for the East End', *Health Service Journal*, July: 28-9.

Bloor, G. and Dawson, P. (1994), 'Understanding Professional Culture in Organizational Context', *Organization Studies*, 15(2): 275-95.

Campbell, J.L. (1996), 'The Reported Availability of General Practitioners and the Influence of Practice List Size', *British Journal of General Practice*, 46 (August): 465-68.

Clegg, S.R. (1989), *Frameworks of Power*, Sage: London.

Dale, J., Green, J., Reid, F., and Gluckman, E. (1995), 'Primary Care in the Accident and Emergency Department:1 Prospective Identification of Patients', *British Medical Journal (BMJ)*, 311: 42330.

Davis, G.F. and Greve, H.R. (1997), 'Corporate Elite Networks and Governance in the 1980s', *American Journal of Sociology*, 103(1): 1-37.

DiMaggio, P.J. and Powell, W.W. (1991), 'The Iron Cage Revisited: Institutional Isomorphism and Collective Rationality in Organizational Fields', in W.W Powell and P.J. DiMaggio (eds), *The New Institutionalism in Organizational Analysis*, London, Chicago University Press.

Hallam, L. (1994), 'Primary Medical Care Outside Normal Working Hours: Review of Published Work', *BMJ* 308: 249-52.

Klein, R. (1995), 'Big Bang Health Care Reform – Does It Work? The Case of Britain's 1991 National Health Service Reforms', *The Milbank Quarterly*, 73(3): 299-337.

Latimer, V. Smith, H. Hungin, P. and George, S. (1996), 'Future Provision of "Out-of-Hours" Primary Medical Care: a Survey of Two General Practitioner Research Networks', *BMJ*, 313 (7052):

Le Grand, J. and Bartlett, W. (eds), (1993), *Quasi-Markets and Social Policy*, Macmillan: Basingstoke.

Light, D.W. (1997), 'From Managed Competition to Managed Cooperation: Theory and Lessons from the British Experience', *The Milbank Quarterly*, 75(3): 297-341.

Lupton, D. (1997), 'Consumerism, Reflexivity and the Medical Encounter', *Social Science & Medicine*, 45(3): 373-81.

Mark, A. and Brennan, R. (1995), 'Demarketing: Managing Demand in the UK National Health Service', *Public Money and Management*, 15(3): 17-22.

Meyer, J.W. and Rowan, B. (1991), 'Institutionalized Organizations: Formal Structure as Myth and Ceremony', in W.W Powell and P.J DiMaggio (eds), *The New Institutionalism in Organizational Analysis*, Chicago University Press: London.

Moore, W. (1995), 'Is Doctors' Power Shrinking?', *The Health Service Journal*, (November): 24-7.

Pfeffer, J. and Salancik, G. (1978), *The External Control of Organizations: A Resource Dependency Perspective*, Harper Row: New York.

Rhodes, R.A.W. (1991), 'Policy Networks and Sub-Central Government', in G. Thompson, J. Frances, R. Levacic and J. Mitchell (eds), *Markets, Hierarchies and Networks: The Coordination of Social Life*, Sage/Open University Press: London.

Salter, B. (1993), 'The Politics of Purchasing in the National Health Service', *Policy and Politics*, 21(3): 171-84.

Scott, W.R. and Meyer, J.W. (1991), 'The Organization of Societal Sectors: Proposition and Early Evidence', in W.W. Powell and DiMaggio, P.J. (eds), *The New Institutionalism in Organizational Analysis*, Chicago University Press: London.

Singer, R. (1995/96), 'Really Working for Patients', *Health Matters*, 24 (Winter): 6-7.

Sixxma, H.J. and Debakker, D.H. (1996), 'Hospital or General Practice: Results of Two Experiments Limiting the Number of Self Referrals of Patients with Injuries to Hospitals in the Netherlands', *Journal of Accident and Emergency Medicine*, 13(4): 264-68.

Wass, A. and Zoltie, N. (1996), 'Changing Patterns in Accident and Emergency Attenders', *Journal of Accident and Emergency Medicine*, 13(4): 269-71.

PART IV

NEW PUBLIC MANAGEMENT
AS CONTESTED TERRAIN

Chapter 11

The New Public Management and Higher Education: A Human Cost?

Elisabeth Berg, Jim Barry and John Chandler

Introduction

Our intention in this chapter is to examine the human cost of the New Public Management (NPM). In order to do this we draw on the literature covering the NPM and higher education as well as a series of semi-structured, in-depth interviews undertaken by the authors in the course of a research investigation into the implications and consequences of the NPM. The interviews were conducted with Heads of Department, Heads of Division, Principal and Senior Lecturers, all in what might be called middle management positions, with responsibility for implementing change.

The focus of the chapter is on 'stress' or mental strain (Karasek and Theorell, 1990), an important dimension of any 'human cost' deriving from change. Our choice of stress, rather than say disaffection or alienation, reflects recent academic preoccupation (cf. Cooper, 2000; Levi, 2000), with 'stress' becoming emblematic of a wide range of problems in contemporary work places. It has even been described as one of the largest work-related diseases today, not least in England (Edworthy, 2000, Karasek and Theorell, 1990, Cooper, G. and Payne, R. 1994, Cooper, 2000, Chandler, Berg and Barry, 2003).

We have commented elsewhere on the lack of definitional clarity regarding the term 'stress' and have criticised conventional psychological approaches to it (Clark, Barry and Chandler, 2000). We wish, nevertheless, to explore the impact of the NPM in this chapter in relation to what has conventionally been called 'stress' or 'strain', not least because this seems a significant part of the way in which our interviewees both experienced and understood their situation. But before considering the impact of the NPM in higher education and the findings from out interviews, we turn to a brief discussion of some of the literature on stress.

Stress and the New Public Management

Stress as a phenomenon has been commented on in various ways. Psychological and bio-medical research on individuals coping with high pressure, for example, has considered demands on the body, revealing different stress tolerances for different people in different environments (Levi, 2000).

Hans Selye's experiments, which identified what he referred to as a general adaptation syndrome, also considered external pressures on organisms and, prompted him to coin the term 'stress'. Selye used this term to account for the 'generality' or 'stereotypy' of pressure and its long-term effects, or 'wear and tear' over time. The term strain would probably have described more accurately what he meant than the word stress, although Selye's linguistic misinterpretation of the term, partly because of his Austro-Hungarian background (Levi, 2000: vi), seems to have been important. The term stress has certainly endured, proving popular among those concerned with the pressures of work.

Different definitions have pointed to a wide range of problems linked with stress. These include social, political and organisational problems, reduced by many work psychologists to psychological or biological difficulties for the individual (Clark, Chandler and Barry, 2000). Maslach (2000), for example, focuses on burnout, which she sees as a final stage, reached when individuals, exposed to stress over a prolonged period, are no longer able to cope. In emphasising the importance of organisational relationships, she contends that burnout occurs where:

> an individual stress experience [is] embedded in a context of complex social relationships, and... involves the person's conception of both self and others
>
> (2000: 69).

In earlier days when people were considered more likely to be vulnerable to physical threat, stress reactions fulfilled a purpose, preparing the body for a fight or flight response. Yet today stress is seen as comprising both a physiological and a psychological component, whereby individuals are exposed to dangers that are not clearly visible. Yet stress is also considered to be motivating, when expectations are capable of being met or at least within the grasp of those involved. Negative or unhealthy stress, or distress, occurs where there is a discrepancy between demands and abilities or between demands and time; where targets and deadlines, for example, are set unrealistically. It is in these kinds of situations that people can feel mental strain, wear and tear, exhaustion and discomfort.

Mental strain is the concept used in the demand/control model associated with Karasek and Theorell (1990). Here the significant factors giving rise to strain are work demands, or the effort required by the job and the extent of self-control. By emphasising the importance of the organisational environment within which strain is produced this approach also shows how mental strain and stress-related illness can be reduced in the workplace. Karasek and Theorell (1990) expanded the demand/control model to include social support as a third factor that influences the degree of strain.

The expanded model, involving demand, control and social support, is intended to show how people experience different types of job demand, characterised as low or high, in combination with low or high control in conditions of low or high support. The combinations are shown to produce different levels of stress, or mental strain. Here control is defined as decision latitude and 'is interpreted as the worker's ability to control his or her own activities and skill usage, not to control others' (Karasek and Theorell, 1990: 60). People with high demands and low control are exposed to high mental strain, whilst high demands and high control provide a healthier work environment that avoids high mental strain. Several types of social support are identified at workplaces. One of these is socio-emotional support, which buffers psychological strain. Another type is instrumental social support, which 'measures extra resources or assistance with work tasks given by co-workers or supervisors' (ibid, 1990: 71).

Karasek and Theorell's thesis is that certain work situations are capable of producing stress-related factors which can, in turn, lead to heart or other problems for those involved. They develop the factors linked with 'stress' use the notion of mental strain as their key concept:

> Strain may be viewed as the discrepancy between the individual's desire to cope with a challenge and reality. Implicitly this type of strain can be eliminated by a reduction in expectation level: the person would be happier not even trying to succeed in the face of difficult challenges. This approach, however, can justify repressive environments
>
> (ibid, 1990: 95).

Their methodology is quantitative and prioritises measurement, with health problems like high blood pressure, breathing difficulty, chest pain and heart weakness are measured and related to psychosocial job dimensions. Tests on men who had suffered a myocardial infarction in different job positions were used, for example, to investigate the influence of different variables such as age, race, education, systolic blood pressure, cholesterol and smoking, together with the decision latitude associated with the job, the psychological demands and the physical exertion required. They have also used secondary sources for both women and men to test the relation between job strain and heart problems. Their focus is not specifically work organisation; rather it is job positions in relation to other factors which, they argue, can give rise to physical symptoms (1990: 117-57). It would seem, from their work, that people need freedom of action if they are to avoid mental strain and illness. This means, to take an example from our empirical work reported on shortly, that academics can, if their work becomes more controlled, move from a situation characterised by high job demands and high control to one where they face high job demands and low control, constraining their freedom of action – thereby increasing the chance of mental strain and illness.

Our approach, however, emphasises the importance of the wider social context, as well as the immediate work environment. For if the concept of stress is a social construction and work pressure is socially created, as is being suggested here, it follows that the NPM may be an important conditioning factor, where demands for enhanced control and strident managerial influence are used to increase efficiency and generate higher performance. This leads us to wonder how far academics have been affected by the NPM, and whether the organisational changes it has brought have impacted directly on demand, control and social support, and with what consequences. In order to address these questions we seek to apply Karasek and Theorell's model to higher education in England. However, we do so, not by applying the quantitative approach favoured by Karasek and Theorell, but through semi-structured interviews aimed at understanding how the respondents themselves define their situation, which might include self-reports of the experience of 'stress'. It may be thought that such self-reported 'stress' should not be taken at face value. Elsewhere we have written about the problematic nature of the term 'stress' and of psychological approaches to it in particular, but in so far as respondents do use the term as a synonym for strain or dissatisfaction we feel it is an important feature of the social situation and tells us something about what respondents think or feel that is useful at a certain level of analysis.

This is by no means the first study of stress in academic life (Earley, 1994; Fisher, 1994; Kinman, 1996, Utley, 1997 a and b, Chandler, Barry and Berg, 2003), but the central questions addressed in this chapter, following the lead of Karasek and Theorell (1990), are *whether the NPM has led to the increased control* of the work of academics and whether their jobs involve *high or low demand* and *high or low social support*. The empirical work undertaken for the research investigation, and used here to help us explore these questions, is based on in-depth interviews with fifteen female and fifteen male academics in middle management positions. The semi-structured interviews, which were conducted by the authors, took place during 2000 and 2001 in two universities in England, one a traditional university, the other a one-time polytechnic which achieved university status in 1992, with little difference discernible in the experiences of academics, contrary to expectation (Barry, Chandler and Clark, 2001). However, before considering the interview findings, we turn to a discussion of the NPM in higher education in order to set the context.

The New Public Management in Higher Education in England

Development of the NPM in the public sector followed the emergence in the USA of 'entrepreneurial government', designed to steer the course of public sector reform (Osborne and Gaebler, 1992; Du Gay, 1993). As a movement for change the NPM reforms were also seen in a number of different countries as far apart as New Zealand, Australia, Canada and Sweden, where its impact appears to have been most keenly felt, (Hood 1995, Pollitt and Bouckaert, 2000). Its arrival in England was seen in attempts to introduce a series of managerial techniques and control strategies that had their roots in the private sector (Hedlund, 1997; Clarke and Newman, 1997; and Hood, 1995). In higher education the British government introduced league tables, ostensibly to rank the quality and quantity of teaching and research, relying on indicators to loosen the grip of professional autonomy on academic work. As Trow has explained:

the withdrawal of trust in its universities by the government has forced it to create bureaucratic machinery and formulas to steer and manage the universities from outside the system

(Trow, 1994: 11).

Finding themselves in a competitive and entrepreneurial educational market place, universities looked also for administrative efficiencies and rationalised internal operations for economies, under pressure from the DES (Department of Education and Science) to expand student numbers significantly without corresponding increases in financial support (Trow, 1994).

Implementation of the NPM saw increases in control, more measures of output in contrast to input, and a growth in academic workload, with more students clamouring for attention, and less time for research (Trow, 1994; Hedlund, 1997; Fogelberg, Hearn, Husu, and Mankkinen, 1999; Chandler, Barry and Berg, 2003). This was accompanied by an emphasis on monitoring and audit, leading to a growth, rather than a decline, in administration.

As the NPM developed so the emphasis switched from policy making to management skills, with a number of elements of change discernible (Hood, 1995: 95-7). These dimensions challenged the traditional way of understanding public administration, questioned traditional assumptions about how far the public sector could be transformed in order to reflect private sector ideology, and focused on outputs measured by quantitative performance indicators (Smith, 1995; Clarke and Newman, 1997). Universities in England, in line with this approach to managing public services, went through a number of important organisational changes as a result (Chandler, Berg and Barry, 2003; Barry, Chandler and Clark, 2001; and Clark, Chandler and Barry, 1998 and 1999) involving 'neo-Taylorist' forms of managerialism, characterised by Pollitt as cost control and decentralised management (Clarke and Newman, 1997). These organisational changes had an impact on universities as organisational entities as well as on academics and their workload (Ibid). Little wonder, perhaps, that universities in England have been identified in the literature on the NPM as on the verge of something akin to managerial colonisation (Parker and Jary, 1995). A crucial turning point for higher education in England was the Report of the Steering Committee for Efficiency Studies in Universities (1985), known as the Jarratt Report. This was one of the first texts on higher education to express interest in this movement for change by advocating the introduction of managerial techniques. The report was published by the Committee of Vice Chancellors and Principals, and enjoined universities to seek efficiencies through better management. The government position was summed up in the DES Green Paper, which appeared in the same year as the Jarratt Report:

The Government believes that it is vital for our higher education to contribute more effectively to the improvement of the performance of the economy...The future health of higher education – and its funding from public and private sources – depends significantly upon its success in generating the qualified manpower the country needs

(DES, 1985: 3, cited in Bone, 1997: 18).

Managerialism was thus pressed into service to meet not just the needs of universities and government but also 'the country'. Its advocates appeared, in addition, to be dedicated followers of fashion, keen to introduce economies through new employment flexibilities and a new accountability, both of which played down the new insecurities of work (Gregg and Wadsworth, 1999). The implementation of the NPM, through managerial techniques drawn from the private sector, was thus used to intensify the labour of university workforces as well as initiate management by endeavour, in the spirit of the new entrepreneurialism so beloved by Osborne and Gaebler. How much all of this is new – control, accountability, entrepreneurialism and so on – is of course debatable. Echoes of Taylorism, as well as the clarion voices of gurus and consultants, suggests this is at best perhaps a kind of re-tread management, at worst syncretic vulgarity. But what is clear is that interest in these matters is thought to be responsible, in part at least, for the development of heightened insecurity among university staff. This is likely to have implications for the ways in which academic work is experienced as more or less 'stressful'.

All in all then English higher education would seem to offer a suitable test case for an examination of the human consequences of NPM reforms, since England would seem to be at the forefront of attempts to adopt the NPM, with English higher education having experienced its impact like much of the rest of the public sector. In what follows, the human cost of the NPM is thus considered through an examination of the mental strain experienced by academics in middle-management levels, charged with responsibility for delivering the reforms.

Academics in a Pressurised Organisation?

Stressed Environments – High and Low Demand

The academics in our investigation generally viewed the NPM as a government-inspired initiative and understood it as a strategy to cope with increasing numbers of students and diminishing public revenues. In the interviews we conducted with middle managers a variety of strategies to cope with increasing workloads and greater pressure, on both women and men, were mentioned. The most common way to handle the high workload for both the women and the men was to work more intensively. Another strategy, for many of the women and a few of the men, was to extend the working week by working in the evenings and weekends, at home or at the university.

Whilst the stereotype of an academic conveys an image of a person driven more by a critical and reflective mind than feelings, examination shows that academic work involves both reason *and* emotion (Brante, 1984). The daily routine, of

Professors, Readers and Lecturers, involves teaching, marking, administration, meetings and seminars. It is not work where academics constantly experience mental strain or overload the whole time. Occasionally there is time to read and reflect over research and teaching:

> It's not a job when you are constantly on the stress the whole time so there are times when you are on top of things and can cope quite easily, you always know when stress becomes really bad it's not going to last forever. With the younger colleagues it can be more difficult, they have not the experience you have to support a bit more and sit down and talk with them, help them to see the end of the tunnel, whatever
>
>   (Male Academic).

A principal lecturer, and also part-time head of department, experienced his workload as coming in waves. He sometimes worked sixty hours each week but still never felt free from work, especially when he was teaching and was responsible for large numbers of students who needed to discuss their courses with him. His research ambitions were quite low, faced as he was with no time to write articles, which were at the bottom of his priority list:

> I don't get so much time to do research, that's the down side where I am I basically when you came in to a situation like this, if you want to progress with your career. You have to make a decision fairly early on, am I going to focus on research and try to get to Readership, maybe a Professorship, through my research. Or am I going to focus on students, management and administration and things like that and try to get promotion from that side, to a Principal Lecturer. If you try to do everything, you just end up not so far.

From our interviews it appeared that academics worked under pressure, although this is not to say that they actually worked harder than anyone else in contemporary society. The degree of pressure experienced, however, might be thought to depend on a range of mediating factors such as the career phase (Aldrich, 1999) in which they find themselves. A young person with no children at their beginning of their career, for example, may feel little stress or exhaustion. After a few years they may well have more responsibilities and more pressure from both work and family. But our interview data suggests a common experience of what our respondents described as 'stress' across the career cycle, indicating the presence of a highly pressurised work environment.

One female head of department described her workload at around sixty-to-seventy hours each week, another forty five-to-fifty. The first head indicated that nobody in academe worked just thirty-five hours, for which they considered themselves to be paid, adding that she had been away from her work for a couple of months because she had been very close to burnout. She considered it to be very difficult for academic staff to do research, one reason being meagre institutional support. The only way a researcher could survive, she suggested, was by applying for and securing external funding – a highly competitive and time-consuming process, with little prospect of success. Both of these two heads were worried because they had lost staff, with one having only just left. One of our interviewees intoned:

> There are quite high levels of sickness. I think that sometimes staff withdraw from… more management issues… I think they would rather stay at home and do their research. We lose staff – they actually leave. We have lost four in the last couple of years, nearly all of which would, I think, say that their main worries were with the institution, not the department.

Her way of coping was to work harder and to work with different tasks sequentially. She knew older Lecturers and Professors who could not stand the pressures and had said that they would seek early retirement, whilst the younger ones had indicated that they were already applying for other jobs. Her recollection was that they did not want to leave but felt that they could not stay, as the working conditions were not satisfying: 'Well, we've had two members of staff who have left because of lack of support to research'. Academic staff expected to work with and be involved in research, but the university appeared incapable of fulfilling such expectations. The research situation was seen as problematic indeed, due largely to a lack of resources.

The problem was not just the amount of work; it was also to do with the kind of work the university could offer. Our interviewees saw research as one of the most important tasks, but one that was often de-prioritised or sacrificed in the face of financial pressure. A male Principal Lecturer commented that there was always too much to do, leading to feelings of stress:

> The main stress we have is that there are times of the year when we have time so that we constantly must decide, which parts of the job we have to do and which parts of the job you are going to do well and which of the job you are not going to do well because you have not the time.

The same person explained how he went from one deadline to the next, continuously, and that if there were several things to do and the deadlines were close then he found himself unable to do them all to the best of his ability. He had to rush to finish one task after another in quick succession, finding himself prioritising endlessly. Taking such decisions made him feel stressed and forced him to make decisions about the future direction of his career and whether he should attempt to prioritise research, teaching or management. Having so little time for reflection it was unclear to him whether he took these kinds of decision himself or by default.

Another Principal Lecturer described a situation where he felt enormously pressurised and had worked especially hard for one semester only to find that he had not recovered before the start of the next:

I can say that I went through a very fairly stressed experience, I felt much stressed in the last semester. When I came back to work this semester, thinking consciously, saying to myself, I am not going to be in that state again'.

Academic work was thus located in what our respondents described as a stressful environment, characterised by a high pace of work and constant pressure. But are the academics concerned also losing control over their work?

Stressed Environments – High and Low Control

This pressurised environment seemed to be connected, in the view of our respondents, with a highly controlled work situation where control is seen as decision latitude and 'interpreted as the worker's ability to control his or her own activities and skill usage ...' (Karasek and Theorell, 1990: 60). There has been greater use of managerial control strategies such as target setting in higher education, alongside a speeding up of information flows, especially through systems like email and mobile telephones, as well as through institutional audit and peer review. A male Principal Lecturer from England sought to avoid managerial controls by avoiding mobile phones and having email at home:

I do not want them to contact me at any place and anywhere so I refuse to have one. For the same reason, we have a computer at home, I have been resistant to have Internet at home so the head of the department cannot actually get hold of me at home and send me extra work to do over the weekend. I try to avoid technology in my personal life.

The use of technology in universities has increased. In certain respects it has become intrusive although at the same time it seems to have been helpful, making work much easier. The use of email constructs dialogues other than face-to-face interaction, which can speed up the work and put more pressure on people, producing so-called techno-stress, which derives from enhanced expectations of response (Edenius, 1996). Shared expectations can result in a dialogue that would, by telephone or letter, have taken a few weeks. The increasing speed of communication is one reason why work has changed, with expectations moved up a gear. So-called new technology is intrusive in other ways too. There are reactions towards new technology, for example, which add to the pressure for employees. A male head of department described his strategy to avoid stress:

Partly by not making the university my entire life, I try to only work here; I do not take my work home. If I work twelve-hour days here, fine, but I try to separate the two halves of my life. So when I am at home I have my own social life and interests outside of my academic discipline.

This man had also made a choice to separate his work and private life by not having email or a mobile phone at home. It was his way of saying that he had taken control of his life; he was the one who was in charge. Yet academic work is not easy to somehow cut off or detach oneself from. Indeed, most of the academics we interviewed found it easier to mark essays, read and keep up with the literature and draft papers at home. What this man felt was that he had too much to do at work and that his private life would not exist unless he took precautions.

One Head of Department felt that the academic job had lost its attraction because academics were unable to work in the same way as they did previously, at home with preparation and research and then at their workplaces a couple of days each week. The growing administration tied people to their workplaces. She also indicated that 'everything has to be monitored', for the Quality Assurance Agency for Higher Education (QAAHE). She described QAAHE as an intrusion that generated much of her work. This was something that seemed never to stop. It produced a great deal of administration, bureaucracy and high stress levels for everyone:

> I think it started with the subject review process because we had two stages, we had an internal subject review involving a lot of people in the university, we got a couple of people outside the university as well. It wasn't the national quality audit people it was an exercise with the university quality department in charge and that was stressful and been in just the last three weeks that I began to realise that a number of reasons why it was stressful, we all say it was stressful, and I was exhausted at the end of it. It was stressful because I felt it was intrusive.

According to Weber (1978), while the bureaucratic type of administrative organisation is, from a technical point of view, capable of achieving the highest degree of efficiency, it is also associated with formal rationality, which dominates human spirit, as means come to overshadow or obscure ends. Higher education does not have a tradition of quality inspections and reviews with observation of teaching. Yet monitoring of teaching has increased, with more administrative routines, marking, double marking and external peer review. One head of department felt that research and teaching should be monitored but indicated that this did not mean that it did not put great pressure on those involved.

Some of our interviewees talked of workload committees and timetables that kept an annual record, or track, of everybody's teaching hours and essay/exam marking responsibilities. There was a standard, agreed, tariff, which gave the average time it should take to mark an essay, a practical report or a thesis. They also had a record of how much 'interviewing and invigilation everybody has to do, plus all the administrative jobs'. One Principal Lecturer had to review all the administrative jobs on her course, because she needed to know what they did and if there were anything they could do differently:

> I am going to try and gain an estimate of how many hours they spend on it [each task]. So then I can sit down and establish whether things are being done

in the most efficient way or not. Maybe additional staff is necessary; maybe the job needs to be done a different way.

So far we have seen how our academic interviewees have experienced high levels of demand and serious threats to their professional autonomy, and that they themselves link this situation with what they describe as 'stress', but what about social support, which is the third element in Karasek and Theorell's (1990) model of mental strain?

Stressed Environments – Social Support – Socio-emotional and Instrumental Support

As in many other workplaces staff in universities compete for scarce resources. Academics, for example, compete for project funding, as well as opportunities to publish in what are considered prestigious journals. But universities are also workplaces where an element of social support, in the form of collegiality, is supposed to exist. If people do not have support from senior and middle managers this might well, according to Karasek and Theorell, expose them to anxiety and mental strain. One of our interviewees, a male academic, experienced a high pressure at work, feeling threatened by a reduction in student numbers and a culture of blame promulgated by senior management:

> It is a culture of blame here, which some managers are aware of but they blame us for that culture of blame. It is really a problem, the teaching staff feeling frustrated, they want to get on with teaching, that's what we are here for, we believe in our subjects and what we are doing. Unless there is a more supporting atmosphere, it gets very discouraging.

Another concern for those in middle management positions was their inability to support colleagues. They indicated that they did not have sufficient resources to be able to help staff when they needed it most. And it was not just staff they wanted to help; they were also concerned about students, who complained at the lack of support. With insufficient resources, those involved felt that they could not do anything to make a difference:

> You never get thanked for anything you do; everything is taken for granted, you only get blamed when something doesn't go how people want. It can be stressful, and a bit lonely at times because you are slightly kept at a distance.

Sometimes, also, competence it was said was 'rewarded' with an increased workload. A Reader revealed what happened when she was perhaps too successful in her work and ended up doing nearly 2.5 jobs:

> What tends to happen, I find, is that if you efficiently do a certain amount of work on time then people ask you to do more things. If you are inefficient, they

don't ask you. If you are reasonably competent, you get more things to do and you take on more things. That then becomes your new baseline workload.

Staff felt they were under pressure, feeling that they could not do everything required of them. One Head of Department experienced growing pressure accompanied by declining support from her senior managers at times when economic problems seemed to be the most important issue under discussion at her Faculty Board. With almost constant reorganisation, staff felt pressurised, particularly as they felt they had no control over events and did not perceive reorganisation as necessary. They felt powerless and extremely stressed as a result. One head of department described it as follows:

> You feel as if you have a perfectly sane argument, which everybody else shares, [yet it is] not taken any heed of. If you feel that you have no control over situations this increases anxiety levels

Of course academics might be expected to receive social support from a variety of sources, including some of their peers, families and friends, and perhaps from sympathetic students. However even if these other means of social support do serve to buoy up a beleaguered academic, the above comments seem to suggest serious strain emanating from a work environment that is inimical to social support in some important respects.

Concluding Thoughts

In this chapter we have provided evidence which suggests that the NPM has changed the character of academic work in favour of enhanced managerial control, characterised by high demands on academic staff, accompanied by increasing control and a lack of social support from management. We have also shown how our respondents see this as leading to what they describe as 'stress', in Karasek and Theorell's (1990) terms.

The appearance of the NPM would seem to have brought with it a growth in administration and bureaucracy in universities. This raises questions about shifts in power relations within the academy and control of academic work. To increase bureaucracy carries a risk for the character of academe. As Max Weber argued:

> No one knows who will live in this cage in the future, or whether at the end of this tremendous development entirely new prophets will arise, or there will be a great rebirth of old ideas and ideals

(Weber, 1992: 182).

Recent changes in higher education have seen an increase in the use of private sector managerial techniques and monitoring, altering the creative character of academic work in the process. This raises a number of questions. How can academics shift from their position of relative autonomy to accommodate more regulated and controlled work patterns, which are measured quantitatively and subjected to scrutiny? And what are the likely consequences? Many academics will, of course, try to find other ways to express their creativity. They are also likely to develop resistances against the new regulation. Academics have enjoyed a privileged position, where the requirement to engage in reflective and critical thought has necessitated the maintenance of professional autonomy. To seek now to manage so independently minded a group is indeed like attempting to herd cats.

Yet it looks as if a critical point is being reached for academics, where the growth of management has provoked frustration and a questioning of academic identities. Higher education has different, wider, goals than the private sector and a range of competing interests and demands to satisfy. The questions raised are thus at the core of what it means to be an academic − where reflection and critical thinking requires the raising of difficult questions and going sometimes against the political and managerial grain. One consequence is to focus on research − where that is possible. The problem is that not everyone succeeds in that competitive endeavour.

Whilst there is recognition of the need for accountability among academics, restricting their relative freedom of action and autonomy may not help to guarantee standards in higher education. The current problems seem to stem from a lack of resources, not least for research, with universities increasingly dependent on external funding. And there is greater competition for external funding, which means that a lot of research potential will likely be lost in the time-consuming and energy-sapping frenetic activity generated by competition. Nor has the mythical 'free-lunch' yet appeared, leaving those academics, fortunate to have secured external funding, to satisfy yet another customer with applied research findings and reports, which are difficult to transform into academic papers. In the long run this may affect collective research effort considerably, as political correctness and the dictates of funding bodies seek at first to steer and then perhaps dictate the direction of academic minds.

Such an analysis might appear predictable, even as a case of self-interested whingeing, from a group of privileged workers. But in exploring the human costs of the NPM in academia our purpose has not been to set academics apart as a group who have suffered more than others. Our research does not seek to make such comparisons. It is likely, however, that to the extent that the NPM has impacted on other groups of public sector workers in similar ways it may well have had similar effects; although there are likely to be differences, too.

In all this one thing is clear: that certain work environments can induce strain, and that this can result, in turn, if the analysis of social psychology/medicine is accepted, in the development of different diseases (Karasek and Theorell 1990). It seems that people need some freedom of action and autonomy if they are to avoid mental strain and illness. Yet it comes across in our interviews that many academics have witnessed a growth in demands and controls, and experienced a lack of social support from managers, leaving them faced with a highly pressurised work situation. Many appear to be actively pursuing early retirement or other work outside academia, and many report themselves as highly stressed. If Karasek and Theorell are correct, then the human cost of the NPM in academia may only be counted years from now, in a haemorrhage of talent and experience, and a debilitated workforce.

References

Aldrich, H. (1999), 'Promise, Failure, and Redemption: A Life Course Perspective on Teaching as a Career', in B.A. Pescosolido and R. Aminzade (eds), *The Social Worlds of Higher Education: Handbook for Teaching in a New Century*, Pine Forge Press: California.

Barry, J., Chandler, J. and Clark, H. (2001), 'Between the Ivory Tower and the Academic Assembly Line', *Journal of Management Studies*, 38(1): 87-101.

Berg, E. (2001), 'To Be Or Not To Be a Lecturer in Higher Education in Sweden', *International Journal of Sociology and Social Policy*, (211/12) 57-74.

Bone, J. (1997), 'Women and the Ethics of Leadership in Higher Education', in H. Eggins. (ed), *Women as Leaders and Managers in Higher Education*, Open University Press: Buckingham.

Brante, T. (1984), *Vetenskapens Sociala Grunder – En Studie av Konflikter i Forskarvärlde*, Kristianstad: Raben & Sjögren.

Chandler, J., Berg, E. and Barry, J. (2003), 'Workplace Stress in the United Kingdom: Conceptualising Difference', in C. Peterson (ed) (2003), *Work Stress: Studies of the Context, Content and Outcomes of Stress – A Book of Readings*, Baywood: Amityville.

Clark, H., Chandler, J. and Barry, J. (2000), 'Work, Stress and Gender: Conceptualisation and Consequence', in J. Barry, J. Chandler, H. Clark, R. Johnston and D. Needle (eds), *Organization and Management: A Critical Text*, International Thomson: London.

Clark, H., Chandler, J. and Barry, J. (1998), 'On Whether it is Better to be Loved than Feared: Managerialism and Women in Universities', in D. Jary and M. Parker (eds), *The New Higher Education: Issues and Directions For The Post-Dearing University*, Staffordshire University Press: Stoke on Trent.

Clark, H., Chandler, J. and Barry, J. (1999), 'Gender and Management in the Organisation of University Life', in P. Fogelberg, J. Hearn, L. Husu and T. Mankkinen (eds), *Hard Work in the Academy*, University of Helsinki Press: Helsinki.

Clarke, J. and Newman, J. (1997), *The Managerial State*, London: Sage.

Cooper, G. (ed), (2000), *Theories of Organizational Stress*, Oxford University Press: Oxford.

Cooper, G. and Payne, R. (eds) (1994), *Causes, Coping & Consequences of Stress at Work*, Wiley: Chichester.

Earley, P. (1994), *Lecturers' Workload and Factors Affecting Stress Levels: a Research Report from the NFER*, NATFHE: London.

Edenius, M. (1996), *Ett Modernt Dilemma: Organiserandet Kring Elektronisk Post* [A Modern Dilemma: Organising Around Electronic Mail], Unpublished Dissertation, Stockholm Universitet: Stockholm.

Edworthy, A. (2000), *Managing Stress*, Open University Press: Buckingham.

Fisher, S. (1994), *Stress in Academic Life: The Mental Assembly Line*, SRHE and OU Press: Buckingham.

Fogelberg, P., Hearn, J., Husu, L. and Mankkinen, T. (eds), (1999), *Hard Work in the Academy*, Helsinki University Press: Helsinki.

Gregg, P. and Wadsworth, J. (1999), 'Job Tenure, 1975-98', in P. Gregg and J. Wadsworth (eds), *The State of Working Britain*, Manchester University Press: Manchester.

Hedlund, G. (1997), 'Kön, Makt, Organisation och Ekonomi i Svenska Kommuner' [Sex, Power, Organization and Economy in Swedish Local Authority], in. G. Jónasdóttir (ed) *Styrsystem och jämställdhet*, SOU 1997:114, A t.

Hood, C. (1995), '"The New Public Management" in The 1980s: Variations on a Theme', *Accounting, Organizations and Society*, 20 (2/3): 93-109.

Karasek, R. and Theorell, T. (1990), *Healthy Work. Stress, Productivity, and the Reconstruction of Working Life*, Basic Book: New York.

Kinman, G. (1996), *Occupational Stress and Health among Lecturers Working in Further And Higher Education: A Survey Report*, NATFHE: London.

Levi, L. (2000), *Stress och hälsa 2000* [Stress and health 2000], Skandia: Stockholm.

Maslach, C. (2000), 'A Multidimensional Theory of Burnout', in G. Cooper (ed) *Theories of Organizational Stress*, Oxford University Press: Oxford.

Parker, M. and Jary, D. (1995), 'The McUniversity; Organization, Management and Academic Subjectivity', *Organization*, 2 (2) 319-38.

Pollitt, C and Bouckaert, G. (2000), *Public Management Reform: A Comparative Analysis*, Oxford University Press: Oxford.

Prichard, C. and Willmott, H. (1997), 'Just How Managed is the McUniversity?', *Organization Studies*, 18 (2): 287-316.

Smith. P. (1995), 'On the Unintended Consequences of Publishing Performance Data in the Public Sector', *International Journal of Public Administration*, 18 (2/3): 277-310.

Trow, M. (1994), Managerialism and the Academic Profession: The Case of England. *Higher Education Policy*, 7 (2): 11-18.

Utley, A. (1997a), 'Axe Threat Outrages Notts Staff', *Times Higher Educational Supplement*, 25th April: 6.

Utley, A. (1997b), 'Bullies in the Common Room', *Times Higher Educational Supplement*, 14th March: 6.

Weber, M. (1978), *Economy and Society: An Outline of Interpretive Sociology* (Volume 1), University of California Press: Berkeley.

Weber, M (1992), *The Protestant Ethic and the Spirit of Capitalism*, Routledge: London.

Whitehead, S. and Moodley, R. (1999), (eds), *Transforming Managers: Gendering Change in The Public Sector*, UCL Press: London.

Chapter 12

A Bit of a Laugh: Nurses' Use of Humour as a Mode of Resistance

Sharon C. Bolton

Introduction

Humour in nursing work is well documented. Nurses use humour as a coping mechanism, to alleviate stress and 'let off steam' (Meerabeau and Page, 1998). Humour acts as a means of easing the often turbulent path of interaction between different hierarchically ordered occupational groups (Coser, 1962) or between nurse and patient whilst carrying out the 'dirty work' of nursing (Lawler, 1991; Warner, 1984; Strauss, 1982). It is also offered as a 'gift' to colleagues and patients to help assuage distress and grief (Astedt-Kurki and Liukkonnen, 1994; Bolton, 2000; Sumners, 1990). For its beneficial effects, humour in nursing is frequently seen as a valuable professional tool. There is little doubt that play, joking and laughter creates and sustains the familial bonds of a close working community whilst also enhancing the status of nurses as warm and caring professionals who undertake a stressful and difficult job.

Discussions, however, tend to focus on what has been described as 'pure' humour (Mulkay, 1988) which reflects the genuine pleasure nurses gain from interaction with patients and colleagues. This type of humour is transparent and benign, which this chapter argues, does not wholly reflect the way humour is used in a nursing community. Data collected as part of a longitudinal study of a particular group of hospital nurses reveals ample examples of 'pure' humour, but also just as commonplace is the presence of a scathing, sarcastic humour which very clearly has a serious point to it. 'Applied' humour such as this has a hidden or veiled purpose (Mulkay, 1988; Fox, 1990) and can be seen as inherently oppositional (Ackroyd and Thompson, 1999; Collinson, 1988; Griffiths, 1998).

Data presented demonstrates how nurses use 'applied' humour as a potent negotiative device, which often serves to alter the balance of power during hierarchically structured interactions. Nurses defy the patriarchal, taken-for-granted, assumption that they must act as hand-maidens to newly-qualified doctors and challenge the recently introduced market mentality which requires that patients be 're-imagined' as customers. In effect, nurses use humour to 'execute the double stance'. Whilst apparently adhering to the 'official definition of the situation' they sustain simultaneous activity that shows, with varying degrees of subtlety, they have not agreed to have themselves 'defined by what is officially in progress' (Goffman, 1961: 133).

Humour as a Mode Of Resistance

The significant part humour plays in organisational life has long been recognised. For instance, Roy's (1973) classic study of shopfloor workers brought attention to the way apparently inane banter between workers is a vital form of communication in that it offers a form of structure and meaning and gentles the 'beast of boredom' to the 'harmless kitten' (1973:215). More recent ethnographic studies, carried out in a variety of workplace settings, confirm the important role of play and laughter. They note that humour crosses organisational boundaries, it may subvert, support or accommodate social forms (Linstead, 1985) and serves many purposes: conformity (Ackroyd and Crowdy, 1990; Thompson and Bannon, 1985); opposition (Collinson, 1988; Westwood, 1984); relief from boredom (Roy, 1973; Burawoy, 1979; Collinson, 1988) or 'letting off steam' (Fine, 1988).

Much of the humour portrayed in accounts of organisational life is laughter and joking produced as little more than a method of offering relief from the seriousness of work (Mulkay, 1988). Management has been swift, however, to recognise its positive effects and note that 'workplay' need not always undermine performance. Humour can create a sense of involvement (Duncan and Feisal, 1989; Barsoux, 1993; Ashforth and Humphry, 1995) and, in the interests of encouraging employee consent to the rigours of the labour process (Burwaoy, 1979), management often ignore, tolerate and even actively encourage playful practices. In this way the informal rules, which generally inform humorous episodes at work, do not stand in opposition to formal organisational rules. That is, they do not create a contradictory relationship but rather have the unintended consequence of furthering organisational goals.

Humour can indeed add 'joy' to work but it can also have a serious point to it and may not always be seen as beneficial to all participants. Many accounts show how teasing and practical-joking amongst colleagues can be harsh and destructive (Ackroyd and Crowdy, 1990; Burawoy, 1979; Collinson, 1988). 'Applied' humour such as this is often used to re-order the hierarchical positions of members of informal work-groups by testing the vulnerability of various group members. Humour used in this way demonstrates the multi-faceted nature of joking relationships. Play and laughter may serve to bind an occupational community together and give relief from the monotony and pressures of work but it can also create long-standing and deep-seated conflicts.

Despite recognition of both the creative and 'dark-side' of humour (Collinson, 1988: 198), and its power to alter informal relationships, it is rare that play, joking and laughter are seen to have any transformative power. In general, humour is underestimated as a form of resistance at work, despite various accounts showing that it can become a critical resource and a powerful means of social control (Ackroyd and Thompson, 1999). During social interaction humour is often employed to deal with difficulties encountered in hierarchically structured situations where the division of 'definitional labour' (Goffman, 1959:21) is not equal: the 'unreal' nature of humour means that actors may attempt to influence the conduct of others in order to upset the established 'working consensus' (Goffman, 1959). As Emerson (1973: 269) states:

> for the very reason that humour officially does not 'count' persons are induced to risk messages that might be unacceptable if stated seriously.

Thus, under the guise of humorous discourse, the delicate balance of human interaction is disturbed and the once dominant party finds they have lost control of the exchange. They are left feeling 'unruled, unreal and anomic' (Goffman, 1967: 135) and unable to re-assert their authority without losing further face.

The power of humour as an effective form of covert resistance lies in the way apparently innocuous banter is able to define and redefine 'non-play' activity (Linstead, 1985). Frequently employees' light-hearted comments are actually of a deeply subversive character and have a 'serious intellectual content' (Ackroyd and Thompson, 1999:111) that is used to register criticism, defiance or discontent concerning certain persons, practices or situations. Even where humour may not be directly aimed at those in authority, joking and laughter are ways in which employees delineate their identity and maintain a sense of self, separate from the workplace (Ackroyd and Thompson, 1999; Collinson, 1988; Westwood, 1984). Teasing, practical-joking and general exchange of light-hearted banter between workers creates spaces where organisational prescription may be evaded and from which management are firmly excluded.

The evidently meaningless character of much of organisational humour often leads to the conclusion that humorous discourse, whilst creating some temporary discomfort for those who are its target, is a futile form of resistance. The framework of interaction may be momentarily disrupted through the use of applied humour but the structures of power and control remain firmly intact (Collinson, 1988; Mulkay, 1988). To dismiss the use of humour as a mode of resistance, however, is to neglect its negotiative potential (Ackroyd and Thompson, 1999; Linstead, 1985). Humour plays on contradiction. Applied humour, especially, identifies weaknesses and creates ambiguity. It upsets the status quo in subtle ways, blurring and obfuscating power relationships. It creates interpretive loose ends that can be picked up time and time again in order to continually reassert dissent. Whilst the use of humour as a mode of resistance makes no claim to over throw structures of power and domination, each interaction which successfully unsettles the 'working consensus' is a micro-revolution (Douglas, 1975) where the 'unreal' of joking and laughter creates the possibility of changing very 'real' hierarchically ordered relationships.

Humour in Nursing Work

Occupational groups such as public sector caring professionals have rarely had the luxury of open defiance. Though supported by professional bodies, a combination of factors prevents them from registering collective resistance. A code of conduct and the importance of their self-image as altruistically motivated 'caring' professionals means that the most obvious forms discontent takes are absenteeism and high staff turnover (Ackroyd, 1993; Peelo et al, 1996). It is argued here that for an occupational group – such as nurses – humour is, and always has been, a vital source of 'misbehaviour'.

Given that the use of humour is a vital critical resource for nurses it is surprising that much of the literature concerning humour in nursing work offers a benign picture of play, joking and laughter. There are studies that show humour used by nurses as a 'modality of resistance' (Griffiths, 1998) but generally laughter in medical settings is applauded for its therapeutic benefits: as a reliever of pain, stress and anxiety, as a diffuser of conflict, as a builder of occupational communities and as a counter to a mechanistic approach to health care (Astedt-Kurki and Liukkonnen, 1994; Bolton, 2000; Harries, 1995; Lawler, 1991; Mallett, 1993; Meerabeau and Page, 1998; Sumners, 1990). Where 'applied' humour is recognised it is viewed as negative and detrimental to professional practice (Carlisle, 1990; Harries, 1995) or as a sort of empty rebellion never directed at those who are the source of nurses' discontent (Coser, 1962). The benevolent use of humour in this way maintains the carefully preserved picture of the nurse as an 'angel of mercy', as a dedicated caring professional. But, without denying the central contribution 'pure' humour makes to the working life of nurses, this portrayal gives only partial insight. As data presented in this chapter shows, nurses use applied humour to vent aggression, anger, hostility and belligerence, successfully subverting the established order and achieving the triumph of the 'informal' over the 'formal' (Douglas, 1975).

A Nursing Community

Qualitative data presented in this chapter was collected as part of a longitudinal study looking at the effects upon the nursing labour process of changes in the management of British public sector services. The focus of the study is a group of gynaecology nurses working in a large North West trust hospital. Fieldwork was conducted over a period of six years, 1994-2000, using semi-structured interviews and observation in two surgical wards and the associated out-patient clinics. Additional valuable data was also collected through informal contact with clerical staff, cleaners, doctors and managers. Indeed, it was often the casual conversations, which provided the greatest insight into the complexities involved in nursing work, as did the observed reactions of nurses to particular incidents and their interactions with doctors, managers and patients.

The specific group of forty-five gynaecology nurses included in this study exemplifies a particularly close occupational community, which may not represent all nursing communities. Over half of the nurses have worked together for an average of fifteen years with the length of service for senior staff being between twenty and twenty-five years. They have worked together for so long they say they feel like a family. They have nicknames for each other and have their own 'knicker department' language that has nothing to do with medical terminology: 'Ethel' and 'Fred' as a means of describing reproductive organs for example.

The gynaecology nurses have created their own traffic rules of interaction that often set them apart from other areas in the hospital. Within the social network of the hospital many of the gynaecology nurses are renowned for their 'in the face' attitude, their 'bolshiness', their 'manic' sense of humour and their close-knit community. They have created their own coping mechanisms, their own methods of 'letting off steam' and their own ways of asserting their collective identity.

The nurses shape and continually strengthen their collective identity through shared banter and game playing (Roy, 1973; Westwood, 1984). The use of humour plays an important part in the creation and preservation of a close working community. The gynaecology nurses appear particularly adept at a sharp, cutting humour, which, at times, appears unnecessarily callous and unkind. This type of humour, however, is not always delivered as a slight or reprimand. The atmosphere on the gynaecology unit tends to be highly emotionally charged and, as one nurse aptly describes it, sometimes they can 'care too much'. At these times a harsh, sarcastic humour is actually offered as a 'gift' to colleagues to help alleviate feelings of distress. A comment such as 'I'm not mopping up after you, you snivelling bitch' is actually 'pure', spontaneous humour, which serves to strengthen and maintain familial bonds. New recruits to the unit comment on how they had to learn the new rules of interaction:

> When I first came on here I didn't know what to do with myself. People were very welcoming, but they do have their own ways that take a bit to get used to. A lot of it I understand now, but they certainly have their own ways of doing things. I've never worked anywhere like it. It's frantic. We have women coming in who are so upset and I feel upset for them and the next minute we are having a laugh about something else. It must appear callous to outsiders but it's not you know. We really care, but you have to get along, you can't dwell on things too much. I can't imagine working anywhere else now.

However, on different occasions this type of humour is directed to 'outsiders'. That is, those who are not accepted as part of the working community and may pose a threat to its continued survival. This is 'applied' humour, which as the title of this chapter suggests, nurses use as an effective mode of resistance. 'Applied' humour manifests itself in varying degrees of subtlety, depending upon circumstance and recipient. At times episodes of play may be derisory and bold, at other times the humour is soft and ironic. The remainder of the chapter investigates a variety of encounters and incidents which display the successful use of humour by nurses as a means of attacking the patriarchal and market ideologies which they see as threatening to their occupational community and their status as public service caring professionals.

Doctors and Nurses

The nurses' peculiar brand of sharp humour seems to be especially effective when dealing with junior doctors (usually male, the female house officers tend to get off lightly). Comments are made concerning a doctor's dress, facial expression, or possible sexual prowess. The nurses have discovered that embarrassment is an effective weapon in their battles with junior doctors and on many occasions the doctor is happy to make a rapid exit from the ward. As a Staff Nurse notes with pride:

> We get some doctors on here who haven't got a clue. They come 'lording' it and then we have to tell them what to do. Their attitude stinks and they are just asking for it – we make them grovel. Actually some are quite sweet, but we can't resist doing it anyway. It's only a bit of a laugh.

The use of humour in this way can be viewed as a sign of resistance by the nurses against the patriarchal system that says a junior male doctor, who they perceive to have less knowledge than they do, is able to have authority over them. A junior doctor comments with awe:

> They're a frightening lot those gynae nurses. I thought midwives could be trouble, but this lot... I'm glad I've nearly finished on here. If they decide that you don't fit in then that's it – and I don't think I fit in. They aren't as bad with all the doctors. Some of them are ok, but there's a particular bunch that when they decide it's play time – watch out!

The nurses' attitude toward junior doctors is now expected and – as this particular junior doctor notes – all newly arrived doctors are warned to take care with 'that lot'.

The division of definitional labour is much more clearly explicated during interaction with more senior doctors. Though nurses no longer walk two steps behind the consultant on the ward round they are still expected to show deference to their status. This is not to say, however, that nurses are prepared to act as 'surrogate mother, wife and mistress' (Salvage, 1985) and quietly acquiesce to all demands made of them. The nurses actively dislike certain senior doctors though the doctors seem serenely unaware of the disdain they engender and continually try to engage in light-hearted banter, especially with senior nurses. The nurses appear to reciprocate dutifully and smilingly acknowledge the consultant's weak attempts at humour. However, after observing several similar interactions it becomes clear that the nurses are truly enjoying the exchange:

> A consultant who regularly visits the ward very late at night arrives wearing theatre greens. He apologises for arriving so late and looking like 'something from the night of the living dead'. To which a nurse soothingly replies 'Oh please don't apologise, it suits you' and the consultant smilingly acknowledges the compliment and his ego is suitably massaged.

At these times the nurses use humour that does not deliberately upset the accepted 'ceremonial order' (Goffman, 1967). Even so, in the eyes of the audience at least, they have successfully reversed the hierarchical ordering of communication. At other times their humour is not so subtle and they make no pretence at maintaining the ground rules of interaction as the following episode illustrates:

> A patient on the ward is particularly poorly and it is quite obvious the nurses are becoming seriously concerned for her welfare. They require assistance from a 'medical' that is not a consultant gynaecologist but a consultant from another department. They 'bleep' various numbers and get no response. Eventually a doctor arrives and approaches the nurses' station on the ward. A senior nurse enthusiastically greets him and starts to relay the particulars of the case whilst directing him to the patient. The doctor looks confused and says 'but I'm not a medical man'. 'What the hell are you then?' demands the nurse. The doctor attempts to reply but the nurse goes on: 'Where's your badge?'. He meekly points to it hanging from his jacket pocket where it appears to hang over his groin. 'What's it doing there?' the nurse asks 'If I'd wanted to identify doctors by their dicks I'd have bleeped the Chippendales'.

This nurse uses humour to vent her anger and frustration but she also uses it to take charge of the situation. She establishes her own 'working consensus' with the visiting doctor. Her references to a male stripper show disregard for his status and serve to dismiss the doctor as less than useless in a medical emergency whilst reaffirming her own status as a health care professional who is trying to offer the best possible care to a patient, despite obvious difficulties.

Keeping the 'Customer' Satisfied

During the period of research one of the most notable changes commented on by nurses is the difference in the attitudes of many patients. Against the backdrop of twenty years of public sector reform the perceptions of the general public have been altered, tenants, students, clients and patients have been 're-imagined' as 'customers' (du Gay and Salaman, 1992). Nurses resent the commercial dimension that has been added to their work and they actively resist complying with the new display rules that dictate they must present their 'smiliest happiest face' to demanding customers:

> Patient's attitudes have definitely changed. We have always had awkward patients but now we get them thinking they are customers and they are in a hotel or something. This patient the other day had some food brought in for her by her family. That's ok. A lot do. But this one wanted this, that and the other. She was driving me mad with her demands. Obviously feeling much better! In the end I just said to her 'I'll tell you what, get out of bed, take over for me and I'll sit and eat this for you and save you all this bother'. I don't

think she thought it was funny and I immediately regretted it but sometimes they get right up your nose.

On occasions like these there is no attempt at subtlety in the use of 'applied humour' and the resentment of nurses is barely veiled. However, nurses are very aware that if they are not always smiling they are seen as 'unkind and uncaring' and this then runs the risk of the patient being 'unsatisfied' and a complaint being made. The nurses accept this as a challenge and offer a parody of customer service. As Goffman (1959: 29) notes some audiences will not allow a sincere performance:

> In service occupations practitioners who may otherwise be sincere are sometimes forced to delude their customers because their customers show such a heartfelt demand for it.

Often on the gynaecology wards there is a form of consensus that 'customer care' is the order of the day and a sort of hierarchy of humour is created with nurses competing for the top position. A Staff Nurse explains:

> Sometimes we all decide we are going to give the 'customers' what they deserve. Only the best! It's a sort of silent agreement, it's never discussed. An incident will occur and put us in the mood for having a laugh and then we all get on with things – you know. Like a patient will ask for a clean sheet and we will tell her that the Trust only allocates one sheet to each patient per week and that we are not allowed to go beyond that. Some patients get really bolshy, but with the Trust not us. We are always short of pillows and one time we told them that the hospital had a mysterious 'pillow pincher'. I mean we really said that tongue in cheek but a lot still believed us – actually it might be true because I can't imagine where all the pillows go!

The overplayed performances of the nurses for the benefit of demanding customers, actually shows their disregard for the patient as 'customer'. Their use of an ironic humour in this way shows a 'subtle aggressiveness', which allows them to 'seize and hold the initiative in the service relation' (Goffman, 1959: 22).

'Don't Let The Bastards Get You Down'

The use of humour obviously helps the nurses release tension and shows their resistance to many of the demands made of them. However, on some days the atmosphere on the wards reflects the nurses' feelings of anger. The usual flashes of humour are absent and nurses appear demoralised and de-motivated. The ward seems almost disabled without the nurses' usual humour, whether 'applied' or 'pure'. One such day occurred when the nurses had been informed that, due to a 'customer' complaint concerning drinking cups of tea at the nurses' station in the ward, they were no longer to be allowed to have a drink whilst on the ward. The reasons given were that it created the wrong image and did not make the ward look 'customer focused'. The nurses were angry because on busy days it often proves difficult for them to take an official break and they then rely on drinking their 'brew' as they work.

> Everyone is upset today. It's like we spend all our time hanging around doing nothing but having a brew. We go without breaks and this is all the thanks we get. I'm really mad about this, we all are. It's just not on. Have you not noticed that it's not the same on here today? Everyone's got long faces. Management will lose out you know. They keep knocking us back and look at the state of everyone in here. They're not in the right frame of mind to deliver a 'quality' service are they? Of course we will still deliver patient care but patients aren't getting the best of us.

The next day however, a particular group of long serving nurses were on the same shift and had obviously made a conscious decision to 'get back to normal' and engage in playful humour. At first they appeared to have to work on their performances a little in order to overcome the previous day's feelings of disappointment, but humour is contagious (Astedt-Kurki and Liukkonnen, 1994) and through 'deep acting' (Hochschild, 1983) the nurses were able to not only alter their outward performance but also their inner feelings. It was not long before the atmosphere on the ward had visibly lightened. One nurse notes how they have always worked together in this way and that their 'down' times are never prolonged:

> I couldn't stand anymore of that. We have to work and get on with things, brews or no brews, so we might as well get on with it. You can't let the bastards get you down can you? Otherwise they have won and taken all the good bits out of the job. They can tell us 'do this' and 'don't do that' but they will never be able to tell us exactly how to behave or how to do our job. Why should they? We are bloody good nurses and they know that, there's a limit to how far they will go. Nursing will always belong to us and I'm just getting on with it the best way I know how.

On occasions such as these, when the staff rota works out that 'the old gang' are together on the same shift, the atmosphere on the ward is dramatically different. The nurses appear to have the confidence in each other to be able to offer their resistance in more open ways. The banter is that much more risqué, the withdrawal from management prescription is that much more obvious, and the noise levels are that much higher. Their interaction with each other, and even with patients, is bold and loud as they reassert their collective identity.

Conclusion

The examples of the use of humour presented in this chapter show how the nurses on the gynaecology unit, in the face of increasing demands, manage to continue to find spaces where they can disregard professional and organisational display rules. Using game playing and a particular brand of humour, they register resistance to the patriarchal structures that bestow superior status to doctors and also to the enterprise culture rhetoric that has reinvented patients as customers. But they also use these spaces quite simply to 'have a laugh' and it is a laughter that serves to bind their occupational community ever more firmly together and to deter possible threats to the well-being of its members.

This is not to say that the use of humour by nurses is detrimental to the interests of management. Nurses may express dissatisfaction with their work but rarely is it accompanied by 'disaffected behaviour' (Ackroyd, 1993). Despite offerings of resistance the nurses on the gynaecology unit have a fierce pride in their status as health care professionals and would do nothing that would directly affect patient care. On the contrary, despite much of its veiled meaning, the ability of nurses to overcome times of emotional stress with humorous episodes can actually work in the hospital's favour. The use of play and laughter allows nurses to re-define a stressful situation (Goffman, 1961) and carry on and do their job. Nevertheless, it is the unwillingness of nurses to 'misbehave' in ways that would tarnish their status as health care professionals that makes humour such an effective form of resistance. Isolated incidents such as those presented in this chapter do little to alter the abiding nature of the hierarchically ordered relationship between doctors and nurses, reverse the 'marketisation' of public services or halt the ever increasing managerialist ethos. They do, however, open up opportunities for voices of dissent to be heard. At times the voices may be quieter than others but there is little doubt, as the junior doctor above notes, that nurses do determine their own ground rules of interaction in opposition to the established norms. Nurses use humour to deliberately upset the 'ritual game' of hierarchically ordered encounters, thus creating interpretative loose ends. Negotiations must take place to re-establish order and as Strauss et al (1973) note 'negotiations breed further negotiations' allowing change to be instituted. Such is the effectiveness of humour as a mode of resistance that nurses successfully challenge existing social forms whilst appearing to be enjoying 'a bit of a laugh'.

References

Ackroyd, S. (1993), 'Towards an Understanding of Nurses' Attachment to their Work: Morale Amongst Nurses in an Acute Hospital', *Journal of Advances in Health and Nursing Care*, 2: 23-45.

Ackroyd, S. and Crowdy, P. (1990), 'Can Culture be Managed? Working with "Raw" Material: The Case of the English Slaughtermen', *Personnel Review*, 19(5): 3-13.

Ackroyd, S. and Thompson, P. (1999), *Organizational (Mis)Behaviour*, Sage: London.

Ashforth, B. and Humphrey, R. (1995), 'Emotion in the Workplace: A Reappraisal', *Human Relations*, 48(2): 97-125.

Astedt-Kurki, P. and Liukkonnen, A. (1994), 'Humour in Nursing Care', *Journal of Advanced Nursing*, 20: 183-88.

Barsoux, J. (1993), *Funny Business: Humour, Management and Business Culture*, Cassell: New York.

Bolton, S. (2000), 'Who Cares? Offering Emotion Work as a 'Gift' in the Nursing Labour Process', *Journal of Advanced Nursing*, 32(3): 580-86.

Burawoy, M. (1979), *Manufacturing Consent: Changes in the Labour Process under Monopoly Capitalism*, University of Chicago Press: Chicago.

Carlisle, D. (1990), 'Comic Relief', *Nursing Times*, 86 (19th September): 38.

Collinson, D. (1988), 'Engineering Humour: Masculinity, Joking and Conflict in Shop Floor Relations, *Organization Studies*, 9(2): 181-99.

Coser, R. (1962), *Life in the Ward*, Michigan State University Press: Michigan.

Du Gay, P. and Salaman, G. (1992), 'The Cult(ure) of the Customer', *Journal of Management Studies*, 29(5): 615-33.

Duncan, W. and Feisal, J. (1989), 'No Laughing Matter: Patterns of Humour in the Workplace', *Organisational Dynamics*, 17(4): 18-30.

Douglas, M. (1975), *Implicit Meanings*, Routledge: London.

Emerson, J. (1973), 'Negotiating the Serious Import of Humour', in A. Birenbaum and E. Sagarin (eds) *People in Places: The Sociology of the Familiar*, Nelson: New York.

Fine, G. A. (1988), 'Letting Off Steam? Redefining a Restaurant's Work Environment', in M. Jones, M. Moore, and R. Snyder (eds), *Inside Organizations: Understanding the Human Dimension*, Sage Publications: Newbury Park.

Fox, S. (1990), 'The Ethnography of Humour and the Problem of Social Reality', *Sociology*, 24, 3: 431-46.

Goffman, E. (1959), *The Presentation of Self in Everyday Life*, Penguin Books: London.

Goffman, E. (1961), *Encounters*, The Bobbs-Merrill Company Ltd: New York.

Goffman, E. (1967), *Interaction Ritual: Essays in Face-To-Face Behaviour*, Aldine Publishing Company: Chicago.

Griffiths, L. (1998), 'Humour as Resistance to Professional Dominance in Community Mental Health Teams', *Sociology of Health and Illness*, 20(6): 874-95.

Harries, G. (1995), 'Use of Humour in Patient Care', *British Journal of Nursing*, 4(17: 984-86.

Hochschild, A. (1983), *The Managed Heart: Commercialization of Human Feeling*, University of California Press: Berkeley.

Lawler, J. (1991), *Behind the Screens: Nursing, Somology, and the Problem of the Body*, Churchill Livingstone: Melbourne.

Linstead, S. (1985), 'Jokers Wild: The Importance of Humour and the Maintenance of Organisational Culture', *Sociological Review*, 33(4): 741-67.

Mallett, J. (1993), 'Use of Humour and Laughter in Patient Care', *British Journal of Nursing*, 2(3): 172-75.

Meerabeau, L. and Page, S. (1998), 'Emotion Management and Cardiopulmonary Resuscitation in Nursing' in G. Bendelow and S. Williams (eds), *Emotion in Social Life*, Routledge: London.

Mulkay, M. (1988), *On Humour: Its Nature and its Place in Modern Society*, Polity Press: Cambridge.

Peelo, M., Francis, B. and Soothill, K. (1996), 'NHS Nursing: Vocation, Career or Just a Job', in K. Soothill, C. Henry and K. Kendrick, K. (eds), *Themes and Perspectives in Nursing*, Chapman and Hall: London.

Roy, D.F. (1973), 'Banana Time: Job Satisfaction and Informal Interaction', in G. Salaman and K. Thompson (eds), *People and Organisations*, Longman: London.

Salvage, J. (1985), *The Politics of Nursing*, Heinemann Nursing: London.

Strauss, A., Schatzman, L., Ehrlich, D., Bucher, R. and Sabshin, M. (1973), 'The Hospital and its Negotiated Order', in E. Freidson (ed), *The Hospital in Modern Society*, The Free Press: New York.

Strauss, A., Fagerhaugh, S., Suczek, B. and Wiener, C. (1982), 'Sentimental Work in the Technologized Hospital', *Sociology of Health and Illness*, 4(3): 255-78.

Sumners, A.D. (1990), Professional Nurses' Attitudes Towards Humour, *Journal of Advanced Nursing*, 15, 196-200.

Thompson, P. and Bannon, E. (1985), *Working the System*, Pluto Press: London.

Warner, U. (1984), The Serious Import of Humour in Health Visiting, *Journal of Advanced Nursing*, 9, 83-7.

Westwood, S. (1984), *All Day Every Day*, Pluto Press: London.

PART V

THE LIMITS OF NEW PUBLIC MANAGEMENT

Chapter 13

Uses and Limitations of Performance Measurement in the Civil Service: An Assessment from the Singapore and New Zealand Experiences

David Seth Jones

Introduction

From the late 1980s, the governments of New Zealand and Singapore embarked upon major public sector reforms in the wake of widespread changes that were being implemented in the public sector in Britain. These reforms as they were applied to the core public sector (the public service in New Zealand, comprising ministries and departments, and the civil service in Singapore consisting of ministries sub-divided into departments) and other organisations responsible for public services, were broadly shaped by the principles of 'managerialism' or New Public Management (NPM). They entailed importing into these organisations business practices associated with the private sector. The 'managerialist' reforms in both countries to a certain extent followed a similar path although in some respects they were divergent.

At the heart of both sets of reforms was performance measurement. It was recognised that reforming the civil service or public service along 'managerialist' lines required accurate, precise and relevant measurement of the quantity, quality, efficiency and effectiveness of public services and programmes. Much work has been undertaken in both countries on how best this can be done. Departments in the civil service in Singapore and the public service in New Zealand have developed a range of performance indicators for the key areas of performance measurement and have, in many cases, set yearly targets based on those indicators. As a measure of the commitment to performance measurement, and typical of many other departments in New Zealand, the Department of Corrections in New Zealand now employees about 100 output quantity and quality indicators (DCNZ,[1] 2001). It was also recognised that for performance measurement and target setting to be an effective spur to performance, it was necessary to concomitantly introduce incentives to achieve better performance.

The first part of the chapter considers, in light of the reforms in New Zealand and Singapore, the main types of performance measurement used, the arrangements under which performance measurement has been undertaken, and the incentives introduced within these arrangements to spur better performance. The second part discusses the limitations and drawbacks of performance measurement as a means for evaluating the work of the civil service or public service, which has become evident in the two countries.

Types and Levels of Performance Measurement

In response to the 'managerialist' reforms, departments in both New Zealand and Singapore have been required to greatly expand the number of performance indicators and targets, and to systematically evaluate their results. The indicators and targets cover the entire spectrum of performance. They measure: (a) output quantity or volume; (b) output quality; (c) efficiency; (d) outcomes or effectiveness (Swiss, 1991: 139-45; Barrow, 1990; Lewis and Jones, 1990).

Output quantity indicators often measure the number of times a key definable activity is undertaken (e.g. number of inspections conducted), or how many people to whom the service has applied (e.g. the number of offenders in a rehabilitation centre or patients attending a government clinic) (Swiss, 1990: 139-43; DCNZ, 2001: 52; BDS[2], 1998a: 2; MOFS, 2001: 309). In Singapore this is done often on a standardised basis, e.g. number of safety inspections per 100 industrial premises (Jones, 1999: 78-83).

Increasingly, in New Zealand and Singapore, departments have developed indicators, which measure specifically the quality or standard of public services. Signifying the commitment to service quality in Singapore has been the employment of quality service managers in departments and the creation of the Service Improvement Unit in the Prime Minister's Office to advise departments on how to upgrade their standards of service (Ibrahim 1996: 32). Widely used service quality indicators in both countries are those which measure timeliness and promptness in service delivery, accuracy in processing applications and claims and supplying information, and ratings in customer feedback questionnaires (DCNZ, 2001: 37-44; BDS, 1998a: 2; BDS, 1998b; Chua, 1996a: 18; Straits Times, 1995: 1).

Performance measurement may also take into account how efficiently resources are managed. The main indicators of efficiency in the Singapore civil service are, of course, costs per unit of output or service; examples being cost per planning proposal vetted and cost per industrial inspection undertaken by the Pollution Control Department in Singapore (BDS, 1998a: 2; MOFS, 2001: 249). In some cases, the cost units are the persons who are the beneficiaries or recipients of a service. Another gauge of cost efficiency which is used in New Zealand, as well as Singapore, for revenue generating services, are cost recovery ratios.

In addition, departments in both New Zealand and Singapore have been encouraged to develop indicators, which go further than measure outputs and efficiency, and measure ultimate outcomes, showing how effective programmes are in achieving their goals (BDS, 1998a: 2; Swiss, 1991: 143-5; Chua, 1991; Carter, 1991: 90). Such outcome measures provide the strategic goals of a department, but require often the collection of an extensive range of data on social and economic conditions (Kibblewhite, 2000: 4). For example, in New Zealand and Singapore, the effectiveness of industrial safety programmes is determined through the frequency of industrial accidents and the severity of those accidents (measured by number of working hours lost in consequence) (MOFS, 2001: 430; DLNZ,[3] 2001: 28). A number of performance indicators in the two countries measure both outputs (either quantity or quality) and outcomes at the same time. In such cases, the quantity or quality of a service automatically determines how effective it is. An example of a dual indicator measuring both output quality and outcome effectiveness adopted by the Prisons Service in Singapore and the Department of Corrections in New Zealand is the incidence of recidivism amongst released prisoners (DCNZ, 2001: 57-67).

Uses of Performance Measurement in New Zealand and Singapore

Performance Contracts in New Zealand

Performance measurement is a central aspect of the reform of the core public sector in New Zealand. It is especially important in the contractual arrangements through which departments are held accountable for their performance. One of these is the annual purchase agreement (sometimes called the purchase contract) between a department and the responsible minister. Under it, the department gives an undertaking each year to deliver a pre-specified (ex ante) quantity and quality of outputs to meet the performance outcomes set by the minister. Related outputs are presented as part of an output class or programme, with each class sub-divided into specific outputs. In return, the minister provides a budget approved by parliament to enable those outputs to be delivered. In so doing the minister is in effect acting as a purchaser of the outputs on behalf of parliament and the taxpayer. The purchase agreement also includes the scheduling of the delivery of the outputs, the system for monitoring performance and the gathering and verifying of results, procedures for amending and updating the agreement if that is necessary during the year, and consideration of the possible risks that may impair the accomplishment of targets. While a good deal of time and preparation is required in drafting a purchase agreement, it can only be finalised after the departmental estimates have been passed by parliament (Palmer and Palmer, 1997: 81-2, 112-14; Schick, 1996: 7-8; Boston, Martin, Pallot and Walsh, 1996: 274-8). In parallel with and overlapping the purchase agreement is the performance agreement drawn up each year between the chief executive of a department and the responsible minister. This agreement focuses specifically upon the responsibilities of the chief executive, including performance targets, for which he/she is held personally accountable (Boston et al, 1996: 110-14; Scott, 1996: 32-6).

The financial and output performance of a department in New Zealand is subject to assessment from a number of quarters. These include the Office of the Controller and Auditor-General and the Finance and Expenditure Committee of Parliament. They undertake a value-for-money audit of each department focusing upon possible inefficiency and waste in the spending of money, as well as assessing the outputs accomplished. (Palmer and Palmer, 1997: 101, 104-7; Boston et al, 1996: 303). In addition, the State Services Commission assesses the performance of departments. It does so not just through the performance results, but also through feedback received from a range of personnel in both the government and the public service, including a self-assessment by the chief executives themselves (Boston et al, 1996: 114-17; Scott, 1996: 32).

Budgeting For Results and Output Plans in Singapore

Performance measurement has also become a salient aspect of public management in Singapore through the introduction in 1996 of a new system of budgetary management known as Budgeting For Results (BFR). Under BFR, departments and other government funded cost centres have been converted into what are termed as autonomous agencies. Autonomous agencies providing services which are readily measurable in terms of quantity of output, known as piece-rate funded (PF) autonomous agencies or departments, are required each year to specify a range of output quantity targets with at least one for each of their programmes. This is done in their annual output plans (BDS, 1998a: 3; BDS, 1998b: 6-8; Lu, 1998; Koh, 1997: 1; Straits Times, 1997b: 25; Singapore Parliament, 1997: 494-5).

Having set the output targets, PF departments are then required in the output plan to estimate the expenditure in meeting those targets. This process involves determining the unit direct cost (known as the piece rate) of each output, which, as mentioned above, is the main measure of cost performance. The direct costs in providing a service, of course, vary according to the volume of output. In addition, the indirect costs to be incurred must be taken into account, such as utility charges, administrative overheads, and legal and other professional services. If it turns out that the unit costs incurred in a programme are consistently less than anticipated, resulting in substantial savings, then the department concerned may be required to lower its unit cost target with a resultant reduction in its budget allocation. The projected expenditure for each output comprises the volume of output multiplied by the unit direct cost, plus the indirect cost. The estimated expenditures for the various outputs of the department are then aggregated, and the sum total then determines its budget allocation (BDS, 1998a: 5; BDS, 1996: 2-3; Singapore Parliament, 1996: 787-90; Teo, 1996: 3; Chua, 1996a: 18; Chua, 1996b: 23).

Alongside their output volume measures, PF departments are required in their annual output plan to identify appropriate indicators of service quality and effectiveness, and to set goals and targets for them, as with the purchase agreement in New Zealand. This is to ensure that in pursuing high workloads, departments remain faithful to maintaining high standards of service and achieving the ultimate goals of their programmes. For timeliness and accuracy rates, and customer satisfaction scores, departments may, and often do, set their target score at between the 70 and 95 percentile within the chosen measure, rather than at 100 per cent (BDS, 1998a: 2). For example, one of the output quality targets of the Drainage Department of the Ministry of the Environment for FY 20001/02 was to process 90 per cent of plans to maintain or build drains with 14 days (MOFS, 2001: 247). Although important in assessing a department's performance, quality and outcome targets cannot directly determine budget allocations, which can only be linked with output volume targets. However, output quality results, but not outcomes, do determine if a department can retain any of its savings, as explained below (BDS, 1998b: 238; BDS, 1996: 2-3).

In return for their commitment to measure performance and meet pre-specified targets, PF departments enjoy substantial discretion in prioritising their programmes, apportioning financial and other resources, and delivering services. Their autonomy also includes powers to approve their own tenders, purchase equipment, hire their own staff except at the most senior level, extend their operating hours and widen their range of services (BDS, 1998a: 1; Singapore Parliament, 1998: 542; BDS, 1997: 1, 21-31, 67-72; BDS, 1996: 2-3; Straits Times, 1997a: 30; Chuang, 1996. p.3).

For departments, known as macro-funded (MF) agencies, whose output volume is not readily commensurable, a different budget formula applies. In their case, the budget allocation is related to general economic performance (projected nominal GDP growth discounted by gains in national productivity) (BDS, 1998a: 5; BDS, 1996: 3). Although their output volume and workload cannot be quantified, MF departments are expected, in the same way as PF departments, to produce an output plan and in it to set service quality and effectiveness targets wherever possible. Even though they cannot directly determine budget allocation, service quality results, as in a PF department, may affect the right of an MF department to retain any savings, as will be discussed below. In return for their commitment to quality and outcome targets and goals, MF departments, like PF departments, enjoy a greater degree of autonomy in managing their programmes and resources (BDS, 1998a: 5; BDS, 1996: 3).

Incentives for Performance

Performance measurement, contractual agreements and output plans may not in themselves be a sufficient spur to improved performance. What may be needed in addition is a system of incentives providing rewards for better performance and entailing sanctions where performance has, without good reason, declined. Both New Zealand and Singapore have recognised the necessity for such and have implemented incentive arrangements. A key incentive common to both countries is the linking of the budget allocation of a department to the output targets, so that funds given are in accordance with the cost requirements of those targets. In order to secure a bigger budget, a department must set and achieve higher output targets. Setting or achieving lower targets will result in a lower budget allocation.

In New Zealand, an incentive to achieve good output results which directly affects chief executives and their colleagues, is the possibility otherwise of public exposure and embarrassment through the system of open reporting and annual parliamentary scrutiny referred to above, which may highlight sub-standard performance (Palmer and Palmer, 1997: 99-101, 104). Another incentive in New Zealand is the link between the performance of a department and the future career and remuneration of chief executives who are hired on five-year contracts.

Performance will determine whether they will be given an extension of their contracts (Boston et al, 1996: 105-6, 117-20). Another inducement for chief executives to achieve higher performance is financial rewards such as merit increments and bonuses in the case of better than expected departmental performance (SSCNZ,[4] 1998; SSCNZ, 2001: 25, 26, 64-5, 67; Boston et al, 1996: 105, 116-19).

In Singapore, as well as the linking of budgets to outputs, an important incentive for better performance under the BFR is that of surplus retention. Instead of returning an unspent budget allocation to the consolidated fund, PF departments may retain part of it, providing they meet 85 per cent of output volume and output quality targets. MF departments may similarly retain part of any savings, provided they meet 85 per cent of output quality targets. In either case, outcome targets are not included (Jones, 1998: 296; Singh, 1998; BDS, 1998a: 7; BDS, 1996: 3; Teo, 1996: 3). Surplus retention reduces the necessity for departments to indulge in unwarranted expenditure in a year-end spending spree, and provides them with a strong incentive to make efficiency savings and reduce unit costs as well as meet output volume and quality targets under the 85 per cent rule (BDS, 1998a: 7; BDS, 1996: 3; Singapore Parliament, 1996: 787-90; Straits Times, 1997b: 27).

Limitations and Drawbacks of Performance Measurement

In both New Zealand and Singapore, performance measurement and evaluation have encountered certain limitations and drawbacks. In some cases the problems that have arisen are inherent within performance measurement of public services *per se*, but others are avoidable with a better system of performance measurement. The problems may be categorised as follows: shortcomings in measurement and interpretation, problems of attribution, lack of balance in the range of indicators, and detrimental effects of performance measurement upon the job roles and attitudes of public servants.

Measurement and Interpretation

When performance measurement is undertaken, it is necessary that measurements are precise, accurate, and where possible quantifiable. The main drawback with performance measurement in the public services, as experienced in New Zealand and Singapore (as well as in other countries), is that many of the outputs and outcomes of public services are not commensurable with precision and accuracy resulting in vague and overly general measures. These include certain line services as well as the core staff services of personnel administration, accounting, legal services, and policy advice.

An example of a vague or overly general indicator in Singapore is an output quality indicator used by the Singapore Meteorological Service measuring the percentage of weather forecasts that are 'accurate' (MOFS, 2001: 98). This begs the question: what is an accurate weather forecast. In the New Zealand public service similarly vague and subjective criteria are used in part to assess the quality of information services. Typical are the reports on prisoners submitted by the Department of Corrections to the courts, District Prison Boards and Parole Boards. Amongst the criteria are whether the reports were 'concise, logical and grammatically correct', included 'all relevant and appropriate information', contained information that was 'well-documented and verified', provided 'a clear statement of recommendations for further intervention', and were of a standard that 'complies with the Code of Ethics of the New Zealand Psychological Society' (DCNZ, 2001: 38, 43). The problem is that such criteria are largely imprecise, ill defined, and subjective, and defy anything like objective measurement.

A further concern drawn from the New Zealand and Singapore experiences is the use of indicators based on non-uniform units of measurement. This often happens when the outputs in question are difficult to measure, making it difficult to interpret the results. An example is the measurement of output quantity for ministerial services used in the New Zealand public service. This is done by enumerating the numbers of replies drafted by public servants to letters sent to ministers, and to requests from ministers themselves for information. Also included is the number of answers drafted by public servants for ministers in reply to parliamentary questions. In the financial year 2000/01, officials in the Ministry of Agriculture and Forestry in New Zealand with responsibility for ministerial support drafted 1041 letters in reply to correspondence sent to the minister (the target was 1000-1400 letters) and 308 answers to parliamentary questions (the target was 170 questions) (MAFNZ,[5] 2001: 62-3). The problem is that the units of measurement are of course far from uniform. Such letters or replies may vary a great deal in length and detail. In addition, whilst some may be readily answered with available information, others may only be answered after a lengthy process of fact finding. Thus it is difficult to gain even a rough appreciation of how much work was involved and working hours spent.

A further problem of interpretation has arisen in the case of the outcome results of certain enforcement activities. A key outcome indicator for all types of enforcement work is the extent of compliance to laws and regulations measured by the frequency of violations. If most violations are identified and reported, then their frequency is an accurate gauge of compliance. Where offences committed cause immediate or direct harm to others, they are likely to be reported by the victim or another concerned individual. However, where violations do not often cause immediate or conspicuous harm to others, what may be termed 'victimless' offences, they may remain unreported and may only be identified by surveillance activities of the enforcement department. Examples are breaches of laws and regulations in such areas as environmental protection, public health, food safety, agriculture and industrial safety. If recorded offences rise, this may indicate more vigilant surveillance rather than declining compliance. If they fall, the reverse could be true. For example, in Singapore recorded infringements of industrial safety regulations dropped markedly from 90 infringements per 100 industrial establishments in 1987 to 39 in 1998. Similar declines occurred in the violations of pollution and food safety regulations (Jones, 1999: 107-10). However, over the same period the degree of surveillance also declined; so the figures may not necessarily indicate that the extent of compliance was increasing. In the case of the enforcement programme in Singapore to curb Aedes mosquito breeding, the number of violations of the relevant regulations over the last ten years has increased but the conclusion that compliance has declined has to be qualified by the extent to which surveillance has been stepped up (Jones, 1999: 120). Such difficulties of interpretation would, of course, be encountered in similar enforcement programmes in other countries.

Where indicators are too general, vague and subjective or for which the results are difficult to interpret, the assessment itself becomes subjective, making it easier for departments to claim that targets and goals were achieved, and less easy for external assessors to prove otherwise. This perhaps explains in part the high success rate claimed by most departments in New Zealand in recent years in achieving the goals and targets set. Adding to the success is the possibility that targets are perhaps set in such a way as to ensure that they can be readily achieved, especially if the purchasing minister has only a limited appreciation of what a department's delivery potential is. It may thus be necessary to evaluate with some caution performance results indicating a high success rate.

Attribution

In two aspects of performance measurement, the question arises about how much the results can be attributed to the department in question. Firstly, outcome measurement may be hampered by the fact that that they are influenced by a range of factors often outside the control of a department (Kibblewhite, 2000: 7; Schick, 1996: 2). An example is the Pollution Control Department in Singapore. A key indicator of its effectiveness is the pollutant standards index, which measures air quality. Its target in 1997 was to achieve an index reading of 50 or less in 60 per cent of the days of that year. As it turned out, this reading was only recorded in 48 per cent of the days. An important reason why it fell short of this target was the extensive forest fires in neighboring Indonesia during 1997, which caused widespread air pollution throughout Southeast Asia (MOFS, 1998: 269; BDS, 1998a: 2; MENVS,[6] 1998: 8). Since then, air pollution resulting from forest burning in Indonesia has from time to time recurred although to a much less serious extent. Thus, the outcome observed may not always be attributed to and so be indicative of the effectiveness of the service provided. It should be noted that the Pollution Control Department has attempted to refine its outcome assessment by giving greater weight to the pollution standards index at times of the year when the pollution from Indonesia is minimal.

The second area of performance measurement where attribution must be qualified are the volume outputs for demand driven services, which are often beyond the control of the department concerned. Examples in Singapore are the output of the schools programme of the Ministry of Education, and the workload of both the Registration Department dealing with the registration of births and deaths, and the Registry of Marriages, which are all influenced by demographic and social changes. In such cases, increases or decreases in demand outside the department's control are the more salient determinants of outputs. In some cases, it may even be difficult to make predictions of the demand over the forthcoming year and so set appropriate targets. It is a well-known fact that amongst the Chinese population in Singapore marriages and births can be affected by whether a particular year within the Chinese tradition is auspicious. All this limits the usefulness of such volume output measures in assessing the performance of the department (BDS, 1998a: 2).

Lack of Balance in the Range of Indicators Used

In both New Zealand and Singapore, certain aspects of performance measurement have not been adequately developed, leading to noticeable imbalances in the range of indicators used. In both countries, as in other countries which have adopted comprehensive systems of performance measurement, important elements in service delivery such as fairness, impartiality, effective problem-solving, and appropriate exercise of discretion, which are not measurable, are given little consideration in output measurement and assessment and yet are vital in many services, such as housing, welfare, and enforcement programmes (Gregory, 2000: 8-9; Kibblewhite, 2000: 6-7; SSCNZ, 1999a: 5, 9, 22). Even in inspection and scientific testing, little consideration is given to the non-measurable aspects of these tasks such as the thoroughness, rigour and professionalism with which they have been undertaken.

In Singapore, whilst output quantity and efficiency indicators are numerous, the range of the quality indicators is quite small. Most of them are generic, measuring timeliness, client or customer satisfaction and in some cases accuracy of information, as already mentioned, with only a few which are service specific indicators. By contrast in New Zealand much work has gone into developing service specific quality measures of varying degrees of precision, but there has been surprisingly little priority given by comparison with Singapore to measuring efficiency through unit output costs and output costs as percentages of total expenditure within a department.

In both countries the main imbalance is between the output and outcome indicators. In New Zealand, this has given rise to a significant critique of its model of public management amongst both local public service leaders and academics. Despite the priority given to determining output quantity and quality, outcome specification and assessment remain weak, demonstrated by the lack of a sufficient range of specific outcomes indicators commensurate with the wide range of outputs that are built into performance and purchase agreements. Outcomes where they are stated, with certain exceptions, tend to be couched in such broad terms as to become almost truisms, and are applied in a one peg fits all manner to a wide ambit of outputs or output classes in the same department. The problem is that when outcome indicators are stated in broad all-encompassing terms it is difficult to determine what are precisely the desired outcomes to be measured and how much of each has been achieved. This makes it doubly difficult to then evaluate output performance, since the key criterion for the appraisal of an output is whether it contributes to a desired outcome, and if it has not, whether the failure is due to the nature of the service itself, or to the quantity or quality of the output (Gregory, 2000: 7-8; Gill, 2000: 5-6, 8; Gregory, 2000: 7-8; Kibblewhite, 2000: 2, 6, 11;

Scott, 2000; CAGNZ,[7] 2002: 54, 59, 61-2; SSCNZ, 2001: 10; SSCNZ, 1999a: 21; SSCNZ, 1999b: 2-10).

This applies also to outputs from policy advice to ministers as indicated in the results of a survey by the New Zealand State Services Commission in 1998/99, showing that only 7 per cent of policy proposals were subject to ex-post review based on outcome impact. Furthermore, since ministers are primarily responsible for policy outcomes, the lack of sufficient outcome assessment makes it difficult to evaluate their performance, so weakening their accountability. Indeed it has been suggested that ministers are not particularly forthcoming in clarifying outcomes and conveying them to chief executives (Gill, 2000: 5-6, 8; Scott, 2000; SSCNZ, 1999b: 4-5).

The limitations of outcome specification and measurement are illustrated by the Ministry of Agriculture in New Zealand. The outcomes stated for many of its programmes are to contribute to strong economic growth, promote external linkages, and to protect and enhance the environment. Whilst these are legitimate overall goals of the ministry, as they stand they do not provide the basis for outcome measurement. More useful measure of outcomes would be the growth in agricultural production and exports, gains in agricultural productivity, the creation of new agricultural businesses and adoption of new technologies, and the reduction in the amount of soil erosion, or pollution of water courses. For some if not all of these outcomes, specific and even quantifiable measurement may be possible and quantifiable targets could be set (MAFNZ, 2001: 43-120).

In Singapore too there is scope for improvement in measuring outcomes and making departments accountable for them. General goals are set for each ministry, which in some cases are reasonably informative and indicate the basic framework of policy. Others though are so broad as to be simply self-evident and of little informative value. Only in a few departments and programmes are specific and quantifiable outcomes stated. Amongst these are the Department of Occupational Safety (frequency and severity of industrial accidents), the Division of Environmental Health in the Ministry of the Environment (incidence of environmentally related diseases) and the Pollution Control Department (indices of pollution in the atmosphere, water courses and coastal waters). However, even for such outcomes, accountability for the results achieved is not made explicit (MOFS, 2001: 240, 249, 430).

The reasons for the imbalance are not hard to find. Outcomes are often not readily commensurable, and even more difficult to quantify. As already mentioned many factors influence outcomes outside the control of the programme concerned, so creating in particular an obvious aversion to setting outcome targets and be held to account for achieving them. In addition, developing outcome indicators and measuring outcome performance requires that much more information be gathered and detailed analysis be undertaken concerning social, economic and other trends. However, the obstacles are not insurmountable. Whilst it may be impossible to identify a specific outcome for some public services, for others it is possible. Moreover, regardless of whether or not appropriate outcome targets can be set, relevant and detailed ex post data may be gathered to signify outcome performance, allowing informative judgements to be made on the effectiveness of output programmes (Gill, 2000: 13-14; Kibblewhite, 2000: 4).

Effects upon the Job Roles and Attitudes of Public Servants

From the New Zealand and Singapore examples, the performance measurement process increases the workload for senior managers in departments, which now must include developing indicators, setting targets, compiling statistics, and analysing and presenting those statistics for the purpose of assessment. This may lead to work overload and a significant diversion from the mainstream tasks which managers are required to carry out. Adding to the workload effects of performance measurement is the encouragement it gives to expand output activities regardless of how necessary or worthwhile they may be. In simple terms, the more output quantity produced the better the organisation appears in its performance assessment. If the additional output is not necessary, then it simply amounts to a waste of resources. An example is the increases in surveillance work in various enforcement programmes in Singapore in the late 1990s, possibly in response to performance measurement under Budgeting For Results (Jones, 1999: 120-1).

Likewise in New Zealand it has been suggested that outputs have become ends in themselves, resulting in the desire to accomplish or exceed targets without consideration of the ultimate benefits. It has been argued that regard for targets as ends in themselves, especially when they are written into formal contracts or plans, is akin to the conformity to rules characteristic of traditional bureaucracy with the same effect, viz. goal displacement – consequences which ironically new public management was intended to overcome (Gregory, 2000: 3-10; SSCNZ, 1999a: 20).

In addition, output measurement of policy advice and ministerial services in ministries and departments in New Zealand may have altered the relationship between ministers and senior public servants, especially chief executives, since the quality of the advice and services provided are measured by their acceptability to the minister. For example, in the Ministry of Agriculture and Forestry the measure of the quality of the policy advice is that it be 'to the satisfaction of the Minister as assessed by a bi-annual questionnaire.' (MAFNZ, 2001: 48). In replies to letters to the minister, the quality service target is that '95 per cent are acceptable for the Minister's signature without amendment' (MAFNZ, 2001: 62-3). The results show that in recent years nearly all the quality service targets for policy advice and ministerial services across a range of ministries and departments based on acceptability to the minister were accomplished. This is not surprising since the measures probably encourage public servants to give advice and provide briefings and answers that suit the political and party interests of ministers. This could undermine their traditional and important role as sources of impartial and independent advice.

An additional concern that has emerged in New Zealand is that performance measurement and other aspects of the new public management model may reduce the possibility for coordination between different departments with related or overlapping functions. Such coordination may be perceived as diverting the department from accomplishing its own particular output targets. Moreover, since the model treats departments as separate entities subject to different agreements and encourages them to have regard for their own interests, the upshot has been a m ore fragmented public service lacking the unified ethos of service and commitment that it previously enjoyed (Gregory, 2000: 20; Gill, 2000: 6-7, 10; Kibblewhite, 2000: 7-9, 12).

Conclusion

Performance measurement has conferred significant benefits upon the public service in New Zealand and the civil service in Singapore. Public service managers have a more focused understanding of the work their departments are required to undertake, and the levels of performance their departments are expected to achieve. It also provides more detailed information of what has been achieved throughout the financial year. This is a step forward in improving accountability and transparency in the public services of both countries.

However, offsetting these gains are major drawbacks in performance measurement, which have been encountered in New Zealand and Singapore, as indicated above. Not least of these are the misleading results when attempts are made to measure non-commensurable activities (especially if measurement entails quantification), and the lack of comprehensive and informative outcome assessment. However, two dilemmas arise: whilst outcome assessment is essential to the improvement of performance measurement many outcomes are not exclusively attributable to a department or programme. In addition, outputs which are difficult to measure are often a vital aspect of a public service. In such cases, it is preferable to undertake a detailed qualitative analysis of the relevant evidence, which may enable informative judgements to be made on how well a service has been provided.

Notes

1   DCNZ in the in-text citations refers to the Department of Corrections, New Zealand.
2   BDS in the in-text citations refers to the Budget Division, Ministry of Finance, Singapore; MOFS in the in-text citations refers to the Ministry of Finance, Singapore.
3   DLNZ in the in-text citations refers to the Department of Labour, New Zealand.
4   SSCNZ in the in-text citations refers to the State Services Commission in New Zealand.
5   MAFNZ in the in-text citations refers to the Ministry of Agriculture and Forestry, New Zealand.
6   MENVS in the in-text citation refers to the Ministry of the Environment, Singapore.
7   CAGNZ in the in-text citations refers to the Controller and Auditor General, New Zealand.

References

Barrow, M. (1990), 'Techniques of Efficiency Measurement in the Public Sector', in M. Cave, M. Cogan and R. Smith (eds), *Output and Performance Measurement in Government: The State of the Art*, Jessica Kingsley: London.

Boston, J., Martin, J., Pallot, J. and Walsh, P. (1996), *Public Management: the New Zealand Model*, Oxford University Press: Auckland.

Budget Division, Ministry of Finance, Singapore (1996), 'Budgeting For Results – Implementation Framework', *Budget Notes*, 2, Budget Division, Ministry of Finance: Singapore.

Budget Division, Ministry of Finance, Singapore (1997), *Autonomous Agencies: FY1996 Performance Review*, Ministry of Finance: Singapore.

Budget Division, Ministry of Finance, Singapore (1998a), *Budgeting For Results Manual for the Singapore Civil Service*, Ministry of Finance: Singapore.

Budget Division, Ministry of Finance, Singapore (1998b), *Autonomous Agencies: FY1997 Performance Review*, Ministry of Finance: Singapore.

Carter, N. (1991), 'Learning to Measure Performance: The Use of Indicators in Organizations', *Public Administration*, 69: 85-101.

Controller and Auditor-General, New Zealand (2002), *Report of the Controller and Auditor General: Reporting Public Sector Performance*, Audit Office: Wellington.

Chua, G.W. (1991), 'Management Accounting in the Civil Service', paper presented to conference, *Budget Management: the Next Lap*, Singapore.

Chua, L. H. (1996a), 'What New Buzzwords in the Civil Service Mean', *Straits Times*, 16 March, Singapore.

Chua, L.H. (1996b), 'Dr Hu on the Changing Role of Civil Servants', *Straits Times*, 5 March, Singapore.

Chuang, P.M. (1996), 'More Accountability for Public Sector Units', *Business Times*, 29 February, Singapore.

Department of Corrections(2001), *Department of Corrections Annual Report, 2000/01*, Department of Corrections: Wellington.

Department of Labour, New Zealand (2001), *Department of Labour Annual Report, 2000/01*, Department of Labour: Wellington, NZ.

Gill, D. (2000), 'The Grass is Always Greener on the Other Side of the Fence: NZ Experience with Public Management Reform', paper presented to workshop *New Zealand Public Management: Lessons Learned and Future Developments*, March 2000, Wellington.

Gregory, B. (2000), 'Getting Better and Feeling Worse? Public Sector Reform in New Zealand', paper presented to workshop, *New Zealand Public Management: Lessons Learned and Future Developments*, March 2000, Wellington.

Ibrahim, Z. (1996), 'Why the Public Service Push to Provide Quality Service', *Straits Times*, 6 May 1996, Singapore.

Jones, D. (1998), 'Recent Budgetary Reforms', *Journal of Public Budgeting, Accounting and Financial Management*, 10 (2): 279-310.

Jones, D. (1999), 'Changes in Surveillance in Regulatory Enforcement Programmes in Singapore', *Asian Journal of Political Science*, 7(2): 100-20.

Kibblewhite, A. (2000), 'Effectiveness: The Next Frontier', paper presented to workshop, *New Zealand Public Management: Lessons Learned and Future Developments*, March, Wellington.

Koh, B.S. (1997), 'Promise of Better Services to the Public', *Straits Times*, 9 April, Singapore.

Lewis, S. and Jones J. (1990), 'The Use of Output and Performance Measure in Government Departments', in M. Cave, M. Kogan and R. Smith (eds), *Output and Performance Measurement in Government: the State of the Art*, Jessica Kingsley: London.

Lu, C.Y. (1998), 'Putting Budgeting For Results Initiative into Action', address to *IQPC Conference: Performance Measures for Government: Changing the Way Public Sector Organizations Operate*, April, Singapore.

Ministry of Agriculture and Forestry, New Zealand (2001), *Annual Report of Ministry of Agriculture and Forestry, 2000/01*, Ministry of Agriculture and Forestry: Wellington.

Ministry of the Environment, Singapore (1998), *Ministry of the Environment Annual Report, 1997*, Ministry of the Environment: Singapore.

Ministry of Finance, Singapore (1998), *The Budget for the Financial Year 1998/99*, Cmd. 2, Ministry of Finance: Singapore.

Ministry of Finance, Singapore (2001), *The Budget for the Financial Year2001/02*, Cmd. 3, Ministry of Finance: Singapore.

Palmer, G. and Palmer, M. (1997), *Bridled Power: New Zealand Government under MMP* (3rd Edition), Oxford University Press: Auckland.

Schick, A. (1996), 'Spirit of Reform: Managing the New Zealand State Sector in a Time of Change', pt. 7, *Accounting For Results, Special Report*, State Services Commission: Wellington.

Scott, G. (1996), *Government Reform in New Zealand*, IMF: Washington.

Scott, G. (2000), 'Public Management in New Zealand: Learning from Experience', transcript of keynote address to workshop, *New Zealand Public Management: Lessons Learned and Future Developments*, March, Wellington.

Singapore Parliament (1996), *Parliamentary Debates: Official Report*, 65, Singapore Parliament: Singapore.

Singapore Parliament (1997), *Parliamentary Debates: Official Report*, 67, Singapore Parliament: Singapore.

Singapore Parliament (1998), *Parliamentary Debates: Official Report*, 68, Singapore Parliament: Singapore.

Singh, J. (1998), 'Public Sector Financial Management Reform in Singapore', address to *IQPC Conference: Performance Measures for Government: Changing the Way Public Sector Organizations Operate*, April, Singapore.

State Services Commission, Singapore (1998), *Annual Report of the State Services Commission, New Zealand, 1997/98*, Wellington: State Services Commission.

State Services Commission (1999a), *Improving Accountability: Setting the Scene*, Occasional Paper no.10, State Services Commission: Wellington.

State Services Commission, New Zealand (1999b), *Looping the Loop: Evaluating Outcomes and Other Risky Feats*, Occasional Paper no. 7, State Services Commission: Wellington.

State Services Commission, Singapore (2001), *Annual Report of the State Services Commission, New Zealand, 2000/01,* State Services Commission: Wellington.

Straits Times (1995), 'Reward for Civil Servants at Counters', Report, *Straits Times*, 25 July, Singapore.

Straits Times (1997a), 'Going Autonomous Results in More Efficient Service', Report, *Straits Times*, 9 April, Singapore.

Straits Times (1997b), 'Focus now is on Outputs rather than Inputs', Report, *Straits Times*, 13 April, Singapore.

Swiss, J. (1991), *Public Management Systems: Monitoring and Managing Government Performance*, Englewood Cliffs: Prentice-Hall.

Teo, A. (1996), 'It Pays for Government Departments to Meet or Exceed Targets', *Business Times*, 5 March, Singapore.

Chapter 14

Making a 'Success' Out of 'Failure': Darker Reflections on Private and Public Management

Tony Cutler

Introduction

The object of this paper is to revisit, hopefully in a distinctive way, a theme that will be familiar to students of New Public Management (NPM). This is the relationship between management in the public and private sectors. This relationship, at least in the countries that have embraced NPM (for an important survey of the different international experience in this regard see Pollitt and Bouckaert, 2000), is an asymmetric one. Whatever the more recent rhetoric in the British context, concerning 'partnership', the public sector has been cast in the junior role. The broad pattern, discussed in detail below, is that (at least postulated) private sector practice has been seen as the basis of recommended management practice in the public sector.

The importation of ideas, techniques and organisational structures from the private sector is related to another central feature of NPM. It is a discourse, which celebrates its success relative to previous approaches to the organisation of public services. As Pollitt and Bouckaert argue (2000:58), 'a good deal of the rhetoric associated with public management reform vividly contrasts the new (=good) with the old (=bad)'. Further they go on to point out that the 'old/bad' is often characterised as 'traditional bureaucracies' (ibid: 59). In turn such 'bureaucracies' can be defined by their isolation from private sector practices and 'related' perceived deficiencies such as 'lack of entrepreneurship'. Naturally then NPM discourse sees borrowing from the private sector as allowing the public sector access to the conditions of 'success' of the former.

It is in this respect that this paper seeks to be distinctive because it focuses on 'failure' and its consequences in the public and private sectors. The thesis advanced is that, in both sectors, 'failure' leads to pressures to change management teams and structures but *not* to abandon a belief in the efficacy of management. To express this effect in terms of a slogan the position could be characterised as, 'the managers have failed, long live management'.

Before discussing how the paper is set out and the thesis developed, it is necessary to elaborate on how the term 'failure' is used here. The definition used is deliberately 'crude' i.e. it takes either explicit targets adopted by government in the case of the public sector; or, in the case of the private sector, an approach to the assessment of corporate performance, 'shareholder value' (SV) (Williams, 2000) which, if by no means 'consensual', can be said to have played a major role in the US and British economies and, arguably, in major economies in continental Europe (see, for example, O'Sullivan, 2000 and Vitols, 2001 for different views of the impact of SV, in particular in Germany).

The adoption of such an approach to the definition of 'failure' invites an immediate objection. It can be plausibly argued that the targets by which 'failure' is defined are, themselves, highly problematic. In both private and public sectors the key targets can be argued to be both tendentious in that they, in effect, favour the interests of certain stakeholders over others; and dubious since they are susceptible to manipulation.

With respect to SV, for example, the tendentiousness derives from the corporate governance premise underlying the position, namely that companies ought to be run in the interests of shareholders. In more specific terms this has been given an operational form in the 'benchmark' that corporations should realise a target rate of return on capital. Such targets again can also be argued to exert negative pressures on terms and conditions of employment (to sustain profit levels by constraining the labour share of value added, see Froud et al, 2000a, but note their discussion of the distributional complexities of shareholder value) and thus threaten the interests of workers. Equally, such pressures provide an incentive to manipulate measured financial performance. These can refer to either 'side' of the rate of return formula. Thus earnings can be exaggerated and/or capital employed understated. Such practices, of course, have become of great topical interest given, amongst others, the Enron and Worldcom cases. At Enron, for example, misrepresentation of corporate performance involved questionable practices in shifting debt from the balance sheet of the corporation to 'special purpose entities' (Chaffin, Hill and Spiegel, 2002) which, inter alia, involved both understating capital investment and hiding liabilities for interest payments. In the case of WorldCom the central alleged misrepresentation was the excessive booking of operating expenses as capital expenditure thus allowing an inflated profit figure to be stated (Budden, 2002).

While SV targets are financial, analogous problems can be discerned with respect to major public sector non-financial targets. For example, a target with a high political profile concerns hospital in-patient waiting lists. Thus the Labour government elected in 1997 committed itself to reducing such waiting lists by 100,000 (National Audit Office, 2001a: 11). As with shareholder value such targets can be claimed to have tendentious effects on stakeholder interests. Thus an emphasis on the reduction of in-patient waiting lists gives an implicit (and, arguably unjustified) priority to elective hospital treatment over other health priorities (Devlin et al, 2002: 225). Equally there is potential for manipulation via the treatment of patients of a 'lower' clinical priority to clear lists. Thus a National Audit Office study found that 52 per cent of consultants responding to a survey on waiting lists, thought that '...NHS waiting list targets meant that they had to treat patients in a different order in 1999-2000 than clinical priority indicated' (National Audit Office, 2001a: 18, but see ibid. for some of the complexities around using clinical priority as a treatment criteria). Equally, though the cited instances are relatively rare, there are reported instances of effective falsification of waiting list data, including delays in adding patients to the list or offering admission dates at very short notice in the expectation that a refusal would allow the hospital trust to suspend the person from the waiting list (National Audit Office, 2001b: 5 and 7).

Given such cogent objections to these performance standards in the public and private sectors what is the rationale for defining 'failure' relative to such (flawed) standards? The treatment is consistent with the principal object of the paper, namely to explore the *response* to 'failure' in the two sectors; this is most easily done by taking the definitions of success and failure broadly accepted as, at least, the 'official' practice in the sector. In particular what the paper seeks to establish is that even when 'failure' (in these terms) is frequent it has not shifted the dominant view that the road to 'success' is managerial. The paper is divided into five parts: the first (selectively) examines the ways in which private sector management has served as a de facto 'model' for the public sector; the second, which relies on the work of Froud and her colleagues (2000a and b), discusses the emergence of shareholder value as a standard for judging corporate financial performance and shows that, in these terms, even under relatively favourable economic conditions, most large corporate enterprises fail to meet the key rate of return targets used by advocates of SV. The third section develops the parallel argument in the public sector by looking at the performance of public sector social services against explicit government targets taking examples from the British public sector. The fourth section examines responses to such public and private 'failure' and argues that there are parallels in that, while structural conditions can frequently be argued to be at the root of 'failures', policy responses in both sectors are 'managerial' referring to 'solutions' such as organisational restructuring or changes in management teams. The conclusion suggests some of the reasons why these common responses are made. It argues that the roots lie in the attenuation of the links between the discourse of management and that of political economy.

The 'Lessons' of the Private Sector

The aim of this section is to trace how, under successive UK governments, the private sector has been seen as embodying standards of management to which the public sector should aspire. Without any pretension to exhaustiveness this process can be seen as embodying three key elements: the use of, usually senior, private sector managers to both report on and recommend changes to organisational practices in the public sector; the increased use of the private sector as a means of delivery of public services; and the importation of organisational and financial structures characteristic of private sector organisations into the public sector.

Obligatory Consultancy

With respect to the first of these features important examples date from the early to mid 1980s. In health, for example, the then Secretary of State for Health and Social

Security, Norman Fowler, appointed the late Sir Roy Griffiths (then Deputy Chairman and Managing Director of Sainsburys) (Harrison, 1988: 60) to lead a group of businessmen to investigate the use of resources in the NHS (Cutler and Waine, 1997: 2). This practice of calling on senior corporate executives to provide such prescriptions for the public sector has continued into the current period. Thus the Labour government invited Derek Wanless to advise on the future form of financing of the NHS. Wanless had been a Group Chief Executive of NatWest bank in the period 1992-99 and, at the time of his appointment, acted as a non-executive director of two companies (Treasury, 2002a). While his report was principally concerned with finance it also included managerial prescriptions on 'efficient use of resources' in the NHS (Wanless, 2002: Ch. 6).

While each of these interventions has their own character a clear underlying premise was (and is) that the public sector must change to conform to actual or at least postulated private sector management practice. This can be illustrated by looking at one of the earliest examples of these key documents, the 1983 Griffiths Report, entitled *NHS Management Inquiry*. The Griffiths team saw the NHS as lacking when contrasted with the private sector. There was, in their view, the absence of a 'clearly-defined general management function throughout the NHS' (Griffiths, 1983: 11). The latter was seen as '...the responsibility drawn together in one person at different levels of the organisation, for planning implementation and control of performance' (ibid). The inquiry team did indicate that this observation was made from the perspective of its 'business background' (ibid). However, this did not lead to any reservations over the appropriateness of such a 'management' function. Inter alia, one of the assumptions of this position was that there was no room for a view of the NHS as a public service that could require a distinctive form of organisation from that prevailing in 'business'. This issue was raised in the report, which pointed to the conception that the NHS was 'different from business in management terms...because [it] is not concerned with the profit motive and must be judged by wider social standards which cannot be measured' (ibid: 10). Naturally such a position would raise difficulties for the required 'management' function since 'control of performance' would be rendered problematic by virtue of the difficulty of measuring 'performance'.

The response to this objection again referred to (postulated) private sector practice. It was argued that the reference to the absence of the 'profit motive' was not relevant because, in the private sector, financial targets do 'not immediately impinge on large numbers of managers below board level' (ibid). However, this line of argument involves a non sequitur. Even if the statement on private sector practice is accepted this only means that a significant number of private sector managers work with non-financial performance indicators. The quality of such indicators could be questionable and, even if they were not subject to significant flaws, there is no necessary implication that they could be successfully replicated in the NHS.

It could be argued that this account is too hard on the inquiry team and contains elements of anachronism. Such an objection could be advanced on the grounds that it has only been with the growth of performance measurement in the public sector that the complexity of evaluation of performance in services such as health has become clearer and has been subject to a critical literature. However, it is not valid to argue that such a critical commentary was not available at the time of the inquiry. For example, a year before the inquiry team began its work, Klein (1982) concluded that developing 'standards and norms which would permit the activities of the medical profession (and other health service providers) to be evaluated' could well be problematic because 'the health care policy area is characterised by complexity, uncertainty and ambiguity' (ibid: 406-7). Klein's thorough discussion of such complexity was not registered in the team's report. In part the failure to engage with the complexity of these issues of performance assessment in public sector services related to the time scale of the inquiry. The announcement of the commissioning of the report was in February 1983 and it was submitted in October of the same year (Harrison, 1988: 60). Not surprisingly it was rather slight consisting of a 24 page memorandum to the Secretary of State (Cutler and Waine, 1997: 2). However, the recommendations were accepted (Harrison, 1988: 64-5) and the implementation of a major organisational change in the NHS, the designation of a general management function, on a thin conceptual and evidentiary basis, is indicative of the superordinate status accorded to private sector management nostrums.

Service Provision

The second major area in which the assumed superiority of private sector management practice is manifested is in service provision. A major Conservative policy, compulsory competitive tendering (CCT) is somewhat ambiguous in this respect. It was introduced in the NHS in 1983 (for catering, cleaning and laundry services) (DHSS, 1983); and for a broad range of services in local government through the Local Government Act 1988 (Cutler and Waine, 1997). This policy required that public authorities put the work covered by regulation or legislation out to competitive tender. Strictly this implied no presumption of the relative merits of public and private sector management since CCT required a mandatory competitive process rather than the privatisation of service provision (ibid: 88-9). However, it is the case that certain aspects of this policy did contain features that involved biases to the private sector. For example, under CCT in the local government services covered, local authorities were required to configure their service departments for CCT work as Direct Service Organisations (DSOs). These were distinct accounting units, which were required to make a target rate of return on capital employed. While, in one sense, this might be seen as a mechanism designed to prevent DSOs winning contracts by providing services below cost, it also imposed conditions that could disadvantage them. This was because private sector organisations could 'loss lead' by cross-subsidising CCT work from profits on other contracts. In principle at least this could lead to DSOs losing contracts and being forced out of the market (for a general discussion of how CCT was consistent with a 'level playing field' between public and private providers see ibid: 95-7).

Under Labour privatisation of provision has been particularly manifested in, arguably, its most controversial policy concerning the management of public sector social services, the Private Finance Initiative (PFI). PFI was originated by Conservatives but the policy was relatively undeveloped until Labour's election victory in 1997; before 1997 no large hospital project had been agreed under PFI (Froud and Shaoul, 2001: 249) while, in its first three years in power, Labour agreed PFI hospital projects to a value of in excess of £3 billion (ibid). Under PFI the public sector purchaser contracts with a private provider to give the public service access to a capital asset (e.g. a hospital) and, usually, the supply of certain services used in the asset (e.g. catering). The public purchaser pays both for the access to the asset (the 'availability' fee, Gaffney et al, 1999a: 50) and for the services provided (the 'service' fee, ibid) and contracts are long term extending over a 25-30 year period. The private sector provider is responsible for building and retains ownership of the asset.

PFI is an alternative to 'conventional' forms of public sector capital investment. Under such forms central government provided the funding for the investment (although this could involve borrowing from the financial markets and thus an increase in public sector debt). Under such schemes while it is standard procedure to employ private contractors in the construction of assets such as hospitals or schools they remain publicly owned. Similarly, while there can be decisions to contract out certain services used in the capital facility, such decisions are quite distinct from the contract to construct the facility.

In one sense the PFI process might appear to be 'neutral' between 'conventional' approaches and PFI. This is because the decision-making process incorporates a comparison between the conventional and PFI options in any given case. However, academic researchers have argued that such comparisons are spurious and loaded against the 'conventional' option. Thus, for example, a major part of the case advanced by advocates of PFI is that significant risks of project failure are effectively transferred to the private contractor. However, in economic evaluations of PFI projects, risk transfer assumptions do not necessarily correspond to the *legal* obligations of the parties. In the case of a PFI hospital in Carlisle, for instance, the possibility that clinical cost savings would not be met was assumed to involve an estimated risk of £5 million that would be the responsibility of the private contractor. However, the *agreement* with the contractor specified no responsibility for achieving such savings and thus no penalty if they were not achieved (Gaffney et al, 1999b: 118-19, see ibid. for further problems with risk transfer in PFI projects).

Such scepticism is reinforced by doubts on the financial logic of PFI. An argument advanced by supporters of PFI is that, by spreading the cost of capital projects, it is possible to increase the scale of such projects and thus deal with past under investment in the public sector. However, as Pollock et al (2001) argue, it would have been possible to finance PFI projects out of current government budget surpluses. As they point out (ibid: 4) the UK budget surplus in 2000/01 alone (£23 billion) would have more than covered the £14 billion of PFI deals signed between 1997 and 2001 (ibid: 4).

Another part of the intense controversy generated by PFI is the criticism that it is likely to give poor 'value for money'. Thus academic researchers have pointed out that PFI projects to build NHS hospitals have involved both marked cost inflation over original estimates and sharp reductions in bed capacity when contrasted with the prior pattern of provision in the areas concerned (for details see ibid: 14). A defence of PFI in this respect is that critics are putting excessive emphasis on bed capacity, which is of questionable relevance in the context of falls in length of stay in NHS hospitals and increasing recourse to day surgery. However, academic commentators have pointed to the conclusion of the government commissioned National Beds Inquiry that no further cuts in NHS bed capacity should be made (ibid: 15). Consequently this opens up the possibility that PFI will combine high regular payments to private providers and dysfunctional facilities which may reduce the level of hospital activity when government policy is aiming to cut waiting lists and waiting times.

This criticism has engendered doubts regarding the rationale for PFI and, given the apparent weakness of the policy, the only rationale might appear to be a government assumption of the superiority of private management skills, which are brought to such projects (for criticisms of such an assumption see ibid: 5). Furthermore the bias against the public sector in such schemes has been illustrated by Pollock et al (ibid) who point to examples such as a capital project in education announced in the 1998 Comprehensive Spending Review which was to be undertaken 'through' a public private partnership once more suggesting that comparison with the conventional public sector option was regarded as superfluous.

Imported Organisational and Financial Structures

A third significant manifestation of the tutelary role of the private sector relates to the importation of organisational and financial structures with at least strong affinities to those operating in private corporations. In the case of health, for example, the NHS reforms effectively constituted provider units in the hospital service as businesses. Working Paper 1, on self-governing hospitals, stated that such a hospital or NHS Trust 'will earn its revenue principally from the services it performs' (Department of Health, 1989a). At least in principle such trusts were to be organisationally distinct from purchasing agencies (initially health authorities and GP fundholders) and the 'corporate' form was reflected in affinities between the financial framework for Trusts and private sector corporations. Trusts were required to value their capital assets and to publish their financial results using a de facto profit and loss account and balance sheet (Department of Health, 1989b).

The corporatisation of providers in health – with the parallels in education, see, for example, Cutler and Waine, 2000 – reflects Conservative initiatives, in particular the 1990 NHS and Community Care Act and the 1988 Education Reform Act respectively, however, this broad structure has been retained by Labour. In the 1997 White Paper *The New NHS: Modern, Dependable* (Department of Health, 1997), for example, it was stated that the NHS 'internal market will be replaced'. However, the purchaser/provider split remains and not only have hospital trusts been retained but the trust 'form' has been extended to the primary sector via the constitution of Primary Care Trusts.

All these aspects have a common character. Borrowing from the private sector reflects a discourse of success. The public sector will learn from the successes of the private sector. However, as will be shown in the next section, if a common approach – at least in the US and UK economies – is used as a standard, the corporate sector is a scene of failure rather than success. This irony is explored in the next section.

Private Sector 'Failure'

In discussing 'failure' in the corporate sector the argument will follow the convention explained in the introduction, namely a commonly held criteria for 'success' or 'failure' will be used as a yardstick. The criteria adopted in this section refer to the use of measures of Economic Value Added (EVA) as a key criterion. It is necessary, therefore, both to explain and situate this standard. EVA can be seen as part of a broader approach commonly referred to as Shareholder Value (SV). In one sense SV refers to the view that the object of corporate activity should be to generate the best financial returns to shareholders. This, of course, is not in any sense novel (see, for example, Parkinson, 1994: 81) but in its contemporary manifestation SV reflects concerns that corporate managers are insufficiently committed and effective in generating such returns.

EVA operates as a broad 'metric' in this respect, i.e. it is a means of measuring corporate performance within an SV framework. As Froud et al (2000b: 81-7) point out EVA is susceptible of a number of variants but there are certain common features. Broadly EVA works by taking a corporate profit figure in any given year (again such figures can be calculated in a variety of ways) and subtracting from this profit figure an estimate of the cost of capital to the corporation. This latter figure has two aspects: a measure of the capital employed in the business; and a de facto target rate of return on capital. In general EVA calculations work on the assumption of an expected rate of return of 12-15 per cent (ibid: 95). Thus, the annual 'cost of capital' is derived by multiplying capital employed by such a rate of return figure. EVA can therefore be positive, i.e. profit exceeds the cost of capital figure, or negative, vice versa. Equally it is common to apply a rhetorical flourish to such EVA calculations. Thus while positive EVA is seen as an instance where SV has been created; negative EVA is portrayed as 'destroying' SV. The metric is linked to the overall objectives of SV because it is designed to operate as a discipline on corporate management. Thus such measures may be used not only at the corporate level but also at a divisional level. The expectation is that negative EVA should trigger actions by management to obviate the unsatisfactory 'value destroying' situation. In particular this includes various forms of 'restructuring' such as merger and acquisition and divestment of divisions/businesses, which are 'under-performing' (Froud et al, 2000a).

Restructuring is seen as a key means of shifting from negative to positive EVA. For example, merger and acquisition could be seen as eliminating the duplication of functions or facilities in the merged companies (Froud et al, 2000a). This is seen as a means of dealing with 'value destruction' by improving profits (through cutting costs) and/or by reducing the capital employed in the business. Divestment can also be seen as having this effect because divisions generating negative EVA due to low profits and/or heavy commitments of capital are sold off thus allowing an improved overall corporate performance.

Given that EVA is seen as a tool, which operates to improve corporate performance, it is necessary to examine how corporations performed when judged by such a standard. In this section the argument uses an analysis given by Froud et al (2000b), which looked at an EVA league table for the largest 200 UK companies for the years 1997 and 1998. Before discussing the results of this analysis, it is necessary to conceptualise this source. The use of the British data is relevant because SV, and thus EVA, has taken a more prominent role in the 'Anglo-Saxon' as against the continental European economies. Indeed for advocates of SV/EVA, economies such as Germany are seen as involving institutional structures that tend to 'destroy' shareholder value. For example, German companies, with 2000 or more employees, under the 1976 Co-Determination Act, are obliged to have half of their supervisory board drawn from employee representatives (Vitols, 2001). The supervisory board is distinguished from the management board; the latter is concerned with day-to-day management of the company while the former is responsible for overall corporate strategy. This structure is seen, by advocates of SV, as likely to 'destroy value' because, for example, it constitutes an obstacle to restructuring. The latter may frequently be expected to involve reductions in employment (Froud et al, 2000b) and equally employee representation on the supervisory board can be seen as allowing for effective resistance to such restructuring (see Vitols, 2001 for examples). Consequently advocates of SV believe that corporate performance (looked at from a 'shareholder' standpoint) is superior in an economy like that of the UK where worker influence over corporate strategy is relatively weak.

Taking the largest 200 companies should also be a reasonable choice in the context of the argument advanced in this paper. These are the companies that offer the highest material rewards to managers and also purport to attract the 'best' managers. Equally, as was indicated above, corporate managers from such large corporations have been those from whom advice on the 'management' of public sector organisations has been sought.

Finally, 1998 in particular is a year where relatively healthy corporate financial performance might be expected. Recessionary conditions might be expected to be more likely to generate negative EVA because profits will be depressed and restructuring measures such as divestments are more difficult in weak trading conditions. However, as Froud et al (2000b: 91) point out, 1998 was a year in which corporate profits were at a cyclical peak.

Consequently this data would appear to be favourable to performance in terms of an EVA standard. The economy concerned is one reflecting institutions seen as amenable to the creation of SV; the largest companies might be seen as at least able to offer the rewards conducive to attracting more competent managers; and the point in the economic cycle taken is favourable to stronger corporate financial performance. However, notwithstanding all this, the EVA results reported by Froud et al (2000a) are notably disappointing (from an SV standpoint). Of the largest 200 companies in 1998 only 87 (43.5 per cent) generated positive EVA; the remaining 113 were thus 'destroyers' of shareholder value (ibid: 91). An indicator of the impact of the relatively favourable conditions in 1998 is that the 1997 figures were even worse with only 59 of the largest 200 companies achieving positive EVA (ibid.). Thus there is a major irony. Public sector managers have been told consistently that they should aspire to the standards achieved by private sector senior management in large corporations. However, even in a 'good' year, the majority of such companies 'fail' in terms of the EVA standard. Later the argument will take up the response to such 'failure' but before addressing this question it is necessary to turn to the experience of 'failure' in the public sector.

'Failure' in the Public Sector

Turning to the public sector there are some aspects of policy, particularly those of the current Government, which facilitate examples at least parallel to those discussed in the last section. In particular a central aspect of the Government's approach, driven by the Treasury, has been to link public expenditure allocations with departmental targets in 'Public Service Agreements' (PSAs). With respect to such targets the Government has shown a clear belief that broad policy objectives can be operationalised in this way. For example, in discussing one of the objectives of the Department for Education and Skills (DfES), the Treasury states that an agreed broad goal is to ensure 'that all young people reach 16 with the skills, attitudes and personal qualities that will give them a secure foundation for lifelong learning, work and citizenship in a rapidly changing world' (Treasury, 2002b). Such a general objective might be seen to raise a familiar caveat, that it is difficult to encompass such qualitative elements in a quantitative measure. However, in setting its public service agreement for the DfES for 2001-4, it clearly thinks otherwise since this broad objective is seamlessly linked to specific quantifiable targets. For example, it is suggested by the Treasury that the DfES should commit itself to Key Stage 2 targets (National Curriculum test results for 11 year olds) in English and Maths (Mathematics) in excess of those which had been previously agreed for the period to 2002. The latter targets were 80 per cent of pupils reaching the expected standard (level 4) in English and 75 per cent in Maths. The precise target for 2004 was not set in this document but is was noted that a specific and 'higher' target figure would be agreed (ibid).

From the standpoint of this paper this approach has certain advantages. It means that given the Government's commitment to quantitative targets there is a correspondingly clear 'official' definition of 'success' (meeting the target) or 'failure' (missing it). Nevertheless it is considerably more difficult to arrive at a summary measure equivalent to EVA analysis described in the previous section. PSA targets are necessarily diverse. Education targets refer, for example, to a variety of age groups and to different dimensions of performance (for example, while many PSAs refer to test or examination performance, others relate to school attendance). This is also the case in health where targets can refer to access to services e.g. waiting times but also to proxies for clinical standards such as emergency readmission rates (Department of Health, 2002a). What this means is that public sector 'failure' cannot be encompassed in a single summary measure and no attempt will be made to undertake what is, arguably, the impossible task of weighting the significance of 'successes' (meeting of targets) as against 'failures' (not achieving the targets). Rather what will be suggested is that, with respect to a number of key targets, it is possible to point to important instances of 'failure'. To set this argument in context there are a number of high profile examples of targets, which *have* been achieved. In the case of health an important PSA, referred to above, was the commitment to reduce NHS inpatient waiting lists by 100,000 over the lifetime of the parliament from the 1.16 million waiting in March 1997. This was achieved by December 2001 when waiting lists had fallen by 108,000 below the March 1997 figure (Department of Health, 2002b). In education a key target was that 50 per cent of pupils should achieve 5 or more GCSEs at A*-C grade. The deadline for achieving this was 2002 but it was reached in academic year 2000/01 (DfES, 2002a).

Nevertheless, it is also possible to find a number of important targets which has either not been attained or where it is doubtful, on current trends, that they will be attained. As was indicated above, the DfES target (for 2002) was that 80 per cent of pupils achieve level 4 in Key Stage 2 tests in English and 75 per cent in Mathematics. The levels achieved in England in 2002 were 75 per cent in English and 73 per cent in Mathematics (DfES, 2002a). A DfES target for 'lifelong learning and employability' was to increase 'the proportion of those aged 19 who have achieved Level 2 or equivalent [in *vocational* qualifications] to 85 per cent by 2002' (DfES, 2002b). The figure for Autumn 2001 was 74.8 per cent and it was stated in the DfES Departmental Report for 2002 that '...we will not meet the Level 2 [target]' (ibid).

In the case of health an interim target (the final target in this respect is a maximum waiting time of 12 weeks by the end of 2003) was that a maximum waiting time of 26 weeks for an *outpatient* appointment be attained by March 2002 (Department of Health, 2002b). In March 2002, 6 per cent of those waiting for outpatient appointments had not been seen in 26 weeks (ibid). An interim target for maximum waiting time for *inpatient* treatment was that no patient be waiting for such an appointment for in excess of 15 months, was set for March 2002 (ibid). Data given in the Department of Health Departmental Report for 2002 does not allow for a definitive 'verdict' on this target since the latest data presented is for December 2001. At that point the numbers waiting 15 months or over were 4,200 and roughly one third of trusts had not reached the 15-month target (ibid). Reflecting its responsibilities for the welfare of children, a PSA for the Department of Health was to increase 'from 4 per cent in 1998 to 15 per cent by 2003-04' the proportion of children leaving care aged 16 and over with 5 GCSEs at grade A*-C (ibid). In the Departmental Report this is rather hopefully described as 'on course' (ibid). However, the attainment level cited for March 2001 is 5 per cent. Thus though the target involves a 375 per cent improvement, with about half the period covered the improvement has been 25 per cent and if the existing trajectory were maintained a 6 per cent outcome would be achieved (under half the target figure).

Thus, while for the reasons given above, it is not possible to apply an overall evaluative metric to public sector performance it is possible to see that there are a number of important 'failures'. In the next section the aim will be to discuss the diagnosis of and response to such 'failure' in private and public sectors.

Responding to Failure

In this section the aim is to trace the dominant response to the frequent occurrence of 'failure' identified in the previous two sections and to suggest an alternative view to this dominant response. To do this, two broad types of explanation need to be distinguished. One can be termed 'managerial'. This is the dominant contemporary response to 'failure' and it broadly consists in the argument that managerial techniques are sound and 'failure' is a function of lack of management competence in the use (or awareness of) such techniques. A clear prescription follows from such a view, what is needed is a mechanism to ensure the replacement of incompetent managers. In contrast, an alternative view is one that emphasises the structural constraints on management practice. This does not imply that management is completely powerless but the logic of the position suggests that management's room for manoeuvre is limited, perhaps severely limited. Of these approaches the managerial is effectively dominant and this can be illustrated by looking at examples from both private and public sectors.

As was pointed out above, Froud et al (2000b) used an EVA 'league table' from the *Sunday Times* to show how, even under relatively favourable economic conditions, the majority of the largest British firms failed to achieve 'positive' EVA. In this work they also cite the commentary given on this result in the *Sunday Times*. This stated that '...shareholders would be better off, if the majority of Britain's biggest companies were either taken over or had new management installed to improve their returns' (*Sunday Times*, 27th September 1998, cited in Froud et al, 2000b: 91). The underlying message is that the problem is the managers and that the answer is to remove the failing incumbents. Further such views are structurally linked with various assumptions of SV. Thus, for example, as was argued above, the relative superiority of the 'Anglo-Saxon' economies in SV discourse is related to a market for corporate control in those economies. In addition to operating as a discipline on management through the *threat* of takeover and the corollary, the change in the senior management team, such a market can be seen as a means of *effecting* a change in such management teams.

There are parallel managerial accounts with respect to public sector 'failure'. To illustrate such a response it is relevant to consider important interventions such as the NHS Performance Ratings. These ratings were initially produced for acute trusts in 2000/01. In 2001/2 the ratings were extended to cover, in addition to acute trusts, specialist trusts (e.g. providing exclusively certain medical specialties such as orthopaedic treatment); ambulance trusts; and mental health trusts (Department of Health, 2002a). In the analysis presented here the focus is on acute trusts because of their links with high profile political targets such as waiting times.

The performance ratings allocated trusts to four performance categories, respectively 3, 2, 1 and 'zero' stars (ibid). This allocation is undertaken by reference to a series of performance indicators. Amongst these are nine 'key targets' (ibid). These include having no patients waiting more than 18 months for inpatient treatment; or 26 weeks for outpatient treatment; or 2 weeks to be seen in hospital if cancer is suspected (ibid: 2). In addition there are a further set of indicators referring to clinical performance; 'patient based' indicators relating to measures such as waiting times in accident and emergency departments; and indicators relating to the management of staff such as sickness absence rates (ibid: 3-4).

There is also a series of descriptors linking to the 'star' categories. While the 'three star' trusts have the 'highest levels of performance' and the 'two star' trusts are 'performing well overall' (ibid: 2), the verdict on the other categories is more sombre. 'One star' trusts are said to give 'some cause for concern regarding particular areas of performance' (ibid) and 'zero star' trusts have shown 'significant areas for concern in the key targets' (ibid: 4). In turn there is a managerial intervention system, which is linked with these performance assessments. Thus 'three star' trusts will have increased autonomy from control (ibid: 8) but, in the case of 'zero star' trusts 'local managers will have to develop immediate plans to improve performance. If this does not happen, the management of the hospital will be put out to franchise' (ibid: 9). As in the private sector, the ultimate 'remedy' is to change the management team.

However, if the managerial response is the dominant one there is an alternative approach. In their examination of corporate performance in EVA terms Froud et al (2000a) point to a series of constraints which, they argue, lead to 'negative' EVA. Similarly they also point to structural advantages, which are conducive to 'success' in these terms. Thus they argue that there is a pronounced sectoral pattern to weak and strong EVA performance. Weak EVA sectors include, for example, hotels, pubs and restaurants, aerospace, defence, electrical equipment and motor industries (ibid: 781). They point out that in the case of hotels, pubs and restaurants a structural constraint is the necessarily high level of capital tied up in material assets (ibid) which, given a benchmark rate of return across all sectors, pushes up the cost of capital set against profit in the EVA calculation. In the case of the other three sectors difficulties in product markets (ibid) depress EVA through the effect on profits.

Conversely, certain sectors such as pharmaceuticals and tobacco exhibit strong EVA performance. This can, in turn, be linked to various structural advantages. In the case of pharmaceuticals patents convey intellectual property rights which abridge competition for the life of the patent (ibid: 780); and the market has been underpinned by strong government commitment to purchase patented drugs which tend to make up an increasing share of overall health care expenditure (Froud et al, 1998). In the case of tobacco strong brands again allow an effective constraint on competition and for premium prices to be charged (Froud et al, 2000a: 780). Thus, what is argued in such accounts is that EVA performance is less related to the agency of management than to the industries in which such managers are operating and the advantages and disadvantages that they confer in attaining such performance targets. There are parallels in the public sector social services. It is a characteristic of such services is that they are frequently universal. A corollary is that the circumstances under which individual 'provider units' such as hospitals and schools operate vary enormously. In the case of hospitals, for example, these include differences in patient case-mix; variations in local labour markets with their impact on the capacity to hire staff; and availability of complementary community services. Such differences can impact on key targets such as reducing waiting times because of their relationship with the capacity of a hospital to treat a given number of patients in a given time period.

Table 14.1   Percentage of Pupils Achieving the Expected Level (or Above) by Eligibility for Free School Meals (FSM) and Key Stage 2 Test Results, England 1999-2001 (% of Pupils at Level 4 or Above)

	All School Avge %	Up to 5% FSM %	5-10% FSM %	10-15% FSM %	15-20% FSM %	20-30% FSM %	30-40% FSM %	Over 40% FSM %
Eng* 1999	71	85	79	73	69	64	57	50
Eng 2000	75	88	83	78	74	69	63	56
Eng 2001	75	88	82	78	73	69	63	57
Maths* 1999	69	83	77	71	68	63	56	50
Maths 2000	72	84	79	74	70	66	60	55
Maths 2001	71	83	77	73	69	64	59	54

* Eng = English; Maths = Mathematics.
Source: DfES 2002c, 2001 and 2000

In the case of education there are major differences in the socio-economic circumstances in which schools are situated. Table 14.1 shows, for example, the connections between a measure of poverty (eligibility for free school meals) and test performance (in this case at Key Stage 2). A corollary of a stress on structural determinants is a scepticism regarding the efficacy of replacing incumbent management. This follows from the logic of the position, if structures condition performance then changing managers is a policy that is not likely to succeed. As was indicated above, the *Sunday Times* panacea for negative EVA was a change in corporate management, in particular via the operation of the market for corporate control. However, as Froud et al (2000b: 91) argue, 'this is a... startling position to take on the British economy where there has been large-scale merger and acquisition activity for the past twenty years': and they point out (Froud et al, 2000a: 773) that, between 1976 and 1995, UK Industrial and Commercial Companies spent the equivalent of half their investment in plant and equipment on mergers and acquisitions. Thus they suggest that these 'orthodox prescriptions' (Froud et al, 2000b: 91) would not appear to be effective.

Table 14.2 Distribution of Performance Rankings: NHS Acute Trusts 2000/01 and 2001/02

	Trust Numbers 2000/01	*Trust Percentages 2000/01* %	*Trust Numbers 2001/02*	*Trust Percentages 2001/02* %
3 Star	35	20.2	46	27.7
2 Star	103	59.5	77	46.4
1 Star	23	13.3	35	21.1
Zero Star	12	7.0	8	4.8

Source: Department of Health 2002a and 2001

Parallel doubts can be raised with respect to the public sector. In the discussion of the NHS performance tables for acute trusts it was pointed out that the 'lowest' two categories ('one' and 'zero' stars) were identified as giving, to varying degrees, cause for 'concern' over their performance. Table 14.2 gives the overall distribution of 'star rankings' for the two years in which these figures have been published on acute trusts. Thus, according to the 'official' view just over a quarter (25.9 per cent) of acute trusts in 2001/2 was giving cause for 'concern' over their performance. Yet, again, the notion that changing the management is the answer seems questionable. After all, managerial solutions have been crucial to the NHS for two decades. As was pointed out above, the Griffiths inquiry triggered the introduction of a general management function into the NHS in the early 1980s. Similarly it is more than a decade since the introduction of a quasi-market in which, to obtain trust status, NHS management teams were expected to show their competence. As with the private sector, this 'orthodox' solution would appear to have been 'tried'. Thus the response to 'failure' is one-sided. Notwithstanding cogent arguments regarding the limits of management agency, if there is an academic debate on the managerial prescription, there is no parallel political debate.

Conclusion

The aim of this conclusion is to examine some of the reasons for and effects of the absence of a political debate on the status of 'managerialism'. This is a broad and complex question and what is presented here can only be a very limited account. However, it can be argued that a crucial feature is what may be termed the suppression of the connection between the discourse of management and that of political economy.

To take the case of the private sector Froud et al (2000a) point out that, as the managerial framework remains invulnerable, then private sector 'failure' leads to 'restructuring' via mechanisms discussed above. However, since restructuring is itself problematic it is not a temporary means of adjustment but rather a *permanent* feature of the economy. For example, in the case of merger and acquisition, problems arise from the logistics of managing companies that have merged (ibid: 787); and such companies generally operate within rather than removing the structural constraints that condition 'failure' in the first place. However, while such restructuring is not a 'solution' it has important social and economic effects. Reduction in employment is a usual corollary and, in turn, this has a variety of effects on the workforce. These range from long-term unemployment to subsequent re-employment on less favourable, comparable or more favourable terms; early retirement on a tolerable pension or on an unsatisfactory pension. Equally, of course, there is the impact on those who remain in employment and, again, varying impacts on terms and condition of employment apply (for a discussion of these issues see Froud et al, 2000a). However, these significant social and economic effects, which appear likely to increase social and economic inequalities, are effectively divorced from the evaluation of managerial responses to 'failure'; there is assumed to be 'no alternative' to restructuring.

There are parallels in the public sector. In education, for example, the setting of targets at all levels and the diffusion of what is seen as 'good' managerial practice are central to Labour's approach to raising 'educational standards' (for a classic example see DfEE, 1998). 'Success' is a function of a good management team; 'failure' indicates a weak team, which must be replaced (see ibid, Ch. 2). However, it is a commonplace observation that social and economic inequalities impact significantly on measured educational attainment and this was discussed earlier. However, the structural constraints posed by such inequalities are marginalised in a policy dominated by managerial prescriptions. This is not to say that Labour has not pursued and achieved (limited) redistribution of income (for a survey of the impact of such policies 1997-2001 see Clark et al, 2002). However, the self-contained status of management means that such policies are not integrated into the discussion of policies on 'educational standards'.

Given this attenuation of the links between broader political economy issues of the distribution of income and wealth and the status of managerialism, a genuine political debate on the role of the latter cannot take place. As long as these circumstances prevail the ironic situation in which the managerial project turns 'failure' into 'success' is likely to continue.

References

Budden, R. (2002), 'Running Scared in the Face of Fraud Allegations', *Financial Times*, 29 June: 16.

Chaffin, J., Hill, A. and Spiegel, P. (2002), 'Buried Partnerships Unearth Grounds for Prosecution', *Financial Times*, 22 August: 14.

Clark, T., Dilnot., A. Goodman, A. and Myck, M. (2002), 'Taxes and Transfers 1997-2001', *Oxford Review of Economic Policy*, 18(2): 187-201.

Cutler, T. and Waine, B. (1997), *Managing the Welfare State: Text and Sourcebook*, Berg: Oxford.

Cutler, T. and Waine, B. (2000), 'Managerialism Reformed? New Labour and Public Sector Managerialism', *Social Policy and Administration*, 34(3): 318-32.

Department for Education and Employment (DfEE) (1998), *Teachers: Meeting the Challenge of Change*, Cmd. 4164, HMSO: London.

Department for Education and Skills (DfES) (2002a), *Departmental Report 2002*, at www.dfes.gov.uk

Department for Education and Skills (DfES) (2002b), *National Curriculum Assessments of 7 and 11 year olds in England 2002 (Provisional)*, at www.dfes.gov.uk

Department for Education and Skills (DfES) (2002c), *National Curriculum Assessments of 7, 11 and 14 year olds in England 2001*, at www.dfes.gov.uk

Department for Education and Skills (DfES) (2001), *National Curriculum Assessments of 7, 11 and 14 year olds in England 2000*, at www.dfes.gov.uk

Department for Education and Skills (DfES) (2001), *National Curriculum Assessments of 7, 11 year and 14 olds in England 1999*, at www.dfes.gov.uk

Department of Health (1989a), *Self-Governing Hospitals*, Working Paper 1 (Working for Patients), HMSO: London.

Department of Health (1989b), *Capital Charges*, Working Paper 5 (Working for Patients), HMSO: London.

Department of Health (1997), *The New NHS: Modern, Dependable*, at www.doh.gov.uk

Department of Health (2001), *NHS Performance Ratings: Acute Trusts 2000/01*, Department of Health: London.

Department of Health (2002a), *NHS Performance Ratings: Acute Trusts, Specialist Trusts, Ambulance Trusts, Mental Health Trusts 2001/02*, Department of Health: London.

Department of Health (2002b), *Departmental Report 2002-3*, at www.doh.gov.uk

Department of Health and Social Security (DHSS) (1983), *Health Service Management: Competitive Tendering in the Provision of Domestic, Catering and Laundry Services*, HC (83) 18, Department of Health and Social Security: London.

Devlin, N., Harrison, A., and Derrett, S. (2002), 'Waiting in the NHS: Part I – A Diagnosis', *Journal of the Royal Society of Medicine*, 95(5): 223-6.

Froud, J., Haslam, C., Johal, S. and Williams, K. (2000a), 'Restructuring for Shareholder Value and Its Implications For Labour', *Cambridge Journal of Economics*, (24): 771-97.

Froud, J., Haslam, C., Johal, S. and Williams, K. (2000b), 'Shareholder Value and Financialisation: Consultancy Promises, Management Moves', *Economy and Society*, 29(1): 80-110.

Froud, J., Haslam, C., Johal, S., Williams, K. and Willis, R. (1998), 'British Pharmaceuticals: A Cautionary Tale', *Economy and Society*, 27(4): 554-84.

Froud, J. and Shaoul, J. (2001), 'Appraising and Evaluating PFI for NHS Hospitals' *Financial Accountability and Management*, 17(3): 247-70.

Gaffney, D., Pollock, A., Price, D. and Shaoul, J. (1999a), 'NHS Capital Expenditure and the Private Finance Initiative – Expansion or Contraction?', *British Medical Journal (BMJ)*, 319, 3rd July): 48-51.

Gaffney, D., Pollock, A., Price, D. and Shaoul, J. (1999b), 'PFI in the NHS – Is There An Economic Case?', *BMJ*, 319, 10th July: 116-19.

Griffiths, R. (1983), *NHS Management Inquiry*, Department of Health and Social Security: London.

Harrison, S. (1988), *Managing the National Health Service: shifting the frontier?*, Chapman and Hall: London.

Klein, R. (1982), 'Performance Evaluation and the NHS: a Case Study in Conceptual Perplexity and Organizational Complexity', *Public Administration*, 60(4): 385-407.

National Audit Office (2001a), *Inpatient and Outpatient Waiting in the NHS*, Report by the Comptroller and Auditor General, HC 221, Session 2001-2002, at www.nao.gov.uk

National Audit Office (2001b), *Inappropriate Adjustments to NHS Waiting Lists*, Report by the Comptroller and Auditor General, HC 452, Session 2001-2002, at www.nao.gov.uk

O' Sullivan, M. (2000), *Contests for Corporate Control*, Oxford University Press: Oxford.

Parkinson, J. (1994), *Corporate Power and Responsibility: Issues in the Theory of Company Law*, Oxford University Press: Oxford

Pollitt, C. and Bouckaert, G. (2000), *Public Management Reform: A Comparative Analysis*, Oxford University Press: Oxford.

Pollock, A., Shaoul, J., Rowland, D. and Player, S. (2001), *A Response to the IPPR Commission on Public Private Partnerships*, Catalyst Trust, at www.catalyst-trust.co.uk

Treasury (2002a), *Biographical Information About Derek Wanless*, at www.HM-Treasury.gov.uk

Treasury (2002b), *Public Service Agreements 2001-2004: Department for Education and Skills*, at www.HM-Treasury.gov.uk

Vitols, S. (2001), 'Varieties of Corporate Governance: Comparing Germany and the UK' in P. Hall and D. Soskice (eds), *Varieties of Capitalism: The Institutional Foundations of Comparative Advantage*, Oxford University Press: Oxford.

Wanless, D. (2002), *Securing our Future: Health: Taking a Long Term View*, at www.HM-Treasury.gov.uk

Williams, K. (2000), ' From Shareholder Value to Present-day Capitalism', *Economy and Society*, 29(1), 1-12.

Index